Modern Migrations,
Black Interrogations

In the series *Studies in Transgression*, edited by DAVID BROTHERTON

ALSO IN THIS SERIES:

Robert D. Weide, *Divide & Conquer: Race, Gangs, Identity, and Conflict*

John C. Quicker and Akil S. Batani-Khalfani, *Before Crips: Fussin', Cussin', and Discussin' among South Los Angeles Juvenile Gangs*

John M. Hagedorn, *Gangs on Trial: Challenging Stereotypes and Demonization in the Courts*

Series previously published by Columbia University Press

EDITED BY PHILIP KRETSEDEMAS
AND JAMELLA N. GOW

Modern Migrations, Black Interrogations

Revisioning Migrants and Mobilities through the Critique of Antiblackness

TEMPLE UNIVERSITY PRESS
Philadelphia • Rome • Tokyo

TEMPLE UNIVERSITY PRESS
Philadelphia, Pennsylvania 19122
tupress.temple.edu

Library of Congress Cataloging-in-Publication Data

Names: Kretsedemas, Philip, 1967– editor. | Gow, Jamella N., editor.
Title: Modern migrations, Black interrogations : revisioning migrants and
   mobilities through the critique of antiblackness / edited by Philip
   Kretsedemas and Jamella N. Gow.
Other titles: Studies in transgression.
Description: Philadelphia : Temple University Press, 2024. | Series:
   Studies in transgression | Includes bibliographical references and
   index. | Summary: "This edited collection applies theories and lessons
   from the study of antiblack racism to the study of migration and
   movement. It locates often hidden legacies, resonances, and influences
   of antiblackness in contemporary migratory regimes"— Provided by
   publisher.
Identifiers: LCCN 2023025390 (print) | LCCN 2023025391 (ebook) | ISBN
   9781439922705 (cloth) | ISBN 9781439922712 (paperback) | ISBN
   9781439922729 (pdf)
Subjects: LCSH: Black people—Migrations. | Immigrants—Social conditions.
   | Emigration and immigration—Social aspects. | Racism against Black
   people.
Classification: LCC JV6225 .M64 2024 (print) | LCC JV6225 (ebook) | DDC
   305.896—dc23/eng/20230909
LC record available at https://lccn.loc.gov/2023025390
LC ebook record available at https://lccn.loc.gov/2023025391

Printed in the United States of America

9 8 7 6 5 4 3 2 1

Contents

Modern Migrations,
Black Interrogations

Black Interrogations

An Introduction

JAMELLA N. GOW AND PHILIP KRETSEDEMAS

This book recounts the experiences of Black people who have migrated, sometimes across national borders and sometimes not, but it is not a book about Black migration. To be more specific, this is not a book that takes the fact of migration for granted and goes about examining the ways that Black people migrate. For this same reason, this is not a book about Black refugees, even though some of its chapters recount the experiences of Black people who have fled for their lives.

This book uses reflections on the Black experience to trouble and progress the habits of thought that have accreted around the concept of "migration" as it's been defined for us by researchers and policymakers and by the pundits of the public spheres of the global North. The legacies of the transatlantic slave trade, the centrality of black morphology to the social ontologies of the modern world, and regimes of racialized violence that operate outside of the law (as well as the "social contracts" presumed by the law) will figure into all of our interrogations. The goals and aims of this book are also informed by Fred Moten's reflections on blackness as "the unasked question."[1] Our aim, as it concerns the field of migration studies, is to break the silence that has stifled the posing of this question, with the understanding that these silences, on the question of blackness, are part and parcel of the antiblack violence that they have enabled and obfuscated. It also bears emphasizing that Moten is not alone in raising this concern. Many scholars have called attention to the long history of silences surrounding the question of blackness in the modern intellectual canon.

This silence can be viewed in light of what Gayatri Spivak has described as the sanctioned ignorance about the relationship between migration and histories of colonial predation that pervade not only migration studies but almost every major subject area of the social sciences and the humanities.[2] As Lucy Mablin and Joe Turner have pointed out, the idea of modernity contributes to these silences, by feeding into the belief that European societies, and their colonial offshoots, are products of a developmental process that is intrinsic to themselves, rather than growing out of their unequal and codependent relationships with the parts of the world that we now call the global South.[3]

This investment in the intrinsically different (and superior) qualities of European societies shares purpose with the rational and rugged individualism that has been romanticized by the Western canon. But in this case, we are dealing with a national character rather than an aggregate of private individuals. These ideas have catered to a gendered paternalism, with Western, industrialized nations playing the role of the benevolent, patriarchal adult that is committed to mentoring the more childlike (and implicitly effeminized) nations of the global South.[4]

It is also important to recognize how the racialized and gendered body comes to be read through the individual as both citizen and nation. Even as masculinity comes to embody the nation in the West, it is frequently women—whether as heteronormative "producers" of citizens or symbolic carriers of national culture—whose bodies become sites for reproducing the nation. While it is white, elite women who are valorized as such, it is Black women and women of color more generally whose presence and ability to reproduce, unless for the purposes of labor, is depicted as a threat to the racialized, gendered, national body.[5] The Western national character, then, must also be read as white, male, and heterosexual—a process that removes BIPOC, women, queer, and trans from beyond the borders of citizenship and national belonging.[6]

When you bring this subtext into view, Spivak's meditations on sanctioned ignorance should also be read in light of one her most provocative statements about colonial-era power relations, that of "white men saving brown women from brown men."[7] To unpack this quote a little, Spivak is calling attention to a gender politics that is advanced in the name of women's rights, but that also reinforces a racial and civilizational hierarchy that was foundational to colonial rule. European colonial powers evidence their cultural superiority by rescuing brown women from their oppressive home cultures. Like Rudyard Kipling's poem "The White Man's Burden" and the bucolic depictions of plantation life that were endorsed by the slave-owning classes (and memorialized in films like D. W. Griffith's film *The Birth of a Nation*), we are presented with narratives that justify racial domination as being in the best interests of dominated populations.[8]

These kinds of narratives are still with us, but they take a more nuanced form in the present day. Instead of white men, rescuing brown and black women, as benign patriarchs, this role is played by coalitions of activists, often in consort with state agencies, who leverage feminist and human rights discourse to legitimate their interventions.[9] It is important to note that these campaigns are often responding to urgent humanitarian crises and they protect vulnerable people who would otherwise receive no help at all. But they also contribute to a phenomenon that Kelly Oliver has coined "carceral humanitarianism,"[10] in which relief efforts become reliant on enforcement solutions that overcriminalize the problems they are trying to correct. As Chandra Mohanty has pointed out, the activists and intellectuals of the global North also have a tendency to conceptualize the oppression of Third World women in ways that affirm the primacy of a white, Western experience of feminism.[11] As a result, they fail to see how histories of colonial domination and the contemporary dynamics of North-South economic dependency and military interventions are also women's issues that require a feminist analysis.

Western feminists' calls for solidarity around reproductive rights and access to birth control provide a compelling example of where Black feminism and Third World feminism diverge. As Black feminists have insisted, Black women have never consistently retained the right to either give birth or keep their own children, even as white feminist politics frame reproductive rights around access to birth control. The right to reproduce and care for children while Black has been shaped by both "controlling images" that serve to villainize Black sexuality and police Black motherhood.[12] Similar narratives around family planning in the global South as a positive feature of development echo this rhetoric around the criminality of Black motherhood in the West.[13] Calls for revoking birthright citizenship in the United States derives from fears of Black sexuality and childbirth, which is then reframed as fear of the nonwhite immigrant seeking citizenship and welfare for their U.S.-born children. Grace Chang explains: "Just as black women have babies in order to suck up welfare, we are told, immigrant women come to the United States to have babies and consume all of the natural resources in sight."[14] Apprehensions of Black and Third World reproduction are thus tightly interwoven with both the logics of development and the racialized and gendered embodiment of the nation as masculine, patriarchal, and white.

We've just described another feature of the sanctioned ignorance that Spivak has written about, which has more to do with the unacknowledged connections between colonization, patriarchal power dynamics, and racism. But it is important, nonetheless, to be mindful about how the silences around these issues dovetail with the silence pertaining to the colonial prehistory of modern migration. Migration scholars have been calling attention to the feminization of international migration for well over two decades.[15] Meanwhile, other migration scholars have called attention to how racialized, non-citizen males are disproportionately targeted for deportation.[16] These gender disparities, in which racialized women become the prototypical face of exploitable, low-wage migrant labor and racialized migrant men are cast in the role of dangerous, disposable others, can be read in light of a history of race-gender power dynamics, traceable to the colonial era, which is normally kept at arm's length from migration studies.

The unasked question of blackness belongs to this same species of silences, though as many scholars have noted, it is not exactly the same thing as the (post)colonial question.[17] For example, the (post)colonial gender troubles raised by Spivak do not apply to black women in quite the same way. As Sojourner Truth made very clear in her poem "Ain't I A Woman," the white males of the colonial era were not inclined to view black women as deserving of being "rescued." Black women were, more typically, excluded from the culture of male chivalry (with all of the patriarchal and paternalist undertones that went along with it).[18] As Saidiya Hartman has explained, this is also why, under antebellum law, it was impossible for a white man to be convicted of raping a black woman, especially an enslaved black woman.[19] Hartman also goes on to reflect on a condition of radical depersonalization that situates the enslaved black body outside of European gender norms. In this era, it was common for white intellectuals to describe black gender relations as a perverse inversion of "normal" (aka white, European) gender norms.[20] But Hartman also describes a more absolute kind of otherness, which leads blackness to become the sign of the subhuman.[21] Bodies that suffered under this sign did not have to be treated like "people." The pleasures that the master derived from the control they exerted over these bodies can be understood as an intoxicating sadism: acting on their desires with no regard for social convention, and with full confidence that they would never be sanctioned for their behavior. This abusive treatment can be reinforced by the objectifying male gaze, but when it comes to black oppression—especially in the antebellum and Jim Crow eras—it is a power that white people of all genders have exerted over black bodies of all genders. Nonetheless, it was enslaved Black women's positionality as object of labor and sexual violence that also led to her vital role in the Black resistance tradition.[22] For Black women, sites of gendered violence also became sites of intersectional struggle in ways that reveal the important perspectives gained from gendered Black theorizing.[23] Once again, race functions as a hidden transcript that transforms the meaning of gender. We also find it important to emphasize that the imbrications of race and gender can unfold in ways that are more or less unique to the black condition.

Another distinguishing feature of (anti)blackness is its chronology, which does not align neatly with the history of European colonization. Several scholars observe, for example, that antiblackness was a feature of the European imagination prior to the colonization of the Americas.[24] Even more important, antiblackness is a problem that continues to unfold in ways that are qualitatively distinct from the histories of colonization, decolonization, and the postcolonial melancholia that followed in their wake. Antiblackness, in its adaptive fluidity, can be used to explain the habitus and social hierarchies of European settler colonies, but it is also very much alive and well in the multicultural liberal-democratic societies of the present day. Joy James, for example, has shown how Black candidates seeking political office in the multicultural democracies of the global North appeal to antiblack tropes in an attempt to appeal to "mainstream" sentiments.[25] Similar observations have been made of the political culture of predominantly Black nation-states, which have undergone their own postcolonial transitions.[26] There are also a number of studies showing how racialized immigrants (including Black immigrants) from postcolonial nations integrate into the societies of the global North in ways that keep their social identities at arm's length from the stigma of blackness.[27] This is not to say that blackness and antiblackness are not historically situated and thus immutable across time and space. Adaptability is an important function of how both race and racism persist.[28] However, we emphasize that within these versions of race, blackness—wherever it emerges—retains a distinctive character apart from generalized Otherness and other specific forms of racialization.

Keeping these examples in mind, antiblackness is better understood as a constantly regenerating and mutating feature of the present-day organization of social relations rather than as a problem that can be uniquely identified with the "transition" from a colonial to a postcolonial or neocolonial social order. In the United States, in particular, the modern silence on the question of blackness seems to have become more entrenched as challenges to the racial order increased in intensity, and as the mechanisms of racial stratification became more complex. Eduardo Bonilla-Silva's theory of color-blind racism, which has been used to explain the racial ideologies of the post–civil rights era, is one of the most influential attempts to explain this process.[29] It bears noting, however, that before color-blind racism came on the scene, there was already a well-established culture of silence on the question of antiblackness and the experiences of Black people.

Although the concept of racism dates to the early twentieth century, it was not originally used to examine the problems faced by Black people.[30] Most of the intellectual currents that laid the foundations for the critical study of race and racism today have an even more recent history, which can be traced to the 1980s.[31] Moreover, as Aldon Morris has shown, most of the justifications about the "inferiority" of Black populations that were advanced by White intellectuals in the late nineteenth and early twentieth centuries were not based on empirical research.[32] Black populations have been understudied for most of U.S. history despite the fact that late-nineteenth-century treatises on eugenics, which had a pervasive influence on federal and local laws and policies, were anchored by ideas about black inferiority.[33] Morris goes on to show that Black scholars attempted to correct this dearth of data by creating their own schools of research that played an instrumental role in getting the social sciences to take empirics more seriously, but they were also excluded from the new research paradigm that they helped to create.[34]

Morris's historiography is centered on the life and times of W. E. B Dubois, and it brings to mind Dubois's fateful observation that the defining problem of the twentieth century was that of the color line.[35] Dubois's prognosis on race and the modern world order is a fitting entry point into the critical intellectual tradition that informs this book. Although Dubois was a disciplined empirical researcher, he understood that blackness posed a problem for the racist imagination that could not be described in practical, measurable terms.[36] Blackness is subjected to a metaphysical judgment that is in a constant state of tension with the state of "race relations" as it actually exists. No matter how intimately entangled the black body is in the lives of White persons, it has no place in an idealized future that is anchored in the aspiration to whiteness. Societal progress is a movement toward a world expunged of blackness, which is why—as Dubois observed—Black people who were deemed a "credit to their race" had to be described as exceptional types who were distanced from the existential problem that blackness posed for White society.[37]

This process, whereby some Black people are provisionally exempted from the excesses of antiblack racism, underscores our earlier observations about the unsettling effect that (anti)blackness can have on gender roles. The Black person who is deemed a "credit to their race" is granted some measure of social status in the eyes of White person. In these assessments there is an objectifying gaze at work that is unique to the terrors of (anti)blackness, but which goes beyond the mere scrutiny of the body.[38] A black body that, under different conditions, could be radically excluded and disposed of, and ultimately killed, is treated—within certain limited set of social parameters—as if they are the legitimate bearers of an occupational status (whether a teacher, a lawyer, a domestic worker, or a groundskeeper), a political status (a citizen), or a socioeconomic status (as middle class, working class, or even upper middle class). Black embodiment is further interwoven with gender through the attribution of certain bodies as morally upright and bodily pure through linkages between color, body size, and Western beauty.[39] The attribution of these qualities to the black body—these qualities of personhood—also allow it to be inducted into the field of "normal" gender roles (the dutiful mother, the respected family patriarch, the bachelor or debutante). Put another way, these people are "credits to their race" only insofar as they model white, middle-class norms of social conduct and comportment for other, less enlightened members of their race. And the special treatment according to these creditable people also, effectively, legitimizes the radical exclusion of the larger majority of blacks who do not meet this standard.

We want to caution the reader that we are describing a cultural subtext for Dubois's writing that does not hold true today, the same way it did when he put his thoughts to paper in the early 1900s. We understand that Blackness is an historically mutable field of symbolic meanings that has been contested and negotiated over time, even as the logics of antiblack racism remain.

It also bears noting that critical analyses of (anti)Blackness have called attention to these mutable qualities, perhaps the best example being Hartman's writing on black fungibility. Hartman uses the concept of fungibility to reflect on the existential condition of radical otherness that haunts these fragile constructions of black personhood.[40] According to Hartman, the fungible body is a radically depersonalized object that can be used for any variety of purposes—as a commodity, as an instrument of physical or emotional labor, or a canvas for sadomasochistic desires. These bodies can be useful or desirable, but they have no meaning intrinsic to themselves, and they pose a "problem" the moment they begin to behave in ways that complicate the ontological primacy of the persons whose lives (and societies) they are being used to enhance.

The puzzling thing about this situation, which makes antiblack racism so difficult to diagnose, is that blackness takes on the quality of a thing that "is not"—a thing that is being perpetually erased, in concept or person, by a tactic that rarely addresses its target by name. Laws that target Black populations can be informed by quasi-scientific treatises on black inferiority that are not directly named by the laws themselves.[41] Extralegal measures can be used to exclude and control black bodies that do not show up in the public record, and if a record is made, it can be retroactively expunged to suit the sensibilities of the times.[42] But these maneuvers do not eliminate the black presence from day-to-day social relations. Black people appear "everywhere" despite being excluded. In the next section we elaborate further on this strange relationship between blackness and White society with some examples from the history of U.S. immigration law.

Seditious Aliens and Slave Rebellions

In the summer of 1798, a French vessel entered the Delaware Bay containing a crew that included a number of men who were identified by the American colonists as "mulattos," as well as other people of African descent.[43] Prior to this incident there had been mounting hostilities between France and the recently established U.S. government, which mainly involved altercations at sea.[44] Concerns about the suspicious vessel had more to do with its ties to the French government than with the racial composition of its crew. But there were also concerns that these incursions by the French might encourage thousands of Black troops from nearby Haiti to invade the United States and attempt to foment a revolution among the U.S. slave population.[45] Although these fears were a little farfetched, the Haitian revolution, which was underway at the time, provided incontrovertible proof that it was possible for enslaved populations to launch a self-organized military campaign. U.S. elites also were aware that there was support for the revolution among the Black enslaved population and that some slaves had even managed to escape to Haiti to fight in the war.[46]

Suffice it to say, the U.S. government was on edge about the possibility of insurrection from a variety of sources. The appearance of the French vessel was the tipping point that has been credited with spurring President John Adams to enact the first of several Alien and Sedition Acts.[47] These acts became infamous for being the U.S. government's first crackdown on civil liberties and immigrant rights, which included an expansion of the government's deportation powers.[48]

The Alien and Sedition Acts also became a staging ground for the first major debate in U.S. history over national security versus civil liberties.[49] President Adams stood for the Federalist position, in favor of national security and a strong centralized government. The primary spokesperson for the civil liberties position was Thomas Jefferson, who was affiliated with the Democratic-Republican Party and was serving as Adams's vice president at the time.[50]

Jefferson was a slave owner. He was also an antislavery moralist, meaning that he was critical of the institution of slavery but was opposed to "radical" proposals for its abolition.[51] Like many U.S. slaveholders, he held to a racist double standard, being an avid supporter of the French Revolution and an equally avid opponent of the Haitian revolutionary cause.[52]

Several years later, Jefferson used popular resentment about the government crackdown on civil liberties as the rallying cry for his presidential campaign. Jefferson won the election and established a Democratic-Republican dynasty that controlled the Executive Office for the next three decades. It also bears noting that Jefferson's electoral victory was aided by the "votes" of enslaved Black people, votes that, according to the laws of the time, were his to cast as suited his interests—along with the interests of all the other slave owners who supported his presidency. These votes were tallied in such a way that every three "slave votes" counted as one vote.[53]

Jefferson's distaste for the deportation powers that were expanded by the Alien and Sedition Acts was rooted in another double standard. What Jefferson mainly opposed was the emergence of a deportation apparatus that would become a permanent feature of a centralized government. But he was not opposed, in principle, to deportation, and privately he endorsed organized schemes that were geared toward the mass removal of Black people from the United States. The American Colonization Society (ACS) was the main vehicle for this agenda, which used the language of "voluntary deportation" and "mass deportation" to describe its plans for creating utopian colonies in the Caribbean or Africa, to which Blacks could be transported in order to form their own self-governing societies.[54] Although these deportation proposals were framed as being in the best interests of the U.S. Black population, they never garnered the support of the Black masses, and historians who have studied the ACS have concluded that the common thread that bound the society's politically diverse membership was its investment in white supremacy.[55] Jefferson was a founding member of the ACS, and the two Democratic-Republican presidents who succeeded him also served as presidents of the ACS.[56]

The details we have just shared draw attention to an antiblack subtext that usually is left out of the story of the Alien and Sedition Acts. When these acts are referenced today, it is usually to recycle a narrative that is not very different from the civil liberties arguments that Jefferson used to rail against the Federalist government in his 1800 election campaign.[57] The social ills of xenophobia and intolerance are pinned on the Federalist position, which initiated the crackdown on immigrant rights. Meanwhile, the antiblack racism that was latent to the pro-immigrant position is concealed by a veil of silence.[58]

This silence is further complicated by the topsy-turvy relationship between the political issues that were at stake in the national security versus civil liberties debate, and the question of Black freedom. For example, although Jefferson was critical of the government's deportation powers, he was not an ally of the Black crew on the French vessel that triggered the expansion of these powers, and he would never have tolerated the extension of civil liberties or U.S. citizenship to these men. And although Adams was swift to respond to the threat of insurrection posed by this vessel containing these "French Blacks," he was not as intransigently opposed to the Black freedom movement as was Jefferson. Like Jefferson, Adams was an antislavery moralist, but unlike Jefferson he did not hold slaves and he was opposed to the expansion of slavery in the United States.[59] During his presidential term, Adams also sent U.S. war vessels to defend the newly formed Haitian Republic from attacks by the French and the British.[60] Adams's interest in keeping a liberated Haiti from falling into the hands of European powers may have been primarily strategic, but whatever the reason, he ended up being a better ally of Haitian democracy than Jefferson.

Instead of concluding that race was irrelevant to all of these maneuvers, it would be more accurate to say that the interests of Black people were irrelevant to the debate over civil liberties versus national security, and that this irrelevance was part and parcel of the dehumanization that typifies antiblack racism. The Black population was going to be subject to terror and displacement within the territory of the United States and be threatened with expulsion from the United States, regardless of how this debate was resolved. Black people factored into the debate only by way of the "slave votes" that were conscripted by their owners to defend a system of rights from which they were excluded. This is a practical example of what Black studies scholars mean when they write about the fungibility and deontological status of blackness.

Black Mobility as a Reckoning and Resistance

We have just described a problem that calls attention to the antiblack common sense that has kept the question of Black freedom separate from that of immigrant rights. These antiblack sentiments also help to explain why Black populations have, historically, been singled out for exclusions and controls that have not been applied to (nonblack) immigrants. But we also want to emphasize that Black populations have been targeted by these controls precisely because they have been persistently mobile, and that this mobility can be viewed both in light of, and despite, the inexplicably cruel system of forced removal that was the transatlantic slave trade.

Fugitive Slave Acts and laws targeting free Blacks are testament to the persistence of Black mobilities in the antebellum era.[61] After the abolishment of slavery in the Americas, exslaves and their descendants migrated throughout the United States, the Caribbean, and other parts of the Americas seeking better fortunes and refuge and creating new communities.[62] Most currents of radical Black politics—including Pan-Africanism, Black Marxism, and other currents of Black postcolonial and anticolonial thought—owe their development to the migrations of Black intellectuals, especially from the Caribbean.[63] Many of the Black intellectuals who challenged White Europeans to confront their colonial histories were also migrants.[64]

The Black experience has to be viewed in light of these interwoven histories of free and forced movement, which is also why Black mobility should be understood as a site of reckoning and resistance. Although Black mobility originates under a regimen of constant surveillance, the historical record shows that Black people thwarted attempts to control their movements at every turn. In the antebellum era, Black people used unauthorized movements as a way to resist enslavement, and in the postbellum era they engaged in similar movements to flee the Jim Crow South and forge transnational alliances.[65] This transgressive history of mobility raised issues, many centuries ago, that prefigure the contemporary movement for open borders but that also raise deeper questions about the racial organization of social life.

Immigrant rights coalitions have attempted to make amends for their silence about this history. Efforts have been made to include the Black immigrant experience, in a more deliberate way, in reports on the struggles of undocumented migrants and asylum seekers, and to call attention to migration and adjustment challenges that are experienced by Black people.[66] Well-meaning as they may be, these inclusive overtures do not interrogate the antiblack beginnings of the U.S. immigration regime. We insist, on the other hand, that it is more important to consider how antiblackness can be used to explain the present-day migration regime, rather than figuring out how to better include Black people in discourses on immigration that take the nonblack migrant as their default starting point.

Rethinking Sovereignty, Borders, and Displacement through Antiblackness

The agonies of Black mobility are also reflected in the complicated relationship between blackness, borders, and displacement. Many voices in the contemporary immigrant rights movement have called for the abolition of borders, borrowing from the language that is famously associated with the nineteenth-century movement to end slavery and, more recently, with the movement for prison abolition.[67] This is yet another example of an overture that posits an analogous relationship between the cause of immigrant rights and Black freedom, but without coming to terms with the qualities that are most singular to the Black condition.

If you accept that the transatlantic slave trade is a defining feature of the Black experience in the West, it should be apparent why the call for open borders (or border abolition) does not get to the bottom of Black oppression. The enslaved Africans' main problem was not that the borders of the Western world were not sufficiently "open" to them. Their problem is that they were ripped out of their home cultures and forcibly transported to another world, where they were incorporated into the total institution of chattel slavery. Furthermore, when it came to the slave trade, the U.S. government's attempts at border control were a benign intervention—at least, that is, from an antislavery perspective—since the goal of these operations was to put an end to the international transport and sale of enslaved people.[68]

After slavery in the United States was abolished, Black people relied on migration as a survival strategy. Black Americans moved north in the Great Migration. Black Caribbean people moved within and outside the Americas.[69] The transnational networks established by these migrations laid the foundations for the remittances that most nations in the global South, including most predominantly Black nations, rely on to keep their economies afloat.[70] As is the case for many aspects of the contemporary migration regime, these remittances are necessary in order for people to survive the ravages of global capitalism, but they also replicate the disparities in economic and political power that are intrinsic to this system.

Moreover, as the United States expanded its own borders westward, even to territories designated by the state as "free" of slavery, free Black Americans were barred from the opportunity that was envisioned by white settlers.[71] In this way, American migratory regimes structured the idea of movement around the exclusion of Black bodies.

David Bacon addresses a comparable problem when he writes about the right to stay home. Bacon came up with this phrase to describe the complaints raised by labor union activists in Latin America who were trying to improve the quality of life in their home communities.[72] These activists were struggling to improve wages and worker rights and government investment in the grassroots economy and local infrastructure, among other issues, so that their community members did not feel that migration was their only choice for a better life. Underlying these efforts is the understanding that, in order for migration to be a decision, the right not to migrate must also be a valid option. People may decide to migrate after carefully weighing the costs and benefits of the decision, but it is a very different thing to migrate because you feel that staying where you are is not an option. When people migrate under these conditions, it becomes increasingly difficult to tell the difference between a migrant and a displaced person. If we focus our attention only on the right to migrate, we normalize the terrifying experience of displacement as a driving force of contemporary migration.

There is the problem of wealthy nations not being as receptive to displaced populations as they should be and could be. This is the problem of the closed border. There is the problem of expulsion, which can be described as a secondary displacement that leads the migrant or the refugee to be removed after they have entered. But there is also the problem of primary displacement, which requires us to face up to the concatenation of social, political, and economic forces that causes people to be uprooted from their homelands in the first place. The Black experience of forced migration focuses attention on this problem.

Even when people migrate under the most desperate of conditions there is a hope, no matter how slim, that things will be better in the new land. The same cannot be said of the transatlantic slave trade. The self-serving narratives of the slaving classes notwithstanding,[73] it is reasonable to conclude that the vast majority of Africans who were sold into slavery would have lived a happier life had they never been violently removed from their homelands and branded as "black slaves" in the New World. There is now a considerable body of evidence showing that many African cultures were at a level of social, cultural, and technological development comparable to that of Europe prior to the establishment of the transatlantic slave trade.[74] If Europeans had not become involved in the capture and commodification of African bodies for forced labor in their colonies, it is likely that African cultures would have continued to develop in ways that were suitable to their own needs and with much less suffering than was caused by the slave trade and the institutions that were designed to "manage" black populations after emancipation. None of this can be conclusively proven, of course. But neither can it be proven that the world system, which evolved out of Europe's colonial exploits, was the best possible developmental trajectory for the entire human species. All of these propositions raise questions about the metanarratives that have made migration, modernization, and socioeconomic progress isomorphic to one another.

Perhaps the most important thing a Black perspective offers the field of migration studies is a healthy agnostic attitude toward the secular mythology that insists that migration is necessarily a good thing for the people doing the migrating. The argument for open borders lends itself to a romanticized idea of the Western industrialized economy as the shining city on the hill— the apex of modern development. Although we agree that the borders of the global North are excessively restrictive, the concern for border abolition overwrites other critical interventions that have called attention to the way the global South has been coercively integrated into the modern world order, which is why we must pay heed to scholars and activists who have insisted on the need for a "delinking" that operates at the level of policy, politics, and orders of knowledge.[75] If the open borders argument does not substantively engage this line of critique, it risks devolving into the desperate plea, "Please let us in!"

The Black freedom struggle, on the other hand, is animated by a very different story, of a people who were taken by force to the city on the hill, whose labor made it shine so attractively for the immigrants who wanted to be let in, and who were thrust into a condition of chronic underemployment and controlled by a complex web of surveillance and carceral practices when they could no longer be used as slave labor. When the voices of this freedom struggle call for abolition, they are not saying "Please let us in," they are demanding to be let go.

If we are going to read antiblack racism into the study of modern migration, we have to come to terms with the genealogical distinction between these two histories of struggle. Even though there are such people as Black immigrants, the Black freedom struggle cannot be seamlessly integrated into the struggle for open borders. There are points of tension to wrestle with that are comparable to the agonistic relationship between blackness and immigrant subjectivity. But this is also why the black condition offers an important vantage point for reconceiving borders and bordering practices. We need to reframe the right to cross borders and the right to stay put within the context of Black mobility. Going a step further, we must also situate borders, border studies, and bordering practices within the context of antiblackness.

There are some important parallels between this line of critique and critical epistemologies that have been innovated by feminist scholars. Dorothy Smith, for example, has explained how women's marginality has been normalized by systems of knowledge that are placeless, abstract, and universal.[76] She has argued that this Archimedean vantage point, which aims to survey all things from a completely detached intellectual perspective, needs to be replaced by experiential knowledges that account for the social location and the knower (and as other theorists have argued, more forcefully, you cannot account for social location without also considering the social-learned coding of the body). Black, Latinx, Asian, Queer, and Indigenous feminist scholars have advanced similar critical epistemologies that interrogate canonical knowledge from different social and experiential vantage points.[77] The idea of a single, authoritative claim on the truth is replaced by a relational dialogue between multiple perspectives that "see things differently" due to the place they occupy in an unequal field of power relations. Intersectionality theory epitomizes this multivalent and relational take on knowledge creation, though many of its precursors can be traced to second-wave feminist theory, critical race theory, and critical legal studies.[78]

One lesson that this critical literature offers is a sensitivity to the mutable and relational qualities of borders. Within the field of border studies, it is already well accepted that borders are not static things, but assemblages of practices that are always being tested and renegotiated.[79] Feminist, queer, and postcolonial perspectives on the border also underscore the social and embodied nature of borders and bordering practices.[80] It is not simply that different kinds of people have different experiences crossing the border. The very composition and enforcement of the border can change radically, depending on the kinds of bodies that approach it. For some bodies, the border checkpoint is just a momentary inconvenience in an otherwise unimpeded trajectory of movement. But for other bodies, the border, and the enforcement powers that go along with it, is an omnipresent reality, even after entering the nation-state. This is not just a question of the policing of the geopolitical borders. It also has to do with the informal ways that institutions and private individuals use gendered and racialized norms to police the borders of their networks, which can dovetail, in unexpected ways, with the policing of geopolitical borders.

These lines of inquiry anticipate many of the changes that are already unfolding in the field of border studies (and can also be credited with influencing some of these changes). For example, border studies scholars are giving more consideration to the way that borders are socially constructed and used not just to demarcate space and place but also to divide and define people, culture, beliefs, and languages.[81] Border studies, as an interdisciplinary field, has also taken such studies a step further and insightfully expanded to examine the ways in which "the *process* of bordering, rather than the border line per se . . . has universal significance in the ordering of society [our emphasis]."[82] As border studies scholars and others insist, the making and maintenance of borders involve the act of creating a difference in both institutional and everyday interactive spaces, not just physical lines of division. Hence, borders function not just as a barrier between inside and outside, but also, more critically, as a process and practice that both defines and divides racialized, gendered, and classed bodies as native/foreign, legal/illegal, or citizen/noncitizen.[83] We believe that this concept can and should be informed by the ways in which the figure of Blackness has been used as both a line of demarcation and a site of exclusion.

Bordering practices can be enacted through the state, the law, everyday interactions, and on the body. Scholars have introduced the concept of bordering practices to more critically delineate the ways in which the boundaries of the nation-state and of social belonging are themselves performative acts implemented at multiple levels of society.[84] The state serves the function of erecting the border, either through the construction of a "wall" or through various systems of filtering entrants, such as visas, citizenship status, and border patrols.

However, state border practices exist not just at its edges of nations but also within them, thus leading to a proliferation of borders and other lines of division.[85] Christensen and Albrecht, for example, point to how "the police engage in multiple practices of bordering that constitute, sustain and modify borders."[86] They insist that policing is a form of border work, particularly in urban centers where migrants and refugees often reside. Urban centers, which are depicted as sites of chaos, disorder, and danger, also become sites of control where police are then encouraged to "bring order." By associating certain spaces as dangerous or in need of control, police and other actors of the state erect borders and mark them as sites of danger and chaos. They also mark those who live within them and cross them as dangerous. Walters, for example, points out that "Borders operate like filters or gateways . . . differentiating the good and the bad, the useful and the dangerous, the licit and the illicit . . . immobilizing and removing the risky elements so as to speed the circulation of the rest."[87] Border-making thus involves the sorting of people and spaces into safe/unsafe, welcome/unwelcome, and legal/illegal.

With the increasing securitization of borders in the post-9/11 era, we have seen the ways in which migrants, refugees, and other movements have become hypercriminalized and surveilled. The U.S.-Mexico border and the waters and lands bordering the EU offer clear examples of the ways in which borders have been sites of danger and violence, as those who cross are depicted as so-called invaders and are negatively racialized as outside threats to the national body. It is important to recognize the ways in which certain kinds of crossing are read through race—where nonwhite crossers are excluded, or at best, valued for their labor and not their citizenship. Further, in this volume, P. Khalil Saucier and Tryon P. Woods's work is instructive in revealing how anti-Blackness pervades both the rhetoric surrounding the border and also the ways in which bordering practices themselves emerge from fears surrounding the specter of the Black body.

Explicating and Interrogating the Borders of (Anti-)Blackness

Border practices are informed not just by race but also by histories of anti-Blackness that delineate certain bodies as fully excluded due to their proximity to Blackness. Bordering practices frequently emerge through the construction of racialized boundaries that determine citizenship, legality, and inclusion. We suggest that Blackness itself serves as a boundary or "border" in two ways. First, as we detailed earlier, Black mobility has itself been perceived as a threat or challenge to the border by virtue of its depiction as a harbinger of chaos and the lack of civilization into an otherwise orderly and civilized society within the nation-state. We see such rhetoric in the fear of African and Muslim migrants who are presently seeking entry into Europe. In the United States, since the nation's early days there has been a fear of Black entry. We discussed, for example, the fear of revolutionary Blacks from the Caribbean, whose actions toward freedom were seen as a threat to U.S/ nation-building and laid the groundwork for the Alien and Sedition Acts. Alongside a fear of Black migration outside the border, there remains a continued unease with the African American subject within the border, whose presence and experiences within the United States have complicated the nation's origin story as a homogenous, racially white democratic republic. We also want to emphasize that antiblack exclusions can be animated by anxieties about sexuality and gender relations. For much of U.S. history, for example, antiblack violence was legitimized in the name of defending white women and the white family norms.[88] Such violence continues to be fueled by anxieties about black fertility and promiscuity (which parallel contemporary fears about Latinx population growth, Latina fertility in particular, which resonates with more recent right-wing discourses on "replacement theory" and "anchor babies").[89]

Second, Blackness itself (or the proximity to it) also functions as a racial border to police other racialized groups by offering a potential pathway to full inclusion. Unlike Black migrants, nonwhite migrants are provided some degree of inclusion into their receiving nations so long as they either remain unwilling to "cross over" into Blackness or are dissuaded from doing so. We can see, for example, how Blackness has served as a bordering practice or dividing line that has determined citizenship (and the ability to exercise it) in the United States. If, as Harris insisted, whiteness was a form of property and citizenship,[90] Blackness can then be read as a lack of both. The so-called one-drop rule, for example, can be read as an emphatically Black bordering practice that laid the foundations on which freedom, mobility, and citizenship in the United States relies. To determine Blackness, and who counts within it, then, is to create a border between whether one has the ability to gain and enjoy citizenship and whether one will be counted as human or subhuman.

Blackness has historically served as a racialized bordering practice that shapes the degree to which migrants—white and nonwhite—can gain inclusion. As race and immigration scholars have pointed out, the traditional assimilation framework, which measures the degree of migrant inclusion, is predicated on measuring a migrant community's racial and socioeconomic distance from Blackness.[91] As these scholars argue, phrases such as "downward assimilation" imply a descent into racialized and classed Blackness and, through such phrasing, deemphasize the sway that race and anti-Blackness continues to have on inclusion. Further, migrants themselves recognize this logic.

Bashi Treitler,[92] for example, describes how migrant ethnic groups partake in "successful" and "unsuccessful" "ethnic projects" in order to fit within or gain positive entry into the racial hierarchy of the United States. As she points out, delegation into Black identity is perceived as a downgrade on the racial hierarchy and may result in partial or full exclusion. As a result, nonwhite migrants' claim to ethnic difference can, within the logic of racialized borders, function as a way to distinguish oneself from Blackness and thus allow for the possibility of upward mobility. The unwritten rule of racial inclusion thus states that nonwhite migrants can hope for at least partial exclusion so long as they do not descend into—or cross the border of—Blackness. For migrants who have gained entry into whiteness, the price, as scholars have pointed out, has been the renouncement of Blackness itself and, in some instances, the obligation to reinforce the racialized border.[93] Thus, Blackness, through its proximity or mere presence, is itself a racialized border with implications for what constitutes the national body and who can endeavor to gain entry into it. As the authors of this volume point out, in various ways, anti-Blackness is not just another dimension of the way mobility and borders are racialized. In fact, Blackness serves as a key starting point for talking about what constitutes borders and inclusion/exclusion.

(Anti)blackness and Migration: Connecting the Dots

Our opening discussion has called attention to the challenges that the Black experience poses for migration studies. Each of the contributions to this book takes up this challenge, using an analysis of (anti)blackness to rethink the way we understand the border, immigrant identity, barriers to integration, and the dynamics of migrant exclusion, to name just a few examples. Before we move on to a summary of the book's contents, we think it important to elaborate a little further on how we understand "blackness" and "antiblackness."

First, the reader has probably noticed that *blackness* and *antiblackness* always appear in lowercase letters in our writing and that *Black* (as well as *White* and *Indigenous*) are written as proper nouns, with the first letter of each world capitalized. We are using these lower- and uppercase references to call attention to the difference between blackness as a depersonalizing condition created by antiblack racism (which eviscerates subjectivity) and blackness as a collective force that uses blackness as an experiential starting point for social identities and social processes, which are used by people who identify as "Black" to create life worlds that, by necessity, have to push back against antiblack racism. In a similar vein, *whiteness* and *indigeneity* are written in lowercase letters (as are *immigrant/migrant* and so forth) because they describe a diffuse social condition or category, and are written as proper nouns when they reference a more clearly defined subjectivity or collective actor. It might be overly simplistic to read the lowercase letterings as describing a structural condition and the uppercase letterings as describing an agency, though this dichotomy may provide a helpful starting point for readers familiar with social science theory.

It bears emphasizing, however, that the lower- and uppercase letterings carry a special meaning when it comes to *Black* and *blackness*. The relationship between (anti)blackness and the Black experience is not quite the same as the structure/agency dichotomy, as it has been discussed by many sociologists, who treat these concepts as qualitatively distinct but reflexively related phenomena. *Black* and *(anti)blackness*, on the other hand, are not just different features of a social landscape—they describe antithetical social realities that are premised on the elimination of the Other. Antiblackness desires a violence against the black body that voids any possibility of agency. Conversely, it is not possible to imagine or inhabit a Black identity without being prepared to inveigh against antiblack desire, in all of its structural and sentimental permutations.

Having acknowledged this much, we left it up to each contributor to decide how to reference this distinction between blackness and Black subjectivity in their own work. Consequently, there is some variation across the chapters in when upper- and lowercase lettering is used, but we think that the more important point is that these letterings signal the difference between racialization as a desubjectivizing condition and an attempt to reclaim an agency in the face of these racist maneuverings. It also bears noting that while *blackness* and *antiblackness* are usually written in lowercase letters, they refer to relatively different phenomena. In this case, there is more of a reflexive and interpenetrated relationship, with *antiblackness* describing the racist sentiments, imaginaries, and ideologies that produce the ocular phenomenon of "blackness" as a badge of inferiority. The resulting condition, of blackness, is experienced by the people with bodies that are labeled as "black" by the racist. Acceptance of one's blackness, as it has been defined by the racist, requires some degree of participation in the replication of antiblack desire, but it is not a sufficient "cause," in of itself, of the forces that propel antiblack racism. Nevertheless, antiblack desire, and the black/nonblack binaries it constructs (which produce blackness as the sign of the fungible, desubjectivized other) can both be distinguished from the collective agencies that we reference through our uppercase letterings for Black mobility, the Black experience, and so forth.

All of this goes to underscore that we have a rigorous conceptualization of the difference between Black subjectivity and (anti)blackness, but we also understand that they are expansive and multifarious concepts that can take on different meanings across temporal-spatial contexts. Each of the authors in this volume treats blackness differently and elucidates how antiblackness emerges in various forms across geographies, timelines, cultures, generations, experiences, and other contexts. The variation of themes elaborated on by the authors also emphasizes the ever-changing categories of blackness and consequent manifestations of antiblackness. At times, treatments of antiblackness may parallel other versions of racialized Otherness or vary from the frameworks or meanings adopted by other chapters in the volume, just as antiblackness co-constructs with the contexts it animates. Still, as we have described here, blackness and antiblackness can be analytically useful to understanding how race and racisms inform mobility, citizenship, sovereignty, borders, and overarching dichotomies of belonging/nonbelonging.

Our treatment of Black subjectivity and antiblackness is also informed by many currents of critical theory, including Black feminist theory, critical race theory, postcolonial studies, and critical currents of migration and refugee studies. It bears noting, however, that Afropessimism has played an especially important role in catalyzing many of the arguments that we have used to frame the book and that are pursued in most of its chapters.

The opening discussion introduced the reader to a number of arguments that have been advanced by Afropessimist scholars, including the thesis on black fungibility and the deontological status of blackness in relation to the modern human, understanding the black/nonblack binary as foundational to the modern racial order, and understanding the transatlantic slave trade as the structural and material precursor to the black/nonblack binary and the blueprint for the regimens of power that have been imposed on black populations since the end of chattel slavery. Many of the scholars we have cited in these opening pages, such as Frank Wilderson, Saidiya Hartman, Calvin Warren, and Jared Sexton, have made important contributions to Afropessimist theory. Other scholars whose work we have discussed in some depth, such as Aldon Morris and Gayatri Spivak, are not Afropessimists though they have produced analyses that invite a dialogue with arguments from Afropessimist theory. Fred Moten, who is the first scholar we mentioned by name, can also be counted in this group, though he has had a rather complex and contentious relationship to Afropessimist theory.

Our use of upper- and lowercase letterings for *Black* and *(anti)blackness* can also be read as an oblique reference to the antagonisms that have been stirred up by Afropessimist theory. From an Afropessimist perspective, blackness can only be understood as a condition of ontological degradation. A meaningful (B/b)lack politics and subjectivity would spell the end of the modern world order as we know it. When we use uppercase lettering for *Black mobility*, *Black migration*, and so forth, we are acknowledging, on the other hand, that there can be such a thing as Black agency in an antiblack world. We want to avoid a carelessly optimistic analysis, which, if left to its own devices, leads down the road of color-blind racism—insisting that we are living in an era in which there no longer any significant structural impediments to Black (social) mobility. But we also think it is important to underline another self-evident fact: that despite seemingly insurmountable odds, Black people have found ways to move of their own accord and to use their mobility as an act of resistance. In a similar vein, Black people are constantly creating and renaming their social identities, launching social movements, and generating knowledge about their experience of race (this book being one such example). Black people have been historically excluded from the modern migration regime, but there is still such a thing as "Black migration" and there are a great many Black people whose experience of blackness has been mediated through their immigrant identities.

Like the Black experience itself, the book's contents express the uneasy tension between domination and resistance without resolving it, and we treat Afropessimism in a similar manner. We do not read Afropessimism to mean that black people are unable to experience joy, or that the struggle for Black freedom is a hopeless cause, but we do accept the challenge that Afropessimism poses to the field of migration studies.

The book begins with a pair of chapters that offer a metatheoretical analysis of scholarship that either misses or obfuscates the role of antiblackness in immigration perspectives. In Chapter 1, Saucier and Woods interrogate the freedom of movement perspective by pointing out the ways in which it ignores the Black experience of im/mobility and how antiblackness, or social death, underlies the rejection and Othering of migrants and refugees. In Chapter 2, Philip Kretsedemas puts Afropessimist theory in dialogue with Gilles Deleuze and Félix Guattari's writing on nomadism to explain how Black mobility can be distinguished from other forms of movement, including that of the migrant and the colonial settler, and also of the transgressive mobilities of Indigenous populations.

The next two chapters take a closer look at the contemporary black migrant experience and the ways that antiblackness figures in immigration policy and scholarship. In Chapter 3, Jamella N. Gow studies the experience of Haitian migrants in south Florida and interweaves Black diaspora and Africana studies to uncover how antiblackness and its gendered dimensions inform immigration policy toward Haitians and how Haitian migrants form political identities and community in the diaspora. In Chapter 4, Hyacinth Udah examines antiblack racism in Australia, using a critical race theory perspective to explain how Australian immigration law perpetuates institutional racism and everyday racism in ways that permeate the lives of African migrants.

The final two chapters examine power dynamics and forms of embodiment and racialization that are singular to the experience of Black female migrants. Both chapters engage this topic through the lens of critical literature studies, using a theoretical framework that is defined by a dialogue between Black feminism and Afropessimism. In Chapter 5, Maya Hislop draws parallels between the ways in which Guinean Nafissatou Diallo and Nigerian Ifemelu (the protagonist of Chimamanda Ngozi Adichie's *Americanah*) each utilize media to navigate antiblack and sexist tropes alongside their immigrant status to testify about or process sexual trauma. In Chapter 6, Paula von Gleich, like Hislop, examines another cultural work—in this case, Yaa Gyasi's *Homegoing*. She explores how, through the lens of Afropessimism and Saidiya Hartman's concept of "fugitive legacy," the legacy of slavery and gendered antiblackness inform the shared genealogies of African Americans and Black Americans.

What unites these chapters are key common themes: the long reach of the transatlantic slave trade into the lives and movement of Black people; the ways in which concepts such as immigration, citizenship, identity, belonging, and mobility are informed by and at times grounded in antiblackness; and how antiblackness must be intersected with other dimensions of difference such as sexism and xenophobia. In these chapters, the authors define *antiblackness* through a variety of lenses and explore the Black experience in ways that encompass multiple Black populations across nationalities. However, each chapter begins with the premise that any study of mobility and inclusion/exclusion must acknowledge the legacies of blackness in shaping those categories of both movement and difference.

NOTES

1. Fred Moten, "Blackness and Nothingness," *The South Atlantic Quarterly* 112, no. 4 (2013): 737–780.

2. Gayatri Spivak, *A Critique of Postcolonial Reason: Toward a History of the Vanishing Present* (Cambridge, MA: Harvard University Press, 1999). Also see Lucy Mablin and Joe Turner, *Migration Studies and Colonialism* (Cambridge: Polity Press, 2021), 2–3.

3. Mablin and Turner, *Migration Studies and Colonialism*, 26–48.

4. Cynthia Gorman, "Feminist Legal Archeology, Domestic Violence and the Raced-Gendered Juridical Boundaries of U.S. Asylum Law," *Environment and Planning A: Economy and Space* 51, no. 5 (2018): 1–18; Connie Oxford, "Protectors and Victims in the Gender Regime of Asylum," *NWSA Journal* 17 (2005): 18–38; Kwok Pui-Lan, "Unbinding Our Feet: Saving Brown Women and Feminist Religious Discourse," in *Postcolonialism, Feminism & Religious Discourse*, ed. Laura E. Donaldson and Kwok Pui-Lan (New York: Routledge, 2002), 62–81.

5. Nira Yuval-Davis, "Gender and Nation," *Ethnic and Racial Studies* 16, no. 4 (1993): 621–632; Patricia Hill Collins, "It's All in the Family: Intersections of Gender, Race, and Nation," *Hypatia* 13, no. 3 (1998): 62–82.

6. Grace Kyungwon Hong, "Existentially Surplus: Women of Color Feminism and the New Crises of Capitalism," *GLQ: A Journal of Lesbian and Gay Studies* 18, no. 1 (2011): 87–106.

7. Gayatri C. Spivak, "Can the Subaltern Speak?" in *Can the Subaltern Speak? Reflections on the History of an Idea* (New York: Columbia University Press, 2010).

8. Cedric J. Robinson, *Forgeries of Memory and Meaning: Blacks & the Regimes of Race in American Theater & Film before World War II* (Chapel Hill: University of North Carolina Press, 2007).

9. Elizabeth Bernstein, "Militarized Humanitarianism Meets Carceral Feminism: The Politics of Sex, Rights, and Freedom in Contemporary Antitrafficking Campaigns," *Signs: Journal of Women in Culture and Society* 36, no. 1 (2010): 45–71; Aparna Polavarapu, "Global Carceral Feminism and Domestic Violence: What the West Can Learn from Reconciliation in Uganda," *Harvard Journal of Law & Gender* 42 (2019): 123.

10. Kelly Oliver, *Carceral Humanitarianism: Logics of Refugee Detention* (Minneapolis: University of Minnesota Press, 2017).

11. Chandra Talpade Mohanty, "Under Western Eyes: Feminist Scholarship and Colonial Discourses," *Boundary 2* 12/13, nos. 3/1 (1984): 333–358.

12. Patricia Hill Collins, *Black Sexual Politics: African Americans, Gender, and the New Racism*, (New York: Routledge, 2004); Dorothy Roberts, *Killing the Black Body: Race, Reproduction, and the Meaning of Liberty* (New York: Vintage Books, 1999).

13. Angela Y. Davis, *Women, Race, and Class* (New York: Random House, 1981); Esther Wangari, "Reproductive Technologies: A Third World Feminist Perspective," in *Feminist Post-Development Thought*, ed. Kriemild Saunders (London: Zed Press, 2002), 298–312.

14. Grace Chang, *Disposable Domestics: Immigrant Women Workers in the Global Economy* (Chicago: Haymarket Books, 2016), 33.

15. Pierrette Hondagneu-Sotelo, "New Directions in Gender and Immigration Research," in *The Routledge International Handbook of Migration Studies*, ed. Steve Gold and Stephanie Nawyn (New York: Routledge, 2013), 180–188; Silvia Pedraza, "Women

and Migration: The Social Consequences of Gender," *Annual Review of Sociology* 17 (1991): 303–325.

16. Tanya Golash-Boza and Pierrette Hondagneu-Sotelo, "Latino Immigrant Men and the Deportation Crisis: A Gendered Racial Removal Program," *Latino Studies* 11, no. 3 (2013): 271–292.

17. P. Khalil Saucier and Tryon P. Woods, "Introduction: Racial Optimism and the Drag of Thymotics," in *Conceptual Aphasia in Black*, ed. P. Khalil Saucier and Tryon P. Woods (Lanham, MD: Lexington Press, 2016), 1–34; Jared Sexton, "Ante-anti-blackness: Afterthoughts," *Lateral* 1 (2012), https://csalateral.org/issue/1/ante-anti-blackness-after thoughts-sexton/.

18. Avtar Brah and Ann Phoenix, "Ain't I A Woman? Revisiting Intersectionality," *Journal of International Women's Studies* 5, no. 3 (2004): 75–86.

19. Saidiya Hartman, *Scenes of Subjection: Terror, Slavery, and Self-Making in Nine-teenth-Century America* (New York: Oxford University Press, 2007), 17–48.

20. Exemplified by the racist stereotypes of antebellum-era "Sambos" and "Mammies." Leigh-Anne Francis, "Playing the "Lady Sambo": Poor Black Women's Legal Strategies in the Post–Civil War South's Civil Courts," *Meridians* 19, no. 2 (2020): 250–270; Arthur Kinney, "Faulkner and Racial Mythology," *Connotations* 5, no. 2–3 (1995): 259–276.

21. Hartman, *Scenes of Subjection*, 17–48.

22. Angela Davis, "Reflections on the Black Women's Role in the Community of Slaves," *Massachusetts Review* 13, no. 1/2, Winter–Spring (1972): 81–100 at 89.

23. Patricia Hill Collins, *Black Feminist Thought: Knowledge, Consciousness, and the Politics of Empowerment* (New York: Routledge, 1991); Combahee River Collective, "A Black Feminist Statement," *Words of Fire: An Anthology of African-American Feminist Thought*, ed. Beverly Guy-Sheftall (New York: The New Press, 1995).

24. Roland Betancourt, "Anti-Blackness and Transphobia Are Older Than We Thought," *Washington Post*, June 16, 2021, https://www.washingtonpost.com/outlook/2021/06/16 /anti-blackness-transphobia-are-older-than-we-thought/; Margaret R. Greer, Walter D. Mignolo, and Maureen Quilligan, eds., *Rereading the Black Legend: The Discourses of Re-ligious and Racial Difference in the Renaissance Empires* (Chicago: University of Chicago Press, 2008).

25. Joy James, "Campaigns against 'Blackness': Criminality, Incivility, and Election to Executive Office," *Critical Sociology* 36, no. 1 (2010): 25–44.

26. Franco Barchiesi, "The Violence of Work: Revisiting South Africa's 'Labour Ques-tion' Through Precarity and Antiblackness," *Journal of Southern African Studies* 42, no. 5 (2016): 875–891; Hanna Garth, "'There Is No Race in Cuba': Level of Culture and the Logics of Transnational Anti-Blackness," *Anthropological Quarterly* 94, no. 3 (2021): 385–410; Antonio Da Silva, Jose Bacelar, and Erika Robb Larkins, "The Bolsonaro Election, Antiblackness, and Changing Race Relations in Brazil," *The Journal of Latin American and Caribbean Anthropology* 24, no. 4 (2019): 893–913.

27. For some examples, see Vijay Prashad, *The Karma of Brown Folk* (Minneapolis: University of Minnesota Press, 2000); Mary Waters, *Black Identities: West Indian Im-migrant Dreams and American Realities* (Cambridge, MA: Harvard University Press, 1999); Tekle Woldemikael, "A Case Study of Race Consciousness Among Haitian Im-migrants," *Journal of Black Studies* 20 (1989): 224–239.

28. Michael Omi and Howard Winant, *Racial Formation in the United States* (New York: Routledge, 1986).

29. Eduardo Bonilla-Silva, *Racism Without Racists: Color-blind Racism and the Persis-tence of Racial Inequality in the United States* (Lanham, MD: Rowman & Littlefield, 2006).

30. John Jackson and Nadine Weidman, *Race, Racism and Science: Social Impact and Interaction* (New Brunswick, NJ: Rutgers University Press, 2005), 105–110, 129–146.

31. Kimberlé Crenshaw, Neil Gotanda, Gary Peller, and Kendall Thomas, eds., *Critical Race Theory: Key Writings that Formed the Movement* (New York: The New Press, 1995).

32. Aldon Morris, *The Scholar Denied: W.E.B. Dubois and the Birth of Modern Sociology* (Berkeley: University of California Press, 2015), 1–14.

33. Jackson and Weidman, *Race, Racism and Science,* 105–120.

34. Morris, *The Scholar Denied*, 119–148.

35. Morris, *The Scholar Denied*, 9.

36. Dubois, *The Souls of Black Folk*, 1–3. Also see Nahum Chandler, *The Problem of the Negro as a Problem for Thought* (New York: Fordham University Press, 2014).

37. Dubois, *The Souls of Black Folk,* 1–2.

38. Which Fanon has famously described: a gaze that undermines the ontological integrity of personhood so that the body of the ex-person become indistinguishable from other malleable, non-human things. Frantz Fanon, *Black Skin, White Masks* (New York: Grove Press, 1952), 3–30.

39. Sabrina Strings, *Fearing the Black Body: The Racial Origins of Fat Phobia* (New York: New York University Press, 2019).

40. Hartman, *Scenes of Subjection.*

41. See Vilna Bashi's account of the antiblack racism, informed by eugenicist ideologies, that was latent to the U.S. immigration laws of the 1920s. Vilna Bashi, "Globalized Anti-Blackness: Transnationalizing Western Immigration Law, Policy, and Practice," *Ethnic and Racial Studies* 27, no. 4 (2004): 584–606 at 590.

42. A good example is the racial covenants that were used, well into the twentieth century, to ensure that white homebuyers would not sell their property to nonwhites and especially to blacks. These covenants were often written into the terms of the lease, but many homebuyers chose to have this language expunged as U.S. public opinion (and the courts) began to challenge the legitimacy of racial segregation. For one account, see Michael Jones-Correa, "The Origins and Diffusion of Racial Restrictive Covenants," *Political Science Quarterly* 115, no. 4 (2000): 541–568.

43. Julius Scott, *The Common Wind: Afro-American Currents in the Age of the Haitian Revolution* (New York: Verso, 2018), 203.

44. Daniel Kanstroom, *Deportation Nation* (Cambridge, MA: Harvard University Press, 2009), 52–53.

45. Kanstroom, *Deportation Nation.*

46. Scott, *The Common Wind*, 30, 58; Gerald Horne, *Confronting Black Jacobins: The United States, The Haitian Revolution, and the Origins of the Dominican Republic* (New York: Monthly Review Press, 2015), 30–53; Leon Pamphile, "The Haitian Response to the John Brown Tragedy," *Journal of Haitian Studies* 12, no. 2 (2006): 135–142.

47. Kanstroom, *Deportation Nation*, 52–55.

48. Kanstroom, *Deportation Nation.*

49. Kanstroom, *Deportation Nation.*

50. Kanstroom, *Deportation Nation.*

51. Fred Kaplan, *Lincoln and the Abolitionists* (New York: HarperCollins, 2017), 157, 280.

52. Horne, *Confronting Black Jacobins*, 30–34, 9–80; Kaplan, *Lincoln and the Abolitionists*, 99–102.

53. Kaplan, *Lincoln and the Abolitionists*, 102–104.

54. Eric Burin, *Slavery and the Peculiar Solution: A History of the American Coloniza-tion Society* (Gainesville: University Press of Florida, 2003); Horne, *Confronting Black Jacobins*, 154; Kanstroom, *Deportation Nation*, 85–86; Kaplan, *Lincoln and the Abolition-ists*, 132–133.

55. Kaplan, *Lincoln and the Abolitionists*, 160.

56. Burin, *Slavery and the Peculiar Solution*, 6–33.

57. Kanstroom, *Deportation Nation*, 63; David Cole, *Enemy Aliens: Double Standards and Constitutional Freedoms in the War on Terrorism* (New York: New Press, 2003), 1–5; Brenda Wineapple, "Our First Authoritarian Crackdown," *The New York Review*, July 2, 2020, https://www.nybooks.com/articles/2020/07/02/alien-sedition-acts-authoritarian-crackdown/.

58. Even when race is raised as a matter of concern, it is connected to the anxieties that presaged the crackdown on immigrant rights and not the racist sentiments of the pro-immigrant faction. See David Cole, *Enemy Aliens: Double Standards and Constitutional Freedoms in the War on Terrorism* (New York: New Press, 2003), 1–5; Kanstroom, *De-portation Nation*, 53. For a rare exception, see Kaplan, *Lincoln and the Abolitionists*, 100–110.

59. Kaplan, *Lincoln and the Abolitionists*, 157, 280.

60. Kaplan, *Lincoln and the Abolitionists*, 138–40.

61. Kanstroom, *Deportation Nation*, 74–83.

62. Elizabeth Thomas-Hope, "Globalization and the Development of a Caribbean Migration Culture," in Mary Chamberlain, ed., *Caribbean Migration: Globalized Identi-ties* (New York: Routledge, 1998); Richard Verdugo, "The Making of the African Amer-ican Population: The Economic Status of the Ex-Slave and Freedmen Population in Post-Civil War America, 1860–1920," *Ethnicity and Race in a Changing World* 5, no. 1 (2014): 17–36.

63. Christopher Cameron, "Haiti and the Black Intellectual Tradition, 1829–1934," *Mod-ern Intellectual History* 18, no. 4 (2021): 1190–1199; Michael Onyebuchi Eze, "Pan Afri-canism: A Brief Intellectual History," *History Compass* 11, no. 9 (2013): 663–674; Paul Gilroy, *The Black Atlantic: Modernity and Double Consciousness* (Cambridge, MA: Har-vard University Press, 1993).

64. Some noteworthy examples include Frantz Fanon, Aimé Césaire, and Léopold Sen-ghor in France and Claudia Jones in the United Kingdom (who, like Garvey, was de-ported from the United States for her politics).

65. Hartman, *Scenes of Subjection*, 65–67; Isabel Wilkerson, *The Warmth of Other Suns: The Epic Story of America's Great Migration* (New York: Vintage, 2010). Also see nn. 40–41.

66. For some examples, see Reema Ghabra, "Black Immigrants Face Unique Challeng-es," *Human Rights First*, February 17, 2022, https://www.humanrightsfirst.org/blog/black-immigrants-face-unique-challenges; Karla McKanders, "Immigration and Blackness: What's Race Got to Do With It?" *American Bar Association*, May 16, 2019, https://www.americanbar.org/groups/crsj/publications/human_rights_magazine_home/black-to-the-future/immigration-and-blackness/; Ibe Peniel, "Immigration Is a Black Issue," *Ameri-can Friends Service Committee* (blog), February 16, 2021, https://www.afsc.org/blogs/news-and-commentary/immigration-black-issue.

67. Dan La Botz, "Ten Arguments for Open Borders, the Abolition of ICE, and an In-ternationalist Labor Movement," *Socialist Forum*, Fall 2019, https://socialistforum.dsausa.org/issues/fall-2019/ten-arguments-for-open-borders-the-abolition-of-ice-and-an-internationalist-labor-movement/; Gracie Mae Bradley and Luke de Noronha Anita Yandle, *Against Borders: The Case for Abolition* (New York: Verso, 2022); Anita Yandle,

"Open Borders, Then Abolish Them," *Abolition and Democracy* (blog), Columbia Center for Contemporary Critical Thought, March 31, 2021, https://blogs.law.columbia.edu /abolition1313/anita-yandle-open-borders-then-abolish-them/.

68. The Coast Guard's first operations geared toward interdicting vessels before they entered U.S. waters targeted slave traffickers. Joanne Van Selm, Betsy Cooper, and Kathleen Newman, *The New "Boat People": Ensuring Safety and Determining Status* (Washington, DC: Migration Policy Institute, 2006) at 71. These border patrol practices, and the laws that authorized them, have been criticized by contemporary scholars—not for their oppressive outcomes, but because they did not go far enough to stamp out the slave trade. Eric Foner, "End of Slave Trade Meant New Normal for America," interview, *Tell Me More*, NPR, January 10, 2008, https://www.npr.org/templates/story/story.php?storyId=17988106.

69. Alejandro Portes and Ramón Grosfoguel, "Caribbean Diasporas: Migration and Ethnic Communities," *The Annals of the American Academy of Political and Social Science* 533, no. 1 (1994): 48–69. Also see nn. 40–41 and 44.

70. Linda Basch, Nina Glick Schiller, and Cristina Szanton Blanc, *Nations Unbound: Transnational Projects, Postcolonial Predicaments and the Deterritorialized Nation-State* (New York: Gordon and Breach, 2000). Amanda Sives, "Formalizing Diaspora-State Relations: Processes and Tensions in the Jamaican Case," *International Migration* 50, no. 1 (2012): 113–128; D. Alissa Trotz and Beverley Mullings, "Transnational Migration, the State, and Development: Reflecting on the 'Diaspora Option,'" *Small Axe* 41 (2013): 155–171.

71. Quintard Taylor, "Slaves and Free Men: Blacks in the Oregon Country, 1840–1860," *Oregon Historical Quarterly* 83, no. 2 (Summer 1982): 153–170.

72. David Bacon, *The Right to Stay Home: How US Policy Drives Mexican Migration* (Boston: Beacon Press, 2014).

73. These justifications tended to alternate between religious appeals and moral-pragmatic appeals to the civilizing qualities of slavery for African peoples. Daragh Grant, "'Civilizing' the Colonial Subject: The Co-Evolution of State and Slavery in South Carolina, 1670–1739," *Comparative Studies in Society and History* 57, no. 3 (2015): 606–636; T. Thomas Fortune, "The White Man's Burden," *New York Age*, April 1899, http://nation alhumanitiescenter.org/pds/gilded/empire/text7/fortune.pdf; Julie Zauzmer Weil, "The Bible was used to justify slavery. Then Africans made it their path to freedom," *The Washington Post*, April 30, 2019, https://www.washingtonpost.com/local/the-bible-was-used -to-justify-slavery-then-africans-made-it-their-path-to-freedom/2019/04/29/34699e8e -6512-11e9-82ba-fcfeff232e8f_story.html.

74. Examples include Fyle Magbaily, *Introduction to the History of African Civilization: Precolonial Africa* (Lanham, MD: University Press of America, 1999), Vol. 1. Walter Rodney, *How Europe Underdeveloped Africa* (London: L'Overture-Bogle Press, 1972); John Middleton, *The World of the Swahili: An African Mercantile Civilization* (New Haven, CT: Yale University Press, 1992).

75. Samir Amin, *Delinking: Towards a Polycentric World* (London: Zed Books, 1990); Walter Mignolo, "Delinking: The Rhetoric of Modernity, the Logic of Coloniality and the Grammar of De-Coloniality," *Cultural Studies* 21, no. 2–3 (2007): 449–514; Anibal Quijano, "Coloniality and Modernity/Rationality," *Cultural Studies* 21, no. 2–3 (2007): 168–178.

76. Dorothy E. Smith, "Women's Perspective as a Radical Critique of Sociology," *Sociological Inquiry* 44, no. 1 (1974): 7–13.

77. Collins, *Black Feminist Thought*; Patricia Hill Collins, "Learning from the Outsider Within: The Sociological Significance of Black Feminist Thought," *Social Problems* 33, no. 6 (1986): 14–32; Chela Sandoval, "U.S. Third World Feminism: The Theory and Method of Oppositional Consciousness in the Postmodern World," *Genders* no. 10 (1991):

1–24; Trinh T. Minh-ha, *Woman, Native, Other: Writing Postcoloniality and Feminism* (Bloomington and Indianapolis: Indiana University Press, 1989); Eve K. Sedgwick, *Epistemology of the Closet* (Berkeley and Los Angeles: University of California Press, 1990); Cheryl Suzack, Shari M. Huhndorf, Jeanne Perrault, and Jean Barman, eds., *Indigenous Women and Feminism: Politics, Activism, Culture* (Vancouver: University of British Columbia Press, 2010).

78. Cheryl Harris, "Critical Race Studies: An Introduction," *UCLA Law Review* 49 (2001): 1215; Vrushali Patil, "From Patriarchy to Intersectionality: A Transnational Feminist Assessment of How Far We've Really Come," *Signs* 38, no. 4 (2013): 847–867.

79. Nancy Hiemstra, "Pushing the US-Mexico Border: United States' Immigration Policing Throughout the Americas," *International Journal of Migration and Border Studies* 5, no. 1/2 (2019): 44–62; Margath Walker and Alisa Winton, "Towards a Theory of the Discordant Border," *Singapore Journal of Tropical Geography* 38, no. 2 (2017): 245–257.

80. Leandra Hinojosa Hernandez, "Feminist Approaches to Border Studies and Gender Violence: Family Separation as Reproductive Injustice," *Women's Studies in Communication* 42, no. 2 (2019): 130–134; Nancy Naples, "Borderlands Studies and Border Theory: Linking Activism and Scholarship for Social Justice," *Sociology Compass* 4, no. 7 (2010): 505–518.

81. Emmanuel Brunet-Jailly, "Theorizing Borders: An Interdisciplinary Perspective," *Geopolitics* 10 (2005): 633–649; David Newman, "On Borders and Power: A Theoretical Framework," *Journal of Borderland Studies* 18, no. 1 (2003): 13–25.

82. Newman, "On Borders and Power," 15.

83. Nicholas De Genova, "Spectacles of Migrant 'Illegality': The Scene of Exclusion, the Obscene of Inclusion," *Ethnic and Racial Studies* 36, no. 7 (2013): 1180–1198. Chris Rumford, "Introduction Theorizing Borders," *European Journal of Social Theory* 9, no. 2 (2006): 155–169; William Walters, "Border/Control," *European Journal of Social Theory* 9, no. 2 (2006): 187–203.

84. Noel Parker and Nick Vaughan-Williams, "Critical Border Studies: Broadening and Deepening the 'Lines in the Sand' Agenda," *Geopolitics* 17, no. 4 (2012): 727–733.

85. Noel Parker and Rebecca Alder-Nissen, "Picking and Choosing the 'Sovereign' Border: A Theory of Changing State Bordering Practices," *Geopolitics* 17, no. 4 (2012): 776.

86. Maya Mynster Christensen and Peter Albrecht, "Urban Borderwork: Ethnographies of Policing," *Society and Space* 38, no. 3 (2020): 390.

87. Walters, "Border/Control," 197.

88. Niambi M. Carter, "Intimacy without Consent: Lynching as Sexual Violence," *Politics & Gender* 8, no. 3 (2012): 414–421; Wilson Kwamogi Okello, "We've Never Seen This": Reckoning with the Impossibility of Black [Males'] Vulnerability to Sexual Violence," *International Journal of Qualitative Studies in Education* (2022): 1–13.

89. Leo Chavez, *The Latino Threat: Constructing Immigrants, Citizens, and the Nation* (Stanford, CA: Stanford University Press, 2013); Evelyn Marrast, "Review of *Killing the Black Body: Race, Reproduction, and the Meaning of Liberty*," *Canadian Woman Studies* 18, no. 4 (1999): 121; Alexandra Villareal, "'Anchor Babies': The 'Ludicrous' Immigration Myth That Treats People as Pawns," *The Guardian*, March 16, 2020, https://www.theguard ian.com/us-news/2020/mar/16/anchor-babies-the-ludicrous-immigration-myth-that -treats-people-as-pawns.

90. Cheryl I. Harris, "Whiteness as Property," *Harvard Law Review* 106, no. 8 (1993): 1707–1791.

91. Vilna Bashi Treitler, "Social Agency and White Supremacy in Immigration Studies," *Sociology of Race and Ethnicity* 1, no. 1 (2015): 153–165; Jemima Pierre, "Black Im-

migrants in the United States and the 'Cultural Narratives' of Ethnicity," *Identities* 11, no. 2 (2004): 141–170.

92. Vilna Bashi Treitler, *The Ethnic Project: Transforming Racial Fiction into Ethnic Factions* (Stanford, CA: Stanford University Press, 2013).

93. Noel Ignatiev, *How the Irish Became White* (New York: Routledge, 1995); Charles W. Mills, *The Racial Contract* (Ithaca, NY: Cornell University Press, 1997).

1

Ex Aqua in the Mediterranean

Excavating Black Power in the Migrant Question

P. KHALIL SAUCIER AND TRYON P. WOODS

> I search for a word or phrase for bringing someone back from
> underwater that has as precise a meaning as the unearthing
> contained within the word exhume. I find words like resurrect
> and subaquatic but not "ex aqua." Does this mean that unlike
> being interred, once you're underwater there is no retrieval—
> that you can never be "exhumed" from water?
>
> —M. NOURBESE PHILIP, *ZONG!*

P oets such as M. NourbeSe Philip are compelled to bend language to accommodate the abyss in Western consciousness in which slavery continues to fester. For our part, we strive here for something complementary to the poet's unraveling of language, a preliminary step toward undoing this ill-formed consciousness, an effort to deviate and depart from that which has formed our pattern of thought, a modest analytic dent in the paradigm through which solutions to these problems are debated.

Our concern in this chapter[1] is with how humanitarian and antiracist engagements with contemporary African migration in the Mediterranean Basin are connected to the racist violence of European border policies and the antiblackness of anti-immigrant discourse. While African migration to Europe is historically connected to long-standing black self-determination against the world-altering violence of Western civilization since at least the dawn of the modern era, contemporary discourse on the Mediterranean displaces this basic expression of black power in favor of an ahistorical "freedom of movement" politic along with the sense of activism that emerges from the work of mourning and memorialization.[2] We examine activist and academic instantiations, and aestheticization, of this freedom of movement discourse, their connection to the essential slaveholding culture of Western civilization, and consequently, the way Western society's antiracist discourse continues to find its sustenance through black social death.

The first half of our chapter, in which we interrogate "freedom of movement" discourse, and the chapter's second half, in which we examine the aesthetics of mourning migrant deaths in the Mediterranean, function as two sides of the same critique about the so-called migrant crisis. The basic contours of our intervention are as follows. Increasing numbers of Africans are choosing to migrate to Europe by crossing the Sahara and the Mediterranean. Many of them perish at sea, while many more encounter detention and deportation at the hands of European border security. We do not contest these facts, nor do we disagree with the basic humanitarian response that contends that border policies are part of the problem, that neoliberal and neocolonial global capitalism compels people to make the hard choices to leave their homelands, that migrants should have the right to move freely to better survive, and that all human life should be equally valuable. We leave it to others to prosecute the details of this basic human rights agenda. Our concern lies with how the humanitarian response is deeply mired in the problem it aims to remedy. To understand how migrant deaths and the migrant humanitarianism that has arisen in response are both part and parcel of the same historical violence, we must move our level of analysis beyond the sociological and the empirical. We are uninterested in debating the utility of sociology, or any other disciplinary formation; the basic pitfalls of the Western order of knowledge have been exhaustively elaborated throughout the black studies corpus, and we have enjoined this critique in other places.[3]

The modern world was formed through racial slavery, and as such, the order of knowledge created in its image remains tethered to this foundational violence. This reality means that antiblackness always functions on multiple levels simultaneously. While the phenomenological reality on planet Earth continues to bear out the basic precepts of antiblackness (that it is best to be white and worst of all to be black), the very conceptual universe available to name this reality is itself a key means by which the reality is reproduced. We seek to elucidate this problem by examining how this antiblack order of knowledge can also function as antiracism. We argue that all social scientific and humanistic inquiry must necessarily grapple with the essential idiom of power governing the structure of humanity. The case of African migrants in the Mediterranean allows us to highlight how the prevailing categories of thought informing migration studies are insufficient for grasping the nature of the world in which black people move. The reason for this has nothing to do with black people; black migrants the world over tend to make decisions and act on them in basically the same ways that everyone else does. The problem lies with the notion that the right to move about is a freedom intrinsic to what it means to be human. This notion is patently ahistorical when it fails to account for its origins in the capture and imprisonment of black people as slaves. This historical context applies to everyone everywhere ever since the dawn of the slave trade. Migration studies, critical or otherwise, that elide this basic historical truth are pretending that the world is something other than what it has been for over a millennium. The fact that blacks remain uniquely eligible for immobilization the world over today has nothing to do with what black people are like or what they do differently from nonblacks; it simply means that the notion of "freedom of movement" *remains* bound to the structure of antiblack violence created by slavery, which uniquely positions black people to be ill-served by both those who seek to harm *and* those who seek to remedy the harm.

One final word of introduction: we must be able to talk about social death. *Social death* is the condition created by racial slavery wherein black people live within a social order that construes them as nonhuman. Social death, like all structures of power created by human beings, is relational: nonblack standing as fully human is premised on black social death. This parasitic relationship between the human and the nonhuman is at the heart of the problem of antiblack antiracism that we examine in this chapter. The realities of social death do not mean that black people are not acting and moving and doing things daily to deal with the infinite permutations of social death. Although these facts of self-determination sociologically disprove the various theses of black inferiority or incapacity, the structure of social death persists. As we endeavor to show in this chapter, the main reason why the structure continues unabated is because people—including, most prominently, academics, artists, and humanitarian activists—remain wedded to its paradigm. Our analysis of mourning in the Mediterranean illustrates this problem. Advocates attempt to recuperate black people as fully human by honoring African migrants who have perished on the Mediterranean crossing. Nobody climbs the ladder of death alone, however, and there is no way of memorializing lost life without getting out of the paradigm created by slaveholding culture in which the relationship between living and dying has been fatally corrupted.[4] In short, our focus in this chapter is not on the question of migrant mobility, which we see as yet another iteration of academic statements on the obvious. Instead, our focus is on the paradigm in which such questions are posed, debated, and resolved.

Freedom of Movement

The study of African movement across the Mediterranean is an investigation into how the modern world's culture of politics remains a variant of slaveholding culture instantiated in the early Mediterranean and Atlantic worlds. Slaveholding serves as a paradigm for the political; that is, it is essential to the way power is achieved and maintained. As with most paradigms, however, it remains largely opaque to even its most astute subjects. Political emancipation for Europeans emerged through the transitions from feudal to capitalist modes of production, taking its modern shape through the state-form and its ideology of political liberty. Since Western thought has formed through this historical process, certain conceptions of the political have come to dominate social thought, functioning as "a basic grammar, a mediation, through which the outlines of social reality have been generated."[5] In short, as Cedric Robinson explains, the political has become a paradigm, and as such, it structures thought about how society is organized *and* about how this social organization can be challenged. All the leading social theories used to study and interpret social phenomena presuppose aspects of the political as reality. "However, they are *contained* explications, that is, they are paradigmatic," says Robinson. "They are exercises through which the political persists rather than instruments by which that persistence might be explained."[6]

Racial slavery supplies the foundation of the paradigm, as well as much of its architecture. As such, it is the key to deconstructing modern society's resident contradictions and its affirming sociopathology—that is, slavery generates the leading social theories of our time, and as a result, subverts our capacity to recognize the nature of social reality and to intelligently create meaningful existential challenges to it. Slaveholding culture's various ideologies are intensified the more concerned they are with the liberal, bourgeois freedoms to which the range of thinkers foundational to Western culture's sense of itself—from Spinoza to Marx, and numerous others, from both affirmative and critical stances alike—have addressed themselves.[7] It is those "freedoms" posited on abolitionist principles of individualism and liberty that spawned the Atlantic regime of antiblackness and continue to drive antiracist humanitarianism in the Mediterranean today.[8] To borrow again from Robinson, the proponents of free movement have "failed to free themselves, to disengage meaningfully from the existential boundaries and force of their own experience. They were (and are) forever in the state clawing out to a thing perceived through the eyes of naïve, desperate infancy."[9] The stamina of slaveholding culture ensures that paradigmatic challenges to the social order are stillborn.

For instance, a look at the Charter of Lampedusa (Carta di Lampedusa)[10] makes plain the condition and horizon of freedom of movement politics.[11] Drafted and approved by over 300 activists and migrants on the island of Lampedusa between January 31 and February 2, 2014, the charter denounces the ways in which militarized forms of policing, along with neoliberal economic policies, stunt trans-Mediterranean migration.[12] Inspired by the ubiquitous concretions of migrant death in the Mediterranean, the charter attempts to achieve inviolability by prioritizing sovereign subjects' right to move, resist, work, stay, and choose where to live. While the signatories of the charter are keen to avoid the pitfalls of humanitarian logic, "with no distinctions made on the basis of nationality, citizenship and/or place of birth," they cannot help but be seduced by the categories of legal and economic thought that evade the relation of domination that is intrinsic to slaveholding culture.[13] Put slightly differently, the charter is held together by a constellation of signifiers (democracy, citizenship) that recursively extend the global black/non-black binary.

Before the charter's call for free movement in the early twenty-first century, there was Hannah Arendt's expositions on freedom in the mid-twentieth century:

> Of all the specific liberties which may come into our minds when we hear the word "freedom," freedom of movement is historically the oldest and also the most elementary. Being able to depart for where we will is the prototypical gesture of being free, as limitation of freedom of movement has from time immemorial been the precondition for enslavement. Freedom of movement is also the indispensable precondition for action, and it is in action that men primarily experience freedom in the world.[14]

Arendt elaborates the central position of mobility in Western social thought. A decade or so before Arendt's formulation given just above, the United Nations codified the "right to freedom of movement" in Article 13 of the Universal Declaration of Human Rights. The charter's assertion of this right as principle thus closely follows the paradigmatic script while entreating a superseding authority that had already been previously compromised by racial slavery. In due course we will consider more fully the ontological claims underwriting the freedom of movement ideology, but first we examine its ahistorical sociology and its aphasia regarding its occluded black subject.[15]

One representative example of the problem at hand is Nicholas De Genova and Nathalie Peutz's notion of the "deportation regime." De Genova and Peutz, in their eponymously named book, as well as in De Genova's numerous single-authored works on migration, construct free movement in terms of its "pernicious regulation" through the sovereign power of nation-states to deport those human beings on the move whom it deems undesirable or otherwise ineligible for inclusion.[16] This formulation is an important attempt at deconstructing the horrors of state power at national borders, wherever they may manifest. At the same time, it instantiates the fungible blackness that lends free movement discourse its coherence.

De Genova and Peutz's "deportation regime" draws our attention *empirically* to an increase in deportations amidst a "global preoccupation with border 'security'" in the wake of the events of September 11, 2001, and the ensuing U.S.-led wars in Afghanistan and Iraq.[17] As has been well-documented, the United States's so-called war on terror has translated into a permanent escalation in its national border enforcement, with historic increases in the pursuit, detention, and deportation of undocumented immigrants.[18] A parallel process of detention and deportation has unfolded in Europe during the same period. The European Commission has been coordinating joint expulsions between member states while at the same time using preemptive detention in the regions of migrant origin or in key transit locales abroad to keep asylum seekers and refugees from entering the European Union in the first place.[19] Neither in North America nor in Europe has there been a commensurate increase in migration or problems attendant to it to which the escalation in migrant detention and deportation is a response. Border "security," as with "law and order" in every form in which it appears, is a politico-symbolic tool for reproducing the racialized space of the nation and for promoting capital during new cycles of accumulation. Partly for this reason, De Genova and Peutz's "deportation regime" also seeks to draw attention *analytically* to the way states are using border enforcement to suture sovereignty and political space at a time when the perception of increased global mobility is seen by some as threatening to the liberal bourgeois polity. The use of deportation as a technique of modern sovereignty is not new, however, with antecedents in the various practices of banishment and expulsion that were features of the regimes of ancient Greece and imperial Rome, and of Europe's Middle Ages as well. Deportation to the colonies was also integral to modern empire-building during the rise of European hegemony. The production of "illegals" as an expression of national sovereignty was a key feature of immigration enforcement throughout the twentieth century as well. Indeed, we may ask, if the "deportation regime" is simply another way of describing how political societies attempt to contain power by routinizing and institutionalizing it, is there anything qualitatively new about the "deportation regime" in the present period? To what new insights, exactly, does the concept direct us?

De Genova's use of Elvira Arellano's story to elaborate the "deportation regime" provides us with some clues. Arellano is a Mexican national living in Chicago who was first deported in 1997 and then arrested again during an immigration raid in 2002. In 2006, in defiance of a final order to report to the U.S. Department of Homeland Security for deportation, Arellano (with her eight-year-old son, a U.S. citizen) took refuge in Chicago's Adalberto United Methodist Church. Arellano's case attracted international attention and inspired the sanctuary movement in support of undocumented immigrants across the United States. As De Genova reports, "Arellano remained confined to the storefront church and a small apartment above it, as well as its modest enclosed parking lot and garden, for the year that followed."[20] DHS held off enforcing Arellano's deportation order until she abandoned her church sanctuary in Chicago to participate in immigrant rights events as an antideportation activist. She was arrested and deported after speaking at a rally in Los Angeles. She returned to the United States in 2014 and now holds a legal work permit as she awaits hearing on her asylum petition.

For De Genova, Arellano's case highlights three facets of the "deportation regime." First, there is the "extravagant and truly unforgiving individualization that comes with deportation."[21] De Genova draws heavily on Giorgio Agamben here, following Agamben's call to identify the point where "techniques of individualization and totalizing procedures converge."[22] Deportation "is precisely such a point of intersection," proclaims De Genova, where the totalizing regime of citizenship, of belonging and exclusion, rights and rightlessness, is applied against particular persons.[23] De Genova asserts that deportation is "irreducibly if not irreversibly individualizing" in that it individuates the immigrant from the kin and community that give people's lives meaning. Insofar as the act of migration is socially produced within specific historical contexts, deportation of individual migrants individualizes these contextual movements.

Second, De Genova views the Arellano case as indicative of how the "deportation regime" imposes a *radical immobilization*—a veritable encirclement, an asphyxiating abrogation of [the right to] freedom of movement."[24] The selective enforcement of immigration laws—the state did not deign to apprehend Arellano from her church sanctuary—merely affirms undocumented immigrants' eligibility for deportation that always haunts their movement. The absence of enforcement of a deportation order is no different from the absence of an order: the disciplinary effect is achieved through deportability as a social condition of possibility.

The third aspect of the "deportation regime" that De Genova draws out of the Arellano case is the claim that border controls normalize a state of emergency for undocumented immigrants. Following Agamben's concept of "bare life," De Genova argues that because immigrants like Arellano are subject to the caprices of border controls, the "deportation regime" advances a fundamental politicization of human existence stripped of all social status. Arellano's "was indeed a life in its barest rudimentary outline, reduced to the most elementary facets with which human existence . . . must, under ordinary circumstances, *sustain itself*."[25] The "deportation regime" politicized her basic standing in society as a mother, calling into question her ability to reproduce her and her son's lives. The reduction of immigrants to bare life, according to De Genova, following Agamben, serves as the "nucleus of sovereign power" wherein "such an inscription is fundamentally an *incorporation* while nonetheless a negation."[26] For De Genova, then, the "deportation regime" is constituted in the contradictory inclusion of persons stripped of full social status.

While every migrant's story is unique, Arellano's case may well index features of the "deportation regime" as many immigrants experience it. De Genova finds himself, however, in an analytical conundrum with her case. He attempts an ontological intervention—what it means to exist within a state of exception—but he fails to properly grasp the structure of ontology in which he is working and in which nonblack immigrants such as Arellano cross borders. As a result, he conflates the sociological and empirical with the ontological. In this sense, De Genova fails to confront the tension between "equally existing" and "existing equally," an abstraction too often neglected in freedom of movement politics. For example, the Mexican migrant and the Black migrant equally exist, but their existence is not equal, for one is imparted a humanity that is withheld from the other. Mere existence does not assure inclusion into humanity, and existence gives no right to the constitution of human space. At best it gives the right to be included into a space always already constituted by others. De Genova's attempt to explicate the paradigm runs aground on the shoals of slaveholding culture precisely because he cannot see where he is going within it. Or, to apply Robinson's terms, the "deportation regime" is a *contained* explication—that is to say, it *is* paradigmatic in that such a concept is the means by which the slaveholding culture at the heart of the political persists, rather than an exercise through which that persistence might be explained. Arellano's "self-selected captivity," as De Genova puts it, contrasts with that of fugitive black slaves.[27] Like migration, fugitivity too has its diverse biographies, but De Genova's use of Arellano's case clashes most directly with the famous slave narrative *Incidents in the Life of a Slave Girl: Written by Herself.*

In *Incidents*, Harriet Jacobs narrates her extraordinary scheme to escape the plantation with her children. At fifteen years old, she was subjected to sexual abuse by both her master and her mistress. To protect herself, she conspired a relationship with another white man, "to be the author of an already marked-out violation, and the 'father' of her children."[28] When it became clear that this protective ruse was short-lived and that there was no position that she could occupy openly that would stop the violation by her slaveholders, Jacobs staged her escape and concealed herself in an attic crawl space above her grandmother's house. Jacobs describes her hiding space as her "loophole of retreat": "The garret was only nine feet long and seven feet wide. The highest part was three feet high, and sloped down abruptly to the loose board floor. There was no admission for either light or air."[29] She survived in this garret for seven years before finally escaping to the North, where she was eventually reunited with her children, eluding her former master's repeated efforts to recapture her.

At the sociological and empirical level, the familiarities between Jacobs's and Arellano's sanctuaries only accentuate the obvious differences. More significant are the ontological differences they register between black and non-black bodies within the world of slaveholding. For Jacobs, the space of self-captivity is both an extension of and a momentary rupture in that which is outside the garret: human bondage and the uses of chattel, the links between property and rape. Jacobs maintains that within the confines of the garret she is *not* enslaved and that her self-captivity is a retreat to emancipation—and yet, she also refers to the space as her dismal cell, her prison, and her dark hole.[30] Jacobs arranges for letters to be sent from New York and Boston to her slave master, prompting him to pursue her where she does not exist, while never looking for her "in the last place they thought of," as she put it, right over their heads in the midst of the plantation.[31] The garret is thus the paradigmatic space of black fugitivity: it is everywhere and nowhere, both inside and outside, captive but not captured, free only within the strict spatial parameters of her temporary concealment. For Hortense Spillers, Jacobs's narrative illuminates how black bodies are "not-quite-spaces."[32] Fugitivity, then, may realize the truth of black mobility, but it also registers the fact that slaveholding's territory is inescapable.

Arellano's space of self-captivity is similarly an extension of that which is outside her Chicago church sanctuary: a set of geopolitical hierarchies organized to construct her otherness and constrain her self-determination. More importantly, however, her resistance to the "deportation regime" borrows its narrative energies from society's grid of associations, from the semantic and iconic connections between the human beings inside the church and those outside of it. The same grid of association is unavailable to black fugitives from state violence, with human misrecognition replacing common identification. Whereas Jacobs's fugitivity relies on subterfuge and concealment, on pain of death (or worse) to her and her children, Arellano's sanctuary is a function of her public displays of protest and resistance. Jacobs must escape not only her master, but civil society itself; Arellano's salvation lies in accessing and engaging civil society. The prevailing public constitutes a state of emergency for Jacobs, while the global public comes to Arellano's aid. Even after Jacobs escapes her garret-prison, American property law ensures she remains a fugitive even in "free" territory; Arellano's refuge-taking, meanwhile, inspires lawmakers and policymakers nationwide to declare their own "sanctuary" cities and campuses. Most acts of resistance by the enslaved are lost to the historical record, and those that are recorded are frequently noted as a bill of sale or an order of execution, lost under the shroud of notoriety, the anonymity of exchange and accumulation, or "the overwhelming debris of the itemized account."[33] On the contrary, not only did Arellano's confrontation with state authority lead to a kind of celebrity status, it was also a shrewd pathway to inclusion without prejudice that may yet prove successful.

Chicago's devotion to its self-proclaimed status as a sanctuary city for immigrants (so proclaimed in 1985 by its first black mayor, Harold Washington) is remarkable given the deathly regard it holds for its black residents. While Arellano was taking sanctuary, thousands of black Chicagoans were being disappeared into the city's clandestine torture site operated by the police department at Homan Square, and from there into the modern-day catacombs of the state's prison system.[34] Police have tortured black residents for decades in Chicago primarily because they could do so with impunity—and yes, police "torture" in Chicago has meant every form of coercion that the United Nations has recognized as torture, including electrocution, plastic bag suffocation and simulated executions, sensory deprivation, beatings, extreme heat, being shackled hand and foot, and being held incommunicado.[35] As evidence of the torture program slowly came to light, Illinois was forced to adopt a moratorium on capital punishment, and eventually to clear its death row entirely in 2003, as many of the capital defendants had been convicted based on coerced confessions. The notorious attempt by the city government to cover up the 2014 murder of Laquan McDonald was followed in short order by a U.S. Department of Justice investigation into the city's police department.[36] The US government found that Chicago police routinely used "excessive force" and violated the basic constitutional rights of the city's black residents.[37] *The Washington Post* reported on a few of the abuses documented in the Justice Department's report:

> Officers are described as running after people who they had no reason to believe committed serious crimes. Some of those chases ended in fatal gunfire. In one case, officers began chasing a man who was described as "fidgeting with his waistband." Police fired a total of 45 rounds at him, hitting and killing him. No gun was found on the man, the report states, and a gun found almost a block away was both "fully-loaded and inoperable." . . . These anecdotes were not limited to fatal incidents. A 16-year-old girl is described as being struck with a baton and shocked with a Taser for not leaving school when she was found carrying a cellphone.[38]

In March 2021, an international commission of human rights experts issued an even more damning report on U.S. state violence against blacks. The commission concluded that the systematic police violence amounts to crimes against humanity, and strongly recommended that the International Criminal Court at The Hague investigate with a view to prosecutions.[39]

This juxtaposition of the position of blackness and the position of the non-black immigrant sheds light on De Genova's emphasis on the individuation, "radical immobilization," and bare life of the immigrant. Each of these features of the "deportation regime" indicates that De Genova is not talking about black people. Antiblack violence is purely gratuitous, and gratuitous violence is never individualized because it does not happen because of anything an individual black person may or may not be doing but rather because a person is identified as belonging to the one group of people constructed ontologically as subhuman. In this historical context, people constructed as black have no ontological ground on which to assert axiological value. Consequently, black people are not signatories to the social contract, and thus they collectively embody the limits of the human. Antiblack violence happens to a people, not to individuated persons. The ontological structure created by racial slavery positions black people as a lethal danger to public welfare and safety. Any acts of violence against black people, therefore, are typically justified as self-defense, are obligatory to ensure the stability of society, and by definition can never be excessive.[40]

> In the paranoia of the police power [against blackness], black children are feared as fully grown adults (Tamir Rice); . . . black therapists aiding their autistic patients are shot for their trouble (Charles Kinsey); . . . black women are body slammed to the ground for crossing the street (Ersula Ore); . . . sleeping black grandchildren become collateral damage during a police raid (Aiyana Stanley-Jones); . . . informing an officer during a traffic stop that you have a legally permitted gun in your glove compartment is interpreted by said officer as an act of aggression, as if you were actually holding the gun (Philando Castile); and heaven help you if you are black and are having a mental collapse of some kind (Quintonio LeGrier, Philip Coleman) or happen to live next door to someone who is (Betty Jones).[41]

These examples from the United States find their corollaries throughout the European context: Adama Traoré (Paris), Mike Ben Peter (Lausanne), Sheku Bayoh (Glasgow), Rashan Charles (London), Tomy Holten (Zwolle), and many more. The list of what black people are doing when they attract lethal violence is quite literally endless. The point is that any black person, at any time and in any place, is "stop-eligible," which means that they carry on their racialized bodies the open-ended justification for being detained, diverted from their path, and bodily violated.[42] In turn, such violence repetitively creates the meaning of blackness as humanity's negation. This gives "radical immobilization" a fundamentally different connotation than that used by De Genova: black people are free to move around the country of their birth—until their very existence is used to justify their killing, which we might see as "radical immobilization" par exemplar.

Given the extent of the antiblack terror campaigns run by police departments across Western society, in the least, it is telling that no place of worship, campus, institution, or municipality has proclaimed sanctuary status for black people. Likewise, Arellano's survival of her confrontation with state power is simultaneously her racialization as a member of the human family, albeit one oppressed by various local and global power differentials. When analysts relegate racial slavery to a time in the past, as they have done consistently in the Mediterranean crisis, they misrecognize the forms it takes in the present. De Genova would do well to compare Arellano's stand against immigration enforcement with Korryn Gaines's stand against law enforcement on August 1, 2016. Harrowing harassment by police on the roadways around Baltimore County led Gaines to seek refuge in her own home when a SWAT team arrived to serve a warrant for a minor traffic infraction. Gaines refused the officers entry, warning them that she would defend her sanctuary with her legally registered shotgun. They responded by shooting her dead and wounding her young son.[43]

European cities, towns, and municipalities also proclaim their sanctuary status for migrants, pointing to a global humanitarian telos. Immigrant sanctuary status, however, is largely symbolic. In the United States, ICE (Immigration and Customs Enforcement) is a federal police agency and has jurisdiction everywhere within the nation-state. Chicago's sanctuary status does not prevent ICE from conducting immigration raids; Arellano was repeatedly deported because of such raids. But the point here is that, depending on where you are positioned within slaveholding culture's hierarchy of value, symbolism may aid you in continuing your struggle tomorrow, as it has with Arellano and the immigrant rights movement, or it may rob you of your tomorrows, as it did with Gaines. De Genova's "radical immobilization" presumes a political subject's existential capacity to traverse space without losing the essential bodily sovereignty that is a central expression of political standing. The law of slavery made clear that the bodies of the enslaved are occupied territory, that blacks have no capacity to give or withhold consent to its uses by whites and nonblacks; as noted earlier, the criminal law today extends the possibility of this bodily occupation to all black people anywhere anytime. Jacobs's efforts to control her own body, and her family's future, sent her into exile within an attic crawl space for almost a decade—she effectively ceased to exist for the duration, an existential purgatory produced by the extant social death of racial slavery. When law enforcement uses SWAT to serve bench warrants for offenses arising from nonviolent misdemeanors, the taking of life that ensues is to be expected because black people and their domestic spaces are illegible in terms of sovereignty, legal rights, or sanctuary. This is the lethality of the antiblack world's symbolism. Arellano, on the other hand, while subject to the caprices of border administration, does not pose the same symbolic threat to civilization. In short, De Genova loses track of the true scale and nature of the material and symbolic power of nonblack nonwhite existence—the abstract "refugee" or "immigrant"—*relative* to the category of blackness.[44]

This is why every attempt to recuperate the freedom of movement in defense of refugees and immigrants—of which De Genova's is merely a symptomatic, not exemplary, instance—is dead on arrival insofar as it does not center the singular commodification of blacks, for centuries the prototypical targets of Western civilization's sociogenic violence and the juridical infrastructure built up around them.[45] As Jared Sexton writes, "Without blacks on board, the only viable political option and the only effective defense against the intensifying crossfire will involve greater alliance with an antiblack civil society and further capitulation to the magnification of state power."[46] It is blackness, not immigrant-ness or refugee-ness, nor generalized processes of racialization, that fully unravels sovereignty's mystified conflation with citizenship and national belonging, leaving African migrants in the Mediterranean literally suspended in aquatic space. Not yet immigrants, and immobilized in vessels unsuited for reaching their intended destination, they are nowhere at all—but this empirical and juridical reality is merely an extension of their ontological condition in an antiblack world. In their case, the human cargo of the ship dissembles the African family, effaces proper human names, and contravenes future possibilities for sanctuary. Africans in motion across the seas are "taken into account as quantities," an accountancy of objects among other entities arriving, or washing up, on civilization's frontier.[47]

De Genova and others write as if "freedom" were identifiable outside of the historical context in which its constraint or negation is its productive feature. De Genova himself is constructing "freedom" in a culturally specific way, and since he is *not* talking about the gratuitous black interdictions, from the Americas to Europe to North Africa, it is understood that the biological imperative to move about unfettered by external constraints is a proprietary characteristic of the putatively nonblack human. That is, "freedom to move" is *antiblack* in the sense that human movement presupposes, in the historical instance (which is roughly the ninth century through the present moment), the captivity of black people. This historical process is an extension of the trap set by the early bourgeois ideological architects of slavery and colonialism. Indeed, to acknowledge the obvious sociological fact of the immobilization of black migrants in the Mediterranean, De Genova is compelled to write a separate and singular essay to deal with the obvious difference that blackness makes to the migrant question—a problematic sequestration of blackness as a parenthetical moment within migration discourse.[48]

Despite an extensive body of work on migration and borders, De Genova addresses the matter of blackness directly for the first time only because of the impact Black Lives Matter has had on racial politics around the world since the 2014 black uprising in Ferguson, Missouri. In a 2017 article De Genova finally asks, "Do black lives matter in Europe?" Although he gives talks around the world on "anonymous black and brown bodies" in the Mediterranean, this article remains singular in all of De Genova's writings for its direct engagement with racial blackness.[49] Why this one blip? De Genova claims that "the first intimations of a European 'migrant' (or 'refugee') 'crisis' arose amidst the unsightly accumulation of dead black and brown bodies awash on the halcyon shores of the Mediterranean Sea."[50] In other words, he locates the origins of the so-called migrant crisis in Europe with the 2015 shipwreck of African migrants off the Libyan coast, killing almost all of the 1,100 people on board, that "served to fix in place a newfound dominant common sense about a 'crisis' of the borders of 'Europe.'"[51]

At first blush, dating awareness of black migration in the Mediterranean to 2015 seems disingenuous given that it had been a matter of widespread public debate since at least the turn of the century. Recall, for example, the extensive attention given to Italy's detention center on Lampedusa and its mass deportation operations in 2004–2005, which drew scrutiny from all of the major international human rights groups, as well as the European Parliament and the UN High Commissioner for Refugees.[52] Upon further consideration, perhaps De Genova is indicating that his work on freedom of movement—after 2005 but prior to 2015—had been complicit in placing blackness under a degree of erasure. His 2010 edited volume *The Deportation Regime*, for instance, includes only one chapter on the Lampedusa deportations, and it is more concerned with a race-neutral evaluation of how "detention and deportation together point to the limits of the state-centric model of sovereignty," without analyzing in any way how racial blackness "enlarges the analytic framework to a transnational space that exceeds the boundaries of the European polity."[53] With the publication of his 2017 edited volume *The Borders of "Europe,"* however, we see that there was no mea culpa intended in De Genova's admission that the "brute *racial* fact of this deadly European border regime is seldom acknowledged."[54] *The Borders of "Europe,"* remarkably, has no sustained critique of "Europe" in relation to the racial construction of Africa across the eras. It is almost as if blackness is a dirty concept that can only be used sparingly in reference to black self-expression (as in Black Lives Matter), or that must always be treated as a suspect analytical and sociological category when deployed by nonblack scholars (appearing under erasure, as in "black").[55]

It seems, then, that blackness comes into view only analytically—albeit tentatively and tepidly—under the weight of spectacular black death. We wrote in our 2014 article on Lampedusa that "given the matrix of violence imposed on blackness, there is a visibility and potentiality to black death that does not attach to black life. As Barbara Browning notes, 'thousands die each year, but word only reaches the [West] when they die en masse.'"[56] Although black migrants perishing in the Mediterranean Basin have made this border zone the most lethal such boundary anywhere in the world, this fact seems only to have spurred a new generation of Western thinkers to contribute their own racialist presumptions to "obliterate the African."[57] The resulting void in critical thought about what this latest scene of black death at sea reveals about the ontological structure of humanity leaves us ill-equipped to interpret the historical impact of these extraordinary losses. Although this tradition was firmly established before his contributions to it in the nineteenth century, G.W.F. Hegel's *The Philosophy of History* stands as a signature insistence on the irrelevance of Africa for understanding world affairs:

> Another characteristic fact in reference to the Negroes is Slavery. Negroes are enslaved by Europeans and sold to America. Bad as this may be, their lot in their own land is even worse, since there a slavery quite as absolute exists; for it is the essential principle of slavery, that man has not yet attained a consciousness of his freedom, and consequently sinks down to a mere Thing—an object of no value. . . . At this point we leave Africa, not to mention it again. For it is no historical part of the world.[58]

Hegel's dismissal of the African and of African culture was calibrated toward legitimating the slave trade, and today's scholars largely relegate it to a notorious past. Two centuries later, however, Hegel lives on in De Genova's facile occlusion of the antiblack violence that generated Europe's emergence as a distinct cultural formation, and in the ongoing parasitic relationship between European civilization and black death. De Genova writes of "the unrelenting *conversion* of European borders into a ghoulish deathscape," and also writes that black migrant deaths in the Mediterranean "have *transformed* [emphasis added] the maritime borders of Europe into a macabre deathscape"—as if there was a time when Europe's borders were *not* a deathscape for black people.[59] The difference between Hegel and De Genova is a difference of degree, not of kind, such that the interval between them is sustained by the steady pace of black social death.

De Genova's 2017 article asking "Do Black Lives Matter in Europe?" is another example of racial reckoning forced by black social movement and at the same time is the latest effort to quarantine critical thought about how global civil society—including academia—depends upon the reproduction of black social death, materially and symbolically. The Black Lives Matter movement compels De Genova *not* to validate BLM in the context of migration, but rather to affirm that "Migrant Lives Matter."[60] The slogan "black lives matter" is itself enough of a truncated challenge to slaveholding culture that it has proven imminently palatable to a wide range of state-corporate forces, from academia to philanthropy to corporate marketing. Dhoruba bin Wahad points out that BLM's accommodation by the status quo would not be so facile if it stood for "Black Liberation Matters" instead.[61] But "black lives matter" is even too much for De Genova to incorporate into his understanding of migration. MLM retains the obvious but implicit reference to black migrants, while adopting the more adroit nonracial nomenclature preferred by the post–civil rights multicultural turn in slaveholding culture. In the long-preferred phrase of the status quo, the dead migrant only "happens to be" inordinately black. This is not a racial analysis; it is how the Western narrative of universality is extended in the post-COINTELPRO and postcolonial era to include and acknowledge race while defusing an analysis of racism as constitutive to the world order, inclusive of the academy's intellectual protocols.[62] De Genova has been a prime shaper of this suppression of blackness in migration studies, as his derisory shows: "And if objective circumstances conspire to ensure that these lives truly do not matter—that these migrant lives are rendered utterly disposable—does it not seem plausible, if not probable, that race has something to do with it?"[63] De Genova does indeed think race "has something to do with it" (a tepid but compulsory acquiescence in today's multicultural academy), but alas, the deceit is in the question, not the answer. In the context of a world historical formation wherein the disposability qua fungibility of black life has long been institutionalized, most fundamentally, in and as the politico-juridical structure of racial slavery and its endless transmutations into the present period, to pose the matter as debatable, even as a question of probability, even rhetorically, is to censure blackness, and by extension "Europe," as unknowable.

Mourning in the Void

If a slave is the essence of stillness, a juridical undynamic human state, fixed in time and space, then today's African migrant moves-in-place within a centuries-old violence that remains as fresh as the latest voyage across the Mediterranean. About 70 percent of the 7,189 migrant deaths recorded worldwide in 2016 occurred in the Mediterranean, and most of those 5,032 migrants were the ones who survived the deathscape of the Sahara to arrive at the North African coastline.[64] The scarcity of autobiographical narratives of this contemporary migration echoes the silence in the archive from an earlier era. As the historiography on the slave trade focused, accordingly, on quantitative matters and on issues of markets and trade relations, so too today's record of Africans on the move is swallowed up by numbers and their toll on the relations between nation-states. This is how the episteme of the Middle Passage reigns over the Mediterranean today, linking holding cells, cargo holds, ship hulls, and barracoons across time and space. This episteme of captivity-in-transit exacerbates the pressure on secondhand accounts, where even the most compassionate journalism appears under the incitement of discourse.

> The boat is taking in water. Nine hours have passed since it left land. It is November, and the water is freezing. Dozens of the 450 people on board are cramped in the bottom hull. Thirty-three-year-old Kamal, from Eritrea, is one of them. He is cold. All he has on are a pair of old pants and a t-shirt. Large waves continually slam against the boat as more water pours in. The boat leans to one side and everyone in the hull moves in the opposite direction to counteract the weight of the water. The boats sways violently. As he hears the terrified screams of the people around him, Kamal is scared for his life. He has, after all, seen television news footage of lifeless African bodies fished from the sea. He remembers asking his smugglers for a life-jacket before they left Libya. The smuggler's answer: "Italia will give you."[65]

Scandal and excess mark the most recent entries in the long history of Africans on the move, the archive of slavery extended to encompass the equally unimaginable form of everyday antiblack practice in the twenty-first century. Before the African migrant-in-waiting even leaves their homeland, they are forced to confront television and internet broadcasts of their own imminent death as "a story about degraded matter."[66] No longer sufficient to merely expose the scandal, accounts such as the previous one measure our capacity to generate a set of descriptions that depart from slavery's archive. "Yet how does one," asks Saidiya Hartman, "recuperate lives entangled with and impossible to differentiate from the terrible utterances that condemned them to death, the account books that identified them as units of value, the invoices that claimed them as property, and the banal chronicles that stripped them of human features?"[67] This question of how to re-narrate the chronicle of a death foretold, of the life lived in loss beyond the ontological coordinates of human loss itself, remains an open one.

Our investigation of this problem now pivots from the freedom of movement discourse in the first half of this chapter to an examination of mourning in the Mediterranean. In the first section, we explored how freedom of movement discourse builds on the conceptual scaffolding of a European theoretical tradition that is unable and unwilling to see its parasitic relationship to black unfreedom. In this section, we encounter antiracist humanitarian activists, artists, and academics who engage the problem of representation that Africans on the move pose for Western aesthetic and intellectual practice. The efforts to memorialize and mourn black migrant deaths in the Mediterranean, however, also function much like freedom of movement discourse does, as exercises through which the political persists, a desperate attempt to preserve this civilization's notions of freedom, democracy, and liberty as if they sprang sui generis from the far-western peninsula of the Asiatic continent. While silence may be the mark of slaveholding's archive of black power, attempts by artists and activists to memorialize lost black lives in the twenty-first century inadvertently suggest that anonymity may be the only way to ethically access an antiparadigmatic politics.

The increased visibility of black death in the Mediterranean has led several domestic and international artists to address the migrant crisis. These exhibitions simultaneously access the consumptive culture of the Western art marketplace and function as public memorials. Examples include Chinese artist Ai Weiwei's *Soleil Lèvant*, an exhibit that uses thousands of salvaged life jackets collected from refugees; Moroccan-French artist Bouchra Khalili's video installation *The Mapping Journey Project*; and the multiple and ever-changing aquatic creations of sculptor Jason deCaires Taylor.[68] In antiracist humanitarian circles, this "migrant turn" in "activist art" serves to memorialize what is happening at sea. It is both a form of protest and an aesthetic challenge to the militarization of borders that is said to have produced the "migrant crisis."[69] Observers uphold these artistic interventions as a means of re-securing humanist solidarity and cultural dialogue. Federica Mazzara, for example, remarks, "Artistic responses to migrant death at sea can produce an important and radical alternative to the necropolitical condition by engaging in acts of contestation of those practices that conceal the violence of the borders."[70] One artistic installation memorializing migrant suffering that has been roundly condemned for undermining antiracist democratic politics is the exhibit by Swiss-Icelandic artist Christoph Büchel titled *Barca Nostra* (Our Boat). The discourse surrounding Büchel's installation exposes how the aesthetics of antiracism beyond the academy reproduce the essential antiblack social antagonism that grips public culture.[71]

Barca Nostra was formerly a migrant vessel that collided with a Portuguese container ship and capsized off the coast of Libya in April 2015, killing more than 800 migrants.[72] Büchel's recovery of the ship and installation of it at the 58th Venice Biennale at the Arsenale in 2019 generated controversy among antiracist activists, artists, and academics for its violent anonymity and its supposed leveraging of black suffering and death for the white culture industry. Placed inconspicuously at the edge of the Arsenale's docks alongside working boats and industrial equipment typical of a functioning marina, the 72-foot unmarked and corroding blue and brick-colored fishing trawler sat upon robust metal stanchions not unlike other vessels undergoing hull repair. Large portside holes in the hull, caused by the boat's fateful collision with the container ship, allowed attendees to peer into the hold. Due to its unassuming artistic display, observers framed *Barca Nostra* as yet another example of a nonblack artist opportunistically appropriating black death and profiting from the raw spectacle while using his privilege to simply push the limits of art. *Barca Nostra*, like many other art exhibits that reckon with race and racism, intensified debates around who has the right to represent black suffering and death. As Elsa Goveia and Jared Sexton have both observed, separated by half a century, nothing is ever made only for black people in a slave society—so to whom is *Barca Nostra* the art installation addressed?[73] What does "collective responsibility" mean in the context of a scene of black death presented to the Western art world's capitalist consumer culture in strictly anonymous terms? How does Büchel's use of the migrant vessel thwart representation of precisely that which has spectacularly captivated the antiracist imaginary? Might *Barca Nostra* be the radical aesthetic needed to point to the ethical ruin latent in antiracist thinking?

In order to excavate the black power embedded within Büchel's allegory about the migrant crisis, we need to examine the gestures of critique that have circulated since the vessel's appearance at the Venice Biennale. *Barca Nostra* is more participatory art than a ready-made installation, an artistic apparatus that generates what Claire Bishop calls a form of "activated spectatorship" in which an observer's encounter with their surroundings prompts larger revelations about the nature of perception itself.[74] In other words, *Barca Nostra* problematizes the regime of the visual, complicating Western culture's own self-confounding aporia. In this sense, *Barca Nostra* works against what Mazzara calls an "aesthetics of subversion"—artwork that challenges the border spectacle and the state-dominant "representational order that prioritizes [*sic*] the anonymity and invisibility of migrants."[75] Because *Barca Nostra* was discreetly arranged, marked only by rope barriers with little to no descriptive material, it has been, and continues to be, criticized for contributing to the border spectacle, rather than working against it. These critics champion an aesthetics of subversion instead, but this attempt at representing the unrepresentable betrays an anxiety about their humanitarian ethos, and resuscitates an investment in the human as an all-encompassing and nonracial category for thought and praxis. The aesthetic complicity between state actors and antiracist humanitarians, therefore, demands closer scrutiny.

In our interpretation of the installation, we position the spectator in relation to the void of representation for which the boat serves as a stand-in. Given that we are still in the "time of slavery" and its perfection, *Barca Nostra* aesthetically marks a temporal abyss that might foster a radical witness to black suffering and death in the Mediterranean, a perspective that would be hard to grasp without Büchel's gesture.[76] This way of reading *Barca Nostra* runs counter to the aesthetics of subversion, which secures the same epistemic contract that it purports to undermine. In much the same manner that De Genova's deportability theory discussed in the first section of this chapter censures blackness, thereby rendering "Europe" unknowable, the aesthetics of subversion is structurally conditioned, and as such, is a paradigmatic reading of the antiblack world rather than an explication of the paradigm that allows us to see the world for what it is. In this way, antiracist signifying practices function as a subsidy to the state-dominant understanding of migrant crisis, and therefore fail to adequately confront that which ontologically conditions the problem of black unfreedom in the first place. Antiracism works to supplement state power by mediating the scopic relationship between the migrant and the state. By forcing representations of the foundational violence of Western civilization into an aesthetic practice privileging identity and individualism, not only do we remain within the known epistemic order but also we are unable to see how such practices are designed to limit our awareness of the order. To borrow from Sylvia Wynter, "Our present mode of aesthetics and signifying practices[,] which institute [antiracism's] psycho-affective field[,] must necessarily function within a parallel yet culture-specific imperative . . . [in order] to secure the social cohesion of the specific human order of which it is a function."[77]

Barca Nostra, alternatively, disrupts the aesthetics of this dynamic by undermining the spectacular form of black death, displacing liberal narratives of identity and representation, and fomenting an existential wash on the structure of humanity. The boat may offer a profoundly ambiguous stand-in for that which exceeds representation, the black social death that is a constitutive pillar of society. The anonymity and fungibility of the migrant-less vessel underscores the historical and ontological truth of antiblackness in the modern world. Crucially, there is nothing for the antiracist to hold onto here—no contextual or subjective anchors—no personal names, places of origin, or dates of life and death, and therefore no identities to memorialize, with which to generate empathy, assign responsibility to state agents, and to foment policy change. The ghost ship docked at the Biennale haunts the everyday activities of Western civil society, not simply the tragic event of a shipwreck and its concomitant state practices of border policing in Europe and neocolonial "human trafficking" out of Africa. As such, *Barca Nostra*'s ahistorical constellation of signs is *the* historical context that matters: it is not a material device to access scenes or events of death, but rather to work *from* death as a structural position in which society itself is reconfigured in all of its violent banality.[78]

The criticisms of *Barca Nostra* affirm our reading of the ship as an installation of social death's analytical and ethical absence in Western aesthetic practice.[79] Critics complain that the migrant is not adequately represented. Before its arrival at the Biennale, the ship that was to become *Barca Nostra* served as an activist touchstone ever since its recovery from the sea floor more than a year after it sank in the Strait of Sicily. The *Comitato 18 Aprile 2015* was established with the aim of preserving the memory of the catastrophic ship-wreck by proposing to create a *Giardino della Memoria* (Garden of Memory) in Augusta, Sicily. The *Laboratorio di Antropologia e Odontologia Forense* (LABANOF) in the Department of Biomedical Sciences for Health of the University of Milan proposed turning the boat into a Museum of Rights.[80] In May 2018, a migrant initiative in Palermo started a petition to claim the recovered shipwreck from the NATO pier of Melilli in an act of symbolic and political appropriation. The activists sought to take possession of the boat and bring it into the public sphere. *Barca Nostra* now sits at the heart of the *Giardino della Memoria* and the Museum of Rights in the port city of Syracuse.[81]

Situating the ship within traditional Western memorial institutions indicates its importance as a balm on the European collective conscience. Upon its arrival, Kamal El Karkouri, director of the *Arco Porco Rosso*, a local Sicilian activist collective, stated that "the boat has been recovered, but we still need to recover the European conscience that drowned in the sea."[82] Critics of *Barca Nostra* further illuminate the dominant racist regimes of representation. For instance, Cairo-based Swiss American curator and artist Alexandra Stock indicates the nature of the outrage surrounding the installation:

> *Barca Nostra* is a performance. It's watching a middle-aged European man metaphorically drape himself in the violent deaths of migrants whom he doesn't bother to name and then, as a second act, attempt to pin some form of vague guilt on his audience. I hate how Büchel tries to implicate visitors to the biennale in this mess, framing the people strolling past the shipwreck as if they're as unaffected by what happened in and on this chunk of metal as they appear. He himself *stripped the work of any context.* There are no signs, no labels; no text anywhere. We're not given anywhere near enough information to engage or contemplate or act or form an independent thought around this work that doesn't involve the artist himself. It's ready-made alright, but all roads lead back to the artist. I don't think the project proves anything beyond how simplistically Büchel himself—not to mention his curator, who made this project possible—views the world.[83]

Similarly, Eleanor Paynter and Nicole Miller allege cultural imperialism, arguing that the installation obscures the migrant struggle altogether:

> *Barca Nostra*, cut loose from its social and spatial histories, appears to follow the path of an imperialist imaginary. As the boat's staging in the Biennale erases the history of the object, it also obscures the processes by which this vessel, in which hundreds drowned, became the Biennale's *Barca Nostra: our boat.*[84]

For Paynter and Miller, the artist's provocation falls flat by virtue of slighting the immediate history of the object:

> So what aesthetic proposition is Büchel making? In the absence of a clear question posed by the work, the ensuing debate risks alienating audiences from the boat's material history, obscuring the gravity of current migration issues. We could also ask who is excluded from the conversation, given the price of entry to the Biennale and the lack of access for many migrants or other marginalized groups to the spaces of art tourism.

Paynter and Miller are further outraged by the ways *Barca Nostra* fails to incorporate and amplify migrant voices.[85] In these critics' mind, the absence of proper place names to identify the specific time and modus of death, as well as the lack of proper names for the individual lives that perished, means that the artist assumes the spotlight on a stage supplied by black suffering. These critics read the staging of anonymity as omission and neglect along the lines of how Western art institutions exclude racialized bodies, and hence, by this reading, Büchel is merely broadcasting his racial privilege. Stock's comments in particular fail to grasp how the ship can signify the utter mundane quality of antiblackness in which European civil society is steeped. She airs the basic unity of the racist and the antiracist: the shared premise that the violence of the modern era produces but one "race," *black*, and to be racialized is thus to be pushed down toward blackness. How does she do this? She presumes that marking "race" is necessary to counter the violence it represents; and in turn, she assumes that the absence of explicit signs of blackness must indicate a perverse and nefarious design. But Stock and other critics are merely outing their own white lens and bringing to light how little removed the antiracist is from liberalism's basic ideology of color-blindness. In other words, Stock expects antiracism to look like the identification of blackness as suffering, because antiracism assumes that not explicitly naming blackness is to reproduce the problem of racism. This is simply the inversion of color-blindness ideology, which maintains that the source of racism is race consciousness and that antiracism entails no longer seeing race at all. If Stock and the other antiracist critics were able to see the world *blackened*, however, they would not need "African migrant ship, 100s die" to see the millions of dead black people across the millennium haunting every seemingly innocuous moment of modern life.

Mazzara is equally disturbed, objecting that it "was not easy . . . to recognize the boat as part of the art exhibit" without migrant names and voices, not to mention that it was placed next to a cafe and portable toilets.[86] Mazzara juxtaposes Büchel's work with the works of other artists who place a premium on identifying and amplifying the stories of migrants. In her view, these other projects are genuinely committed to justice, while *Barca Nostra* is nothing more than a prop for self-indulgent photo ops for Biennale visitors. For example, Mazzara situates Max Hirzel's photographic exhibit/memorial, *Migrant Bodies,* as a prime example of an aesthetics of subversion because it goes beyond the forensics of aquatic death, and because of the great lengths taken by Hirzel to travel to Senegal to inform the family of a migrant who died while attempting to make the journey to Europe.[87] Once again, this approach returns us to the search for proper names beyond the forensics of aquatic death in order to resist state narratives that omit who the migrants were before their confrontation with Fortress Europe—as if the existing ontological structure ever returns that which has been stolen, much like the underwater crypt into which millions of Africans have disappeared. In addition to replicating all its common criticisms, Mazzara also suggests that *Barca Nostra* was not "grounded on research, [and] field work."[88] In other words, she is asserting that *Barca Nostra* worked outside of Western reason, failing to ground itself in the decadent discourse of slaveholding society. If context and names were given and some research was conducted, it seems, the migrant could "come into representation"—to wit, an antiracist politics and political subject could ostensibly emerge from that conjunctural moment and fight for justice.[89]

Mazzara's critique is insidious in its replication of the Western subject's preference for rights and justice within the existing structure at the expense of reckoning with the violence of the structure. Naming is an attempt to convert nonhuman objects into recognizable human value; but without an accounting of the ongoing violence of social death, this maneuver is nothing more than a hermeneutic cover-up. The surfeit of criticism surrounding *Barca Nostra*, in turn, seeks out a racist mindset behind the work, suggesting that a retrograde white privilege is responsible for commodifying migrant death. *Barca Nostra*'s potential for truth-telling is thus thwarted by an obsession with identity cum personhood that misrecognizes how people interact with the boat as backdrop, sharing selfies and otherwise spending their days as art tourists in the shadow of the boat. The installation thus stages the everyday reality of structural antagonism. As a performative installation where the spectators and critics add meaning to the exhibit, *Barca Nostra* compels consideration of freedom beyond the political right to move around, a freedom not dependent on "good" moral citizens, but rather a freedom from freedom's parasitic relationship to violence—in short, a radical autonomy from violence. Critics argue that this performance should have been staged in a way that would shape audience reactions by clearly indicating the meaning of the ship. This complaint itself reeks of white privilege that wants to be shown how to recognize racism, and when and how to feel about it—no surprises, please! *Barca Nostra*, shorn of any warnings, instructions, adverts, or disclaimers, reminds us that black suffering has always served as a backdrop for nonblack life. Elizabeth Alexander offers an observation about the North American context that applies equally to the Mediterranean Basin: "Black bodies in pain for public consumption have been an American national spectacle for centuries."[90] Büchel's critics simply sound sore that they were not adequately warned that *Barca Nostra* would be putting the public on display. Or perhaps their search for the identities of the African victims is betrayed by the exhibit's visual language of anonymity as a desire for their own recovery and repair, in a manner historically consistent with abolitionists of earlier eras.

By withholding reparation's expected narrative, *Barca Nostra* throws the alignment of structure and affect into disarray. Sympathy, responsibility, anger, despair, and hope are unmoored from their stable points of reference and left as open questions. The pictures of people sitting near the boat, enjoying the sun and the water, challenge our comfort that the past is over, and pollute modern antiracist sensibilities that death is not pleasurable. *Barca Nostra*'s demonstration that black death is a constituent element of Western society makes it very difficult to displace the basic meaning of parasitism—that one group's social death sustains another group's social life.[91] For the better part of six centuries, Africans in the Canal of Venice have served as objects of wealth accumulation as well as the necessary antipode for the infinite reconstruction of Europe. The African presence in Europe, and Venice in particular, as slaves passing through the Canal or in the money form generated from the flesh trade, is thus as deep-seated as it is renunciated.[92] Despite the ubiquitous expression of a lived history borne of slavery, colonialism, and looting throughout Western society, the response to *Barca Nostra* is testament that disavowal of this ongoing structural violence remains a feature of antiracism as much as it is of racist culture. Antiracist critique pulls away from a radical understanding of *Barca Nostra*, preferring to see it as an iconoclastic and opportunistic gesture of cultural appropriation. In so doing, antiracists end up reproducing the dialectical relationship they attempt to escape. Naming the dead connects to a redemptive telos of the human as a universal and nonracial category for thought and being. This humanist investment is bankrupt because it falsely claims that all sentient beings are human, thereby discounting the psychic function that the black African plays within the discursive terrain of the Western imaginary, thereby upholding the basic structure of antiblackness that creates the migrant problem in the first place.

In contrast to the condemnation heaped upon *Barca Nostra*, critics have lavishly praised artists who have depicted African migrants in human-replica sculpture form. Jason deCaires Taylor's *Museo Atlántico* presents a submerged museum of hundreds of human figures and architectural forms off the coast of Lanzarote in the Canary Islands.[93] One of Taylor's installations was inspired by Théodore Géricault's famed painting of survivors of a colonial expedition off the coast of Senegal, *Le Radeau de la Méduse* (The Raft of Medusa), exhibited at the Louvre in Paris. Taylor adapts this depiction of survivors to the contemporary Mediterranean crisis in a life-size sculpture of thirteen forlorn migrants huddled on a Zodiac inflatable rubber boat titled *The Raft of Lampedusa*. To make his concrete forms for *The Raft of Lampedusa*, Taylor cast actual black African migrants to Lanzarote in plaster molds. A current resident of Lanzarote, the former migrant Abdel Kader, serves as the model for the centerpiece of *The Raft of Lampedusa*, a figure with his eyes shut at the bow of the boat. Originally from Western Sahara, Kader left his home in Laayoune at twelve years old, enduring several days lost at sea with no food or water before he was saved by a local fishing boat.[94] Critics have praised Taylor's use of actual migrants like Kader, with known names and life histories, for recovering the identities of the victims and staging a face-to-face encounter between victim and spectator that compels observers of the artwork to realize that human existence is embodied and interpersonal. With a remarkable lack of awareness about her own complicity in the erasure of black humanity central to Western civilization, scholar Valérie Loichot asserts, "Taylor returns to the drowned their visibility and establishes their humanity."[95] Here is the doubleness of slaveholding culture: it produces the servile body in order that it may conjure for itself the position of savior-martyr who restores to the slave her lost humanity. Of course, having bestowed a proper name on the objectified human being is in fact a way of denoting the emancipated slave's persistence as a proxy for the human who claims the power to name others. Naming purports to bear witness to a compassionate resuscitation of black injured humanity, when in fact it simply bears witness to itself, to the white master class. Furthermore, it suggests that in order for blackness to be present, it needs to represent something that precedes its social death, something that precedes the structure of humanity; otherwise, it will simply remain an appropriated commodity, a Fanonian "object among other objects." The racial metaphysics of this argument demands consolation for a loss. It shudders at the thought that blackness as social death is configured without full explanation. As a result, it is trapped in perpetual death, as if a full explanation would and could convey the reality, an annotated illustration of those who perished, where, and when. Providing empirical context does not mean that *The Raft of Lampedusa* or *Barca Nostra* suddenly make blackness bearable. The deathly Mediterranean suggests that the modern world is constituted in shipwrecks—*is* a shipwreck—but instead what we get is the continued mis-recognition of the problem in terms of EU migration policy failures, uneven international development, and dispassionate surveillance on the high seas.

In its contextual and subjective anonymity, *Barca Nostra* bucks the promissory note that scholars and activists see and locate in *The Raft of Lampe-*

dusa. It trades the black African migrant's particular identity for the opaque violent banality that structures social life in the West. *Barca Nostra* is an atemporal configuration for slaveholding culture in which the accumulation of pasts that are not over exceeds our desire to fix them in time with proper names. The nameless will narrate what Ralph Ellison might call the invisible presence of the black migrant. For its critics, *Barca Nostra* should be mimetic in order to contribute to antiracism, a form of material reportage. Büchel's installation instead ventures into the twin construction and exploration of reality, stalking those in attendance sipping their coffees and waxing approvingly about the artistic opulence of Biennale exhibits. *Barca Nostra* eschews the liberal antiracist humanitarian format of mimesis that reports back as part of an anthropological optimism inherited from the Enlightenment, a voice within the cosmopolitan democratic milieu of contemporary Western civilization. The lament of critics that humanity could mark with precision what it has done and seek redemption for its deeds if only context and names were affixed to the installation is part of the inversion of slaveholding culture's antiracist reliance on fungible blackness. The desire for names and context sustains the regime of historicity in which black people remain suspended as subhuman beings. Naming abolishes the slave's ahistorical time; in this way, anonymity does not connote submission to the master's narrative of a people without history, but rather unhinges being from slaveholding culture's teleology of names.

The bareness of *Barca Nostra* serves as a sort of Fanonian tabula rasa that cannot and should not be reduced to humanistic politics and sentiments.[96] Naming does little to shatter the affective environment of Negrophobia past and present; it aims to impose order on the chaos that black struggle poses to Western civilization, as opposed to exploring what can be invented within the disorder.[97] To the human, being nameless is a sign of lack, an absence of sociality. If antiblackness *is* sociality, and has been for nigh on a millennium, however, then namelessness is accurate at the ontological and epistemological levels, and therefore, social recognition cannot be the only forum for freedom and liberation. In the end, our radical reading of the installation looks askance at the leading use of *Barca Nostra* as a prop for antiblack exculpability, an anxiety about the inability of the black migrant to appear. Memorializing loss in the Mediterranean attempts aesthetically to *preserve* being, not transform its conditions of possibility.

Conclusion

Even though it happens disproportionately to blacks, it is not only black people who migrate under the risk of death. The difference lies in the structural realm: while nonblack people may share with blacks the experience of migration or violence, at the structural level what nonblacks all have in common is that they are not black. In a world structured by a negative categorical imperative—"Above all, don't be black"—this fact acts as a psychic buffer for nonblack peoples, a confirmation of existence, and, time and again, a source of political sustenance and mobilization.[98] Antiracist discourse on the Mediterranean crisis moves in the opposite direction. Presented in all its rawness, *Barca Nostra* evades the strictures of democratic cosmopolitan reform, as the angst surrounding its appearance affirms. The violence of liberal humanitarian regimes is laid bare. Named or not, the boat is at once generic and specific as to the injured capacity of black mobility.

The inability of retrieving the millions of black lives lost under the sea is at once the impossibility of resurrecting a nonviolent humanity. There is no human prior to the violence. As discomfiting as it may be to the descendants of both slavers and enslaved, what was before is long gone. What will come afterwards has yet to be made. To get there, we still need to figure out, as M. NourbeSe Philip puts it, how to tell "the story that must be told that cannot be told, which in turn becomes a metaphor for slavery—*the* story that simultaneously cannot be told, must be told, and will never be told."[99] We are interested in exploring this impossible imperative, as it were, and in this endeavor we find the search for something like a "black theory of mobility," or the search for a critique of migrant mobility when we're confronted with antiblackness, to be quite beside the point. It is certainly the case that black people's movements have made and unmade the world many times over, from Africans' pre-Columbian voyages across the Atlantic in canoes using the oceanic currents rather than the wind, to the deeply influential African presence in the proto-European world of the Mediterranean Basin, to the intercontinental networks practiced by black sailors, deserters, and maroon communards fugitive to the New World plantation societies from Venezuela to Virginia, to the ineffable diversity of ways black people continue to make a way in this antiblack world.[100]

The impulse to encompass all of this under a discrete theory of black mobility goes back to the slave narratives and the ascription of a so-called black "pattern of movement" that is at once psychic and geographic.[101] The journey from oppression into humanity, we are told, travels through interior fields and across exterior political spaces that become both metaphorical and phenomenological evidence of some determinate subjective agency that is "black" and unbowed. This narrative of overcoming will continue to enamor others, and indeed is not our tale to tell. For our part, we will keep our eye on the violence. Beyond the political right to move around, beyond a freedom based on morality, there is ultimately a freedom from freedom's parasitic relationship to violence. We are some way off from realizing this radical autonomy from violence; so for now, what we can do is rigorously torment the "bad" racists and the "good" antiracists alike for their shared investments in anti-blackness.

NOTES

1. Previously published as "Ex Aqua: The Mediterranean Basin, Africans on the Move, and the Politics of Policing," *Theoria* 61, no. 141 (2014): 55–75.

2. See, for example, Charles Heller, Lorenzo Pezzani, and Maurice Stierl, "Towards a Politics of Freedom of Movement," *Communications* 104, no. 1 (2019): 79–93.

3. See work by Toni Cade Bambara, Lerone Bennett Jr., Cheikh Anta Diop, John Henrik Clarke, W.E.B. Du Bois, Vincent Harding, Joyce Ladner, Cedric Robinson, Walter Rodney, Chancellor Williams, and Carter G. Woodson. See, as well, P. Khalil Saucier and Tryon P. Woods, eds., *Conceptual Aphasia in Black: Displacing Racial Formation* (Lanham, MD: Lexington, 2016), and P. Khalil Saucier and Tryon P. Woods, eds., *On Marronage: Ethical Confrontations with Antiblackness* (Trenton, NJ: Africa World Press, 2015).

4. The Akan proverb "Owuo atwedee baakofoo mforo" means "Death's ladder is not climbed by just one person."

5. Cedric Robinson, *The Terms of Order: Political Science and the Myth of Leadership* (Chapel Hill: University of North Carolina Press, 1980), 3.

6. Robinson, *The Terms of Order*, 4.

7. Although Spinoza and Marx had divergent takes on bourgeois notions of liberty, their philosophical treatments of the matter functioned within the paradigm generated by slaveholding culture. Neither thinker recognized the extent to which humanity as European culture constructed it since the Middle Ages has been parasitic on the violent expungement of African humanity. As such, they contributed to the paradigm's elaboration and legitimation.

8. Robinson, *The Terms of Order*, 5. Antiracist humanitarianism is constituted by a wide variety of ideologies that range from liberal progressivism to radical resistance. Abolitionism as a readily identifiable ideology is usually associated with resistance to racial slavery in the Western slaveocracies of the eighteenth and nineteenth centuries. In fact, abolitionism began with the ending of slavery and bondage for Western Europeans in the early Middle Ages and was, for all intents and purposes, completed before the expansion of the African slave trade throughout the Mediterranean region in the fourteenth and fifteenth centuries. The development of abolition as a centerpiece of Western civilization was unprecedented in human history; most societies have featured various kinds of bondage and servitude, with debate largely relegated to how one might avoid bondage, not about whether it should exist or not. In Western society, however, the fruits of abolition—central cultural concepts of the possessive individual and its liberties—developed as the capacity to enslave objectified others. In this sense, then, abolitionism first appeared as an antiblack racial project and was the necessary cultural precondition for racial slavery, not its antidote. This fact goes some way to explaining why it has been that abolitionism in each successive period of historical transition has produced retrenchments in power and not its redistribution, including in the twenty-first-century Mediterranean Basin. We fully elaborate this historical argument in our forthcoming *African Migrants, European Borders, and the Problem with Humanitarianism* (Manchester: Manchester University Press).

9. Robinson, *The Terms of Order*, 185.

10. The Charter of Lampedusa reaffirms the World Charter of Migrants of 2011.

11. See also Alessandra Sciurba and Filippo Furri, "Human Rights Beyond Humanitarianism: The Radical Challenge to the Right to Asylum in the Mediterranean Zone," *Antipode* 50, no. 3 (2018): 763–782.

12. Nicholas De Genova, "Live from Lampedusa: The Freedom of Movement," *Opendemocracy*, June 9, 2014, https://www.opendemocracy.net/en/5050/live-from-lampedusa-freedom-of-movement/

13. De Genova, "Live from Lampedusa."

14. Hannah Arendt, "On Humanity in Dark Times: Thoughts about Lessing," in *Men in Dark Times* (New York: Harcourt, Brace, and World, 1968), as cited in Nicholas De Genova, "The Deportation Regime: Sovereignty, Space, and Freedom," in Nicholas De Genova and Nathalie Peutz, eds., *The Deportation Regime: Sovereignty, Space, and the Freedom of Movement* (Durham, NC: Duke University Press, 2010), 33.

15. See, for example, Saucier and Woods, eds., *Conceptual Aphasia in Black*.

16. De Genova, "The Deportation Regime," 34.

17. Nathalie Peutz and Nicholas De Genova, "Introduction," in Nicholas De Genova and Nathalie Peutz, eds., *The Deportation Regime: Sovereignty, Space, and the Freedom of Movement* (Durham, NC: Duke University Press, 2010), 4.

18. Deepa Fernandes, *Targeted: Homeland Security and the Business of Immigration* (New York: Seven Stories, 2007).

19. Rutvica Andrijasevic, "From Exception to Excess: Detention and Deportations across the Mediterranean Space," in Nicholas De Genova and Nathalie Peutz, eds., *The Deportation Regime: Sovereignty, Space, and the Freedom of Movement* (Durham, NC: Duke University Press, 2010), 147–165; and Serhat Karakayali and Enrica Rigo, "Mapping the European Space of Circulation," in Nicholas De Genova and Nathalie Peutz, eds., *The Deportation Regime: Sovereignty, Space, and the Freedom of Movement* (Durham, NC: Duke University Press, 2010), 123–146.

20. De Genova, "The Deportation Regime," 35.

21. De Genova, "The Deportation Regime," 35.

22. Giorgio Agamben, *Homo Sacer: Sovereign Power and Bare Life*, trans. Daniel Heller-Roazen (Palo Alto, CA: Stanford University Press, 1998), 6.

23. De Genova, "The Deportation Regime," 35.

24. De Genova, "The Deportation Regime," 36.

25. De Genova, "The Deportation Regime," 38.

26. Agamben, *Homo Sacer*, 6; De Genova, "The Deportation Regime," 38.

27. De Genova, "The Deportation Regime," 36.

28. Christina Sharpe, *Monstrous Intimacies: Making Post-Slavery Subjects* (Durham, NC: Duke University Press, 2010), 10.

29. Harriet A. Jacobs, *Incidents in the Life of a Slave Girl: Written by Herself* (New York: Signet, 2010), as cited in Katherine McKittrick, *Demonic Grounds: Black Women and the Cartographies of Struggle* (Minneapolis: University of Minnesota Press, 2006), 37.

30. McKittrick, *Demonic Grounds*, 40.

31. McKittrick, *Demonic Grounds*, 42.

32. Hortense Spillers, *Black, White, and in Color: Essays on American Literature and Culture* (Chicago: University of Chicago Press, 2003), 223.

33. Spillers, *Black, White, and in Color*, 210.

34. See, for example, Flint Taylor, *The Torture Machine: Racism and Police Violence in Chicago* (Chicago: Haymarket Books, 2019).

35. Flint Taylor, "Chicago's Homan Square: Torture by Any Other Name," *Huffpost.com*, May 17, 2015, https://www.huffpost.com/entry/chicago-homan-square-tort_b_6843750.

36. See Donald F. Tibbs and Tryon P. Woods, "Requiem for Laquan McDonald: Policing as Punishment and Abolishing Reasonable Suspicion," *Temple Law Review* 89, no. 4 (Summer 2017): 763–780.

37. See "Justice Department Announces Findings of Investigation into Chicago Police Department," *Justice News*, January 13, 2017, U.S. Department of Justice, https://www.justice.gov/opa/pr/justice-department-announces-findings-investigation-chicago-police-department.

38. Mark Berman and Matt Zapotsky, "Chicago Police Officers Have Pattern of Using Excessive Force, Scathing Justice Dept. Report Says," *The Washington Post*, January 13, 2017, https://www.washingtonpost.com/news/post-nation/wp/2017/01/13/justice-dept-to-announce-results-of-investigation-into-chicago-police/.

39. *Report of the International Commission of Inquiry on Systemic Police Violence Against People of African Descent in the United States*, March 2021, https://inquirycommission.org/website/wp-content/uploads/2021/04/Commission-Report-15-April.pdf.

40. Bryan Wagner, *Disturbing the Peace: Black Culture and the Police Power after Slavery* (Cambridge, MA: Harvard University Press, 2009), 6–7.

41. Tryon P. Woods, *Blackhood Against the Police Power: Punishment and Disavowal in the "Post-Racial" Era* (East Lansing: Michigan State University Press, 2019), 157.

42. Margaret Raymond, "Down on the Corner, Out in the Street: Considering the Character of the Neighborhood in Evaluating Reasonable Suspicion," *Ohio State Law Journal* 60, no. 1 (1999): 99.

43. For an analysis of the Gaines case in terms of the law of self-defense, see Tryon P. Woods, "The Implicit Bias of Implicit Bias Theory," *Drexel Law Review* 10, no. 3 (2018): 631–672.

44. Jared Sexton, "People-of-Color-Blindness: Notes on the Afterlife of Slavery," *Social Text* 103 (Summer 2010): 48.

45. Sexton, "People-of-Color-Blindness," 48.

46. Sexton, "People-of-Color-Blindness," 48.

47. Spillers, *Black, White, and in Color*, 215.

48. Nicholas De Genova, "The 'Migrant Crisis' as Racial Crisis: Do Black Lives Matter in Europe?" *Ethnic and Racial Studies* 41, no. 10 (2018): 1765–1782.

49. See Nicholas De Genova, "Anonymous Black and Brown Bodies: The Productive Power of Europe's Deadly Border" (Transnational Migration: Borders and Global Justice Conference, Prague, May 30, 2018), https://www.youtube.com/watch?v=3gVqLNrX9Jo.

50. De Genova, "The 'Migrant Crisis' as Racial Crisis," 1.

51. De Genova, "The 'Migrant Crisis' as Racial Crisis," 1. Subsequent forensic excavation of the shipwreck has revealed that the initial reports of as many as 850 migrants on board were incorrect. See https://abcnews.go.com/International/wireStory/mediterraneans-deadliest-shipwreck-deadlier-59924635.

52. See Rutvica Andrijasevic, "Lampedusa in Focus: Migrants Caught Between the Libyan Desert and the Deep Sea," *Feminist Review* 82 (2006): 120–125.

53. Andrijasevic, "From Exception to Excess," 149.

54. De Genova, "The 'Migrant Crisis' as Racial Crisis," 2.

55. De Genova, ed., *The Borders of "Europe,"* 21, 263.

56. P. Khalil Saucier and Tryon P. Woods, "Ex Aqua: The Mediterranean Basin, Africans on the Move, and the Politics of Policing," *Theoria* 61, no. 141 (December 2014): 55–75, at 71; Barbara Browning, *Infectious Rhythm: Metaphors of Contagion and the Spread of African Culture* (New York: Routledge, 1998), 2.

57. Cedric Robinson, *Black Marxism: The Making of the Black Radical Tradition* (Chapel Hill: North Carolina University Press, 2000), 72.

58. G.W.F. Hegel, *The Philosophy of History* (New York: Dover, 1956), 96, 99, as cited in Robinson, *Black Marxism*, 75–76.

59. De Genova, "The 'Migrant Crisis' as Racial Crisis," 3, 2.

60. De Genova, "The 'Migrant Crisis' as Racial Crisis," 3.

61. See "'BLM' Means Black Liberation Movement Not Black Lives Matter with Dhoruba bin-Wahad," *I Mix What I Like*, July 24, 2020, https://imixwhatilike.org/2020/07/24/dhorubabinwahadhistory/.

62. For the uninitiated, COINTELPRO was the FBI's Counter-Intelligence Program against political activists, from labor to civil rights. COINTELPRO led to numerous high-profile assassinations of black leaders such as Dr. Martin Luther King Jr. and Fred Hampton, as well as a slew of low-profile but just as impactful methods of sabotaging black social movement. See Ward Churchill and Jim Vander Wall, *The COINTELPRO Papers: Documents from the FBI's Secret War Against Dissent in the United States*, 2nd ed. (Boston: South End Press, 2002); William F. Pepper, *An Act of State: The Execution of Martin Luther King* (London: Verso, 2008).

63. De Genova, "The 'Migrant Crisis' as Racial Crisis," 3.

64. Hassan Ghedi Santur, "Maps of Exile," in *Warscapes* (Storrs, CT: OpSet Press, 2019), 70.

65. Santur, "Maps of Exile," 70.

66. Saidiya Hartman, "Venus in Two Acts," in P. Khalil Saucier and Tryon P. Woods, eds., *On Marronage: Ethical Confrontations with Antiblackness* (Trenton, NJ: Africa World Press, 2015), 53.

67. Hartman, "Venus in Two Acts," 49.

68. A host of exhibitions that focus on migration, and Mediterranean migration specifically, have been organized across Europe and the United States. Most recently, the Phillips Collection in Washington, DC, opened *The Warmth of Other Suns: Stories of Global Displacement* (June–September 2019). Others include documenta 14 (2017) in Athens and Kassel; the 58th Venice Biennale, and the Valencia Institute of Modern Art (IVAM) exhibit *Entre el mito y el espanto* (2016). To this may be added MoMA's ongoing Citizens and Borders series (which showed Bouchra Khalili's *The Mapping Journey Project* in 2016, as well as *One-Way Ticket: Jacob Lawrence's Migration Series and Other Visions of the Great Movement North* in 2015) and Judith Barry's 2018 mural *Untitled: (Global Displacement: nearly 1 in 100 people worldwide are displaced from their homes)*, which was exhibited on the Isabella Stewart Gardner Museum's façade in Boston. See also *Manifesta 2018*, the roving European biennial of contemporary art.

69. See T. J. Demos, *The Migrant Image: The Art and Politics of Documentary during Global Crisis* (Durham, NC: Duke University Press, 2013); Federica Mazzara, "The Role of Art in Subverting the '"Ungrievability"' of Migrant Lives," *PARSE* 10 (2020): 7.

70. Mazzara, "The Role of Art in Subverting the 'Ungrievability,'" 5. Following Iain Chamber, Mazzara understands artistic practices as encouraging "critical mourning." See Ian Chambers, *Culture after Humanism: History, Culture, Subjectivity* (Routledge, 2013).

71. We should note that Büchel worked in collaboration with the Assessorato regionale dei beni culturali e dell'identità siciliana, the Comune di Augusta, the Comitato 18 Aprile 2015, and other parties.

72. The fishing boat, which normally would have a crew of fewer than twenty men, was carrying well above its capacity. Migrants were locked up in the hold and the machine

room. After colliding with a Portuguese freighter that was attempting to come to its rescue, the boat sank with its imprisoned human cargo.

73. Elsa Goveia, *Slave Society in the British Leeward Islands at the End of the Eighteenth Century* (New Haven, CT: Yale University Press, 1965). Goveia's was a pioneering study of the institution of slavery and the first to put forth the concept of a "slave society" encompassing not just the slaves but the entire community. Jared Sexton, "The Rage: Some Closing Comments on "Open Casket," *Contemptorary.org*, May 21, 2017, https://contemptorary.org/the-rage-sexton.

74. Claire Bishop, *Installation Art* (London: Tate, 2005), 102.

75. Federica Mazzara, "The Role of Art in Subverting the "Ungrievability" of Migrant Lives," *PARSE* 10 (2020): 9. See also Federica Mazzara, *Reframing Migration: Lampedusa, Border Spectacle and Aesthetics of Subversion* (Oxford: Peter Lang, 2019).

76. Saidiya V. Hartman, "The Time of Slavery," *South Atlantic Quarterly* 101, no. 4 (2002): 757–777; Anthony Farley, "Perfecting Slavery," *Loyola University of Chicago Law Journal* 36 (2004): 225–256.

77. Sylvia Wynter, "Re-thinking 'Aesthetics': Notes Towards a Deciphering Practice," in *Ex-iles: Essays on Caribbean Cinema*, ed. Mbye B. Cham (Trenton, NJ: Africa World Press, 1992), 244.

78. David Marriott, *Whither Fanon? Studies in the Blackness of Being* (Stanford, CA: Stanford University Press, 2018), 228.

79. We might note at this point that we are entirely uninterested in Büchel's *intentions* in creating the *Barca Nostra* installation the way that he did. If ever there was a historical reality to verify the aphorism that the path to hell is paved in good intentions, it would be Western abolitionism.

80. "Augusta, trasferimento del barcone del naufragio del 18 aprile 2015 a Milano. Il 'Comitato 18 aprile': 'Utilizzare quei 600 mila euro per salvare vite umane,'" *Siracusa Times*, December 18, 2017, https://www.siracusatimes.it/augusta-trasferimento-del-barcone-del-naufragio-del-18-aprile-2015-a-milano-il-comitato-18-aprile-utilizzare-quei-600-mila-euro-per-salvare-vite-umane/.

81. Giuseppe Marinaro, "Un Giardino della memoria ad Augusta per la vittime delle stragi in mare," *Agenzia Italia*, June 20, 2021, https://www.agi.it/cronaca/news/2021-06-20/strage-migranti-2015-giardino-memoria-augusta-12984067/.

82. Marinaro, "Un Giardino della memoria ad Augusta per la vittime delle stragi in mare" (author's translation).

83. Alexandra Stock, "The privileged, violent stunt that is the Venice Biennale boat project," *Mada Masr*, May 29, 2019, https://madamasr.com/en/2019/05/29/feature/culture/the-privileged-violent-stunt-that-is-the-venice-biennale-boat-project/. Emphasis added.

84. Eleanor Paynter and Nicole Miller, "The White Readymade and the Black Mediterranean: Authoring 'Barca Nostra,'" *Los Angeles Review of Books*, September 22, 2019, https://lareviewofbooks.org/article/the-white-readymade-and-the-black-mediterranean-authoring-barca-nostra/.

85. See Marc Stierl and Nina Schwarz, "Amplifying Migrant Voices and Struggles at Sea as a Radical Practice," *South Atlantic Quarterly* 118, no. 3 (2019), 661–669.

86. Mazzara, "The Role of Art in Subverting the 'Ungrievability,'" 15.

87. Mazzara, "The Role of Art in Subverting the 'Ungrievability,'" 12.

88. Mazzara, "The Role of Art in Subverting the 'Ungrievability,'" 15.

89. Stuart Hall, "New Ethnicities," in *Stuart Hall: Cultural Dialogues in Cultural Studies*, ed. David Morley and Kuon-Hsing Chen (New York: Routledge, 1996), 442.

90. Elizabeth Alexander, "'Can you be BLACK and look at this?': Reading the Rodney King video(s)," *Public Culture* 7, no. 1 (1994): 78.

91. Orlando Patterson, *Slavery and Social Death: A Comparative Study* (Cambridge, MA: Harvard University Press, 2018).

92. See, for example, T. F. Earle and K. Lowe, *Black Africans in Renaissance Europe* (Cambridge: Cambridge University Press, 2005).

93. Jason deCaires Taylor, *The Underwater Museum: The Submerged Sculpture of Jason deCaires Taylor* (San Francisco: Chronicle Books, 2014).

94. Jason deCaires Taylor, "The Raft of Lampedusa Abdel," accessed August 12, 2021, https://www.youtube.com/watch?v=lYE6G0hpASQ.

95. Valérie Loichot, *Water Graves: The Art of the Unritual in the Greater Caribbean* (Charlottesville: University of Virginia Press, 2020), 144.

96. Too often, Frantz Fanon's notion of tabula rasa is understood to be in the service of a redemptive teleology (namely humanism), rather than as an axiological and epistemological pursuit that functions without appeal to the concepts and terms of the structurally empowered. In fact, it is Fanon's desire that it operate independent of recognition or any analysis that is dialectic in form. For our purposes, *Barca Nostra* illustrates an aesthetic project or a new symbolic form that exceeds both the racist *and* the anti-racist. Following Marriott's understanding of tabula rasa, we read *Barca Nostra* as "taking responsibility for a new form of spirit, as the discovery of a differentiation that is also the abyssal rupture of the bond between the universal and its various incarnations"; Marriott, *Whither Fanon*, 362.

97. Marriott, *Whither Fanon*, 254–257.

98. Lewis Gordon, *Her Majesty's Other Children: Sketches of Racism from a Neocolonial Age* (Lanham, MD: Rowman & Littlefield, 1997), 63.

99. Philip, *Zong!*, 206.

100. Ivan Van Sertima, *They Came Before Columbus: The African Presence in Ancient America* (New York: Random House, 1976); Julius S. Scott, *The Common Wind: Afro-American Currents in the Age of the Haitian Revolution* (London: Verso, 2018). In *African Migrants, European Borders, and the Problem with Humanitarianism*, we delve further into the role of black radical autonomous movement throughout the rise of Europe and the expansion of slaveholding culture.

101. A black "pattern of movement" is ascribed to Ralph Ellison. In fact, Ellison employed the phrase as simply a descriptive mapping of the movement between individual awareness of experience and a collective expression of patterns common to the group—*not* as an attempt at positing a grand explanation for how black people in general become legible to themselves and to the larger society as human. In other words, Ellison objected to how the academic industry of meaning-making (led in this instance by Henry Louis Gates Jr. and the formation of an African American literary canon) sought to formalize the varieties of black cultural expression into a theory of identity. See Ralph Ellison, "The Essential Ellison," interview, *Yard Bird Magazine* (1978): 155. The key passage of "pattern of movement" from this interview is reproduced in Ronald A. T. Judy, *(Dis)Forming the American Canon: African-Arabic Slave Narratives and the Vernacular* (Minneapolis: University of Minnesota Press, 1993), 49–50. See, alternatively, Henry Louis Gates Jr., *The Signifying Monkey: A Theory of African-American Literary Criticism*, 25th anniv. ed. (New York: Oxford University Press, 2014). For a critique of Gates and African American studies, see Sylvia Wynter, "How We Mistook the Map for the Territory, and Re-Imprisoned Ourselves in Our Unbearable Wrongness of Being, of *Désêtre*," in *Not Only the Master's*

Tools: African-American Studies in Theory and Practice, ed. Lewis R. Gordon and Jane Anna Gordon (Boulder, CO: Paradigm, 2006), 107–172; and Tryon P. Woods, *Blackhood Against the Police Power*. At another, but related, register, Ellison's "pattern of movement" also reminds us of Fanon's indelible insight that at a descriptive level any decolonization is a success—Fanon's point being that until and unless there is the creation of a new human, decolonization is everywhere incomplete.

2

The Immigrant's Other

PHILIP KRETSEDEMAS

> Because it is a systematic negation of the other person and a
> furious determination to deny the other person all attributes of
> humanity, colonialism forces the people it dominates to ask
> themselves this question constantly: "In reality, who am I?" . . .
> It must in any case be remembered that a colonized people is
> not only simply a dominated people. Under German
> occupation the French remained men; under the French
> occupation, the Germans remained men. In Algeria there is
> not simply the domination but the decision to the letter
> not to occupy anything more than the sum total of the land.
> The Algerians, the veiled women, the palm trees and
> the camels make up the landscape, the *natural*
> background to the human presence of the French.
>
> —FRANTZ FANON, *THE WRETCHED OF THE EARTH*

Frantz Fanon's reflections about the uniquely oppressive nature of colonial domination underscore a point made by other meditations on the black condition.[1] When he insists that French people under German occupation during World War II still remained "men," Fanon is implying that colonized Algerians—and colonized Africans more broadly—were treated as something other than "men." He is not describing the dilemma of "emasculated males," who suffer a degradation that uses masculinity as its frame of reference.[2] He is describing a kind of otherness that does not register as having a coherent gendered meaning, which is why Algerian bodies, camels, and palm trees could be viewed as if they were interchangeable features of a natural/nonhuman landscape.

Fanon has been rightly criticized for catering to misogynistic tropes or, at least, for failing to challenge them.[3] In the passage I have just quoted, for example, he refers to "the Algerians" and then to "veiled women," who are also presumably Algerian but who are distinguished, by gender, from "the Algerians," who define the racial and national idea. Effectively, "veiled women" are reduced to a subcategory of an Algerian identity that is normatively male. These androcentric tendencies in Fanon's choice of words also show up in his insistence that the "French remained men" under the German occupation (and vice versa), despite the fact that he is describing the occupation of an entire country, which would have to include the women of that country.

But as I have already noted, Fanon is also using these observations to describe a troubled relationship to gender norms that is singular to the black experience. His writing evokes a social ontology in which whiteness, humanity, gender, and sexual "normality" all signal and reflexively inform one another. Contemporary Black feminist, Queer, and Afropessimist scholars have explored this relationship between sexuality and racialization in more depth,[4] describing an imaginary and a field of sociostructural relations in which blackness marks the nether zone of normal sexual desire and reproduction.

This problem is comparable to the troubled relationship between blackness and immigration. Blackness has been alienated from the immigrant/citizen binary, in much the same way that it has been alienated from normalizing discourses on gender and sexuality. In order to frame this problem properly, it is important, first of all, to push back against the idea that the immigrant and the citizen are fundamentally different social types. Although the immigrant and the citizen are locked in a hierarchical relationship, they can also be located within the assimilationist ideal that is central to the political mythology of the modern nation-state, and of the United States in particular.[5]

The immigrant has also been associated with qualities that are "genetic" to the modern individual.[6] They undertake migrations that can be described as freely chosen calculated risks, in the same way that any self-interested individual might weigh the costs and benefits of a particular path of action. Viewed in this light, the immigrant is not necessarily the citizen's other; the immigrant is a "citizen in training" who occupies a different rank than the citizen but has a similar investment in the social ladder on which they are both located. The immigrant's other, in contrast, lies outside of this chain of associations. This other kind of other is neither citizen nor migrant. They have a fundamentally different relationship to the land and to their mobility. A good starting point for thinking about this kind of otherness is the contrast between the immigrant and the native.

The etymology of the word *native* can be traced to the early colonial era. In this time, *native* carried connotations of bondage and stagnation.[7] Migration, on the other hand, was associated with merchants, evangelizers, military troops and other persons who were able to fix their gaze on the native from a position of civilizational superiority; similar to the French colonial view of the Algerian. Within this universe of meaning, the migrant/explorer is the superior type, who moves of their own accord.[8] The native is the inferior type, who is encountered in their habitat, burdened by traditions, superstitions, and rituals that keep them fixed in place.

This distinction between mobility and stasis is also reflected in the contrast between the slave and the migrant. The U.S. lawmakers of the antebellum era understood that the transatlantic slave trade was not a migration regime. In their eyes, slavery concerned the importation of tradable goods, not the migration of rights-bearing people.[9] Practically speaking, this meant that the slave was governed by a different body of laws than the immigrant. This legal distinction also carried profound implications for how the mobility of the slave and the immigrant was reconciled to the scientific racism of the eighteenth and nineteenth centuries. The immigrant was, at least, eligible for citizenship whereas the slave was categorically excluded from this consideration. The immigrant could be inserted in narratives that depicted their mobility as self-willed, and which judged their deservingness in light of other traits that underscored their agency, like their industriousness, their moral fiber, and their loyalty to the national idea.[10] The mobility of the slave, on the other hand, was necessarily controlled by others.[11] Furthermore, as Calvin Warren has explained, the black slave (and the manumitted "free black") was excluded from social membership not simply by the letter of the law but by an existential judgment on their status as a (sub)human being that preceded and overdetermined the interpretation of the law—establishing a condition of ontological degradation that continued to haunt the black body long after the dismantling of chattel slavery.[12]

In the remainder of the chapter, I explore this tortured relationship between blackness, migration, and nativity and offer some insights for a theory of Black mobility. Although I have begun the chapter by using nativity as a point of contrast for the citizen/immigrant binary, I am going to show that the Black condition (and Black mobility) must also be distinguished from that of the racialized native. Of course, there are Black people, especially on the African continent, who have legitimate claims to indigeneity. It is also very common for Black people in North America and elsewhere to claim an immigrant or citizen identity or some combination of both, which are, in some cases, also combined with claims to indigeneity (in the case, for example, of those who identify as Black and American Indian[13]).

But if (anti)blackness is viewed through the lens of the transatlantic slave trade and the evolutionary hierarchies that defined the modern concept of race, it is not possible to root the meaning of blackness in a precolonial African past. Rather than being defined through reference to a pre-Columbian "land," "culture," or "peoples," blackness is irreducibly modern. It describes an experience of otherness that has been uniquely stamped by the violent displacements that cleared the way for the modern social order. Even if it is acknowledged that the European history of antiblackness predates the modern era,[14] blackness is still enmeshed in a painful, antithetical relationship to European modernity, defining that which the European-modern "is not."

I aim to show that this understanding of black otherness points toward a kind of mobility that has been stripped of any assurance of territorial belonging. Whereas the native is stigmatized for their immobility, the black condition is typified by an agonistic mobility that is fluid and unfree. The White or nonblack citizens are beneficiaries of a privileged mobility that is anchored by their territorial belonging. Black mobility, on the other hand, can be described as an experience of being radically uprooted. Blackness becomes salient when the informal organization of power that is constantly reinscribing the subhumanity of the black body manages to eat through all of the social roles and (legal) statuses that are meant to anchor a person in a given social structure.

The remainder of the chapter is devoted to exploring the defining features of this experience, using the social types of the citizen, the immigrant, and the native-indigene as a point of contrast. In the next sections of the chapter, I use excerpts from the stories of fugitive slaves to describe a Black experience of mobility that is radically different from that of the modern citizen-subject but remains umbilically connected to the modern world from which it is presumptively excluded. At the end of the chapter, I provide a more detailed discussion of how Black mobility differs from other kinds of transgressive mobilities—especially those proposed by radical Indigenous scholars—by putting some of the insights from Afropessimist theory in dialogue with Gilles Deleuze and Félix Guattari's writing on nomadism.

Exploration versus Escape

William Bartram was one of the more influential European American explorers of the eighteenth century. He is best known for his book *Travels through North & South Carolina, Georgia, East and West Florida, the Cherokee Country, Etc.*, which was published in 1791 and had a significant impact on both the scientific community and the literary circles of his day.[15] *Travels* is, largely, an account of the physical environment that Bartram adventured through, which was interpreted through the lens of his training, as a botanist, ornithologist, and natural historian.[16] Consider the following excerpt:

> We passed for several miles on the left by islands of high swamp land, exceedingly fertile . . . They consist of a loose black mould, with a mixture of, sand, shells and dissolved vegetables. The opposite Indian coast is . . . , a perpendicular bluff, ten or twelve feet high, consisting of a black sandy earth, mixed, with a, large proportion of shells chiefly various species of fresh water Cochlea . . . and Mytuli. Near the river on this high shore, grew Corypha palma, Magnolia grandiflora, Live

Oak, Callicarpa, Myrica cerifera, Hybiscus spinifex, and the beautiful evergreen shrub called Wild lime or Tallow nut. This last shrub grows six or eight feet high, many erect items rising, from a root; the leaves are lanciolate and infire, two or three inches in length and one in breadth, of a deep green colour, and polished; at the foot of each leaf grows a stiff sharp thorn.[17]

Although he often traveled alone, it is important to situate Bartram's journal entries socially. Bartram's writing reflects the habitus of the White, male intelligentsia of the American colonies and that of a broader European reading audience. His writing provides empirical verification for the taxonomic ordering of the natural world that had been pioneered by Carl Linneaus, which also carried implications for the ordering of the social world.[18] Race crops up in Bartram's writing, as it does in Linneaus's treatises, as an innocuous and objective descriptor of human difference:

Being desirous of continuing my travels and observations, higher up the river, and having an invitation from a gentleman who was agent for, and resident at a large plantation, the property of an English gentleman, about fifty miles higher up, I resolved to Pursue., my researches, to that place; and having engaged in my service a young Indian, nephew to the White Captain, he agreed to assist me in working my Vessel up, as high as a certain bluff, where I was by agreement, to land him, on the West or Indian shore, whence he designed to go in quest of the camp of the White Trader, his relation. Provisions and all neccessaries, being procured, and the morning pleasant, we went on board and stood up the river.[19]

This excerpt from Bartram provides a good example of how racial distinctions between "Indians" and "Whites" are used as a cartographic shorthand that helps to structure Bartram's narration of his travels. He proceeds "up river" to the "property of an English gentlemen" and later to the "camp of a White Trader," and he is accompanied through the wilderness that separates these white encampments by a "young Indian" who guides his way. Bartram also makes a distinction between the "Indian shore" of the river and a Western shore that is presumably "non-Indian" and in closer proximity to white civilization.

In Bartram's travel log, Indian-ness functions as a way of marking the distinctions between a white and nonwhite social geography, as well as describing a benign non-European otherness (in the form of the Indian guide) that facilitates Bartram's journey through lands that lie outside the reach of white civilization. But Bartram's presence also transforms this cartography. Through his travel writings, Bartram converts the wilderness into a territory that is intelligible to the mostly male, upper-class, propertied intelligentsia of Europe and the American colonies. It also bears noting that Bartram embarked on some of his journeys to survey lands that were to be ceded by American Indian tribal governments to British colonists.[20] All of this goes to underscore how Bartram's naturalist account of American lands was mediated through his location in a structure of social relations that was intent on securing these lands for white settlers.

The fugitive slave narrative of Henry Bibb, which was written almost seventy years after Bartram's *Travels*, describes a very different relationship to American society and American lands.[21] For Bartram, there is a functional relationship between his mobility and his writing. He travels for the purpose of surveying the land and documenting his observations for others to read. Bibb, on the other hand, experiences mobility as an agonizing condition that is constantly interrupting his writing. In his preface, for example, he confesses that

this work has been written during irregular intervals, while I have been travelling and laboring for the emancipation of my enslaved countrymen. The reader will remember that I make no pretension to literature; for I can truly say, that I have been educated in the school of adversity, whips, and chains. Experience and observation have been my principal teachers, with the exception of three weeks schooling which I have had the good fortune to receive since my escape from the "grave yard of the mind," or the dark prison of human bondage.[22]

In place of Bartram's philosophical, ornithological, and botanical education, Bibb declares an "education in the school of adversity, whips and chains." The contrast between these two kinds of education underscores Bartram's race and class privilege relative to Bibb's. But it is just as important to note that Bibb's education, like his experience of mobility, is more transparently sociological than Bartram's.

Bartram documents his travels through a natural wilderness. Bibb, on the other hand, is trying to navigate his way through an oppressive field of social relations. Put another way, Bibb is describing a relational field that has been produced by networks of power and privilege between unequally positioned social actors. Bibb is concerned with deciphering the interests of social actors—reading between the lines of their stated intentions—and strategically conforming to the social norms and performance expectations of a given social setting. Whom can he trust? How can he behave like a "normal" person in public settings, while concealing his status as an escaped slave?

The end result is a narrative that is gripped by the necessity of becoming mobile, in order to get free, while remaining painfully aware of how this mobility can be jeopardized by the slightest misstep. This sensibility is reflected in the summary of events that precedes each of his chapters, like that of Chapter 4, which reads, "My first adventure for liberty.—Parting scene—Journey up the river.—Safe arrival in Cincinnati.—Journey to Canada.—Suffering from cold and hunger.—Denied food and shelter by some.—One noble exception.—Subsequent success.—Arrival at Perrysburgh.—I obtained employment through the winter.—My return to Kentucky to get my family."[23]

Later in this same chapter of his book, Bibb offers these reflections on his journey northward:

There were no questions asked me while on board the boat. The boat landed about 9 o'clock in the morning in Cincinnati, and I waited until after most of the passengers had gone off of the boat; I then walked as gracefully up street as if I was not running away, until I had got pretty well up Broadway. My object was to go to Canada, but having no knowledge of the road, it was necessary for me to make some inquiry before I left the city. I was afraid to ask a white person, and I could see no colored person to ask. But fortunately for me I found a company of little boys at play in the street, and through these little boys, by asking them indirect questions, I found the residence of a colored man. . . .

He invited me in, and I found him to be a true friend. He asked me if I was a slave from Kentucky, and if I ever intended to go back into slavery? Not knowing yet whether he was truly in favor of slaves running away, I told him that I had just come over to spend my christmas holydays, and that I was going back. His reply was, "My son, I would never go back if I was in your place; you have a right to your liberty.' I then asked him how I should get my freedom? He referred me to Canada, over which waved freedom's flag, defended by the British Government, upon whose soil there cannot be the foot print of a slave.

I travelled on until I had arrived at the place where I was directed to call on an Abolitionist, but I made no stop: so great were my fears of being pursued by the pro-slavery hunting dogs of the South. I prosecuted my journey vigorously for nearly forty-eight hours without food or rest, struggling against external difficulties such as no one can imagine who has never experienced the same: not knowing what moment I might be captured while travelling among strangers, through cold and fear, breasting the north winds, being thinly clad, pelted by the snow storms through the dark hours of the night, and not a house in which I could enter to shelter me from the storm.[24]

For Bibb, as for Bartram, race is intimately connected to cartography. The distinction between "White property" and "Indian lands" that crops up in Bartram's narrative is replaced, in Bibb's narrative, by a distinction between safe and unsafe spaces. In the excerpt just above, for example, Bibb shares his concerns about asking a White person for tips on where he could shelter. The "little boys" who point him in the direction of a "colored man's" house may have been black, or Bibb may have felt that their age exempted them from the distrust he would normally reserve for white adults. In any event, he ends up at the house a "colored man" who shelters him for the night and gives him advice on how to flee to Canada, though Bibb rejects the suggestion of seeking shelter from an abolitionist (who was likely a white person) whose house was on his travel route.

One way to sum up the distinguishing features of these two travel logs is that Bartram is describing an act of exploration whereas Bibb is trying to escape. This distinction between exploration and escape describes two radically different orientations toward mobility. As I have already noted, these orientations are rooted in two very different relationships to American colonial society. Bartram is surveying lands that will, eventually, be claimed by this society, whereas Bibb is trying to free himself from an apparatus of social control that is endemic to this society.

Bartram's mobility can be described by hierarchical schema in which higher/lower distinctions inform the social meaning of the civilized/primitive distinction or the distinction between cultivated and uncultivated lands. All of the living things (including people, plants, and wild animals) that Bartram describes in his travel log can be located in an evolutionary taxonomy that, as some scholars have observed, is a secular translation of the medieval Great Chain of Being.[25] The key question that one asks, when using this categorical system, is "How proximate should this creature be placed relative to the Supreme Being?" Bibb's mobility, on the other hand, is better described by a horizontal or lateral schema organized around distinctions between freedom and capture. The key question that Bibb seeks to answer in every scenario is not "How civilized or superior is this person or thing?" but "Will this path of action allow me to continue an open-ended trajectory of movement, so that I can escape my life of chains?"

I hope the contrast that I have made between Bibb's and Bartram's experience of mobility is clear enough. But as instructive as it may be, this contrast does not get to the heart of the troubled relationship between blackness and immigrant mobility. Thus far, I have only contrasted the mobility of a White citizen[26] to that of an escaped Black slave. There is still the question of how to distinguish Black mobility from that of the immigrant. To answer this question, it will be necessary to take a closer look at the predicament that sets Black people to flight.

Robert Park offers an insight into this predicament with his reflections on "Racial Assimilation in Secondary Groups, with Particular Reference to the Negro." Park uses the words of Charles Francis Adams to great effect when he quotes this:

> We are confronted by the obvious fact, undeniable as it is hard, that the African will only partially assimilate, and that he cannot be absorbed. He remains an alien element in the body politic. A foreign substance, he can neither be assimilated nor thrown out.[27]

One of the curious things about this statement is that the "African" is described as a "foreign substance" in the context of an essay that is trying to explain why Black populations face barriers to assimilation unlike those faced by any other migrant or racialized group. The thing that is taken for granted by this statement, and which neither Park nor Adams gets around to explaining, is what makes the "foreign-ness" of Black populations so difficult to assimilate? It is important to keep in mind that the "African" population that Adams addresses in his speech was composed, predominantly, of Black people who are native-born U.S. citizens, which is why his reference to the "foreignness" of these people should be understood as a euphemism for a quality that does not hinge on the "nativity" or "foreign-ness" of a person's national origins. So what exactly is "foreign" about this U.S.-born Black population?

My answer to this question is that "foreign-ness" is being used by Adams as shorthand for the social ontology that underlies the categorical distinction between White and Black. Viewed in this light, Black people are not "foreign" to the United States so much as they are "foreign" to modern civilization. If you read Adams's statement through the lens of the Social Darwinist ideology of the times, it also follows that this "foreign-ness" has more to do with innate and inherited traits than with legal status and nationality. Put more simply, Black people are biological aliens. Adams caters to this way of seeing by alluding to the absolute difference that separates white and black (which is why Blacks, in his view, can never be completely assimilated into U.S. culture). But he ends by noting that while people of Black/African-heritage cannot be assimilated, neither can they be "thrown out." These closing words evoke a strangely intimate relationship between whiteness and black otherness. Blackness may describe an absolute difference, but it is a difference, nonetheless, that is inextricably bound up with the history of the U.S. social order from which Black people have been excluded. This acknowledgment is an apt starting point for reflecting on the qualities that distinguish Black mobility from the White citizen, the non-Black immigrant, and American Indigenous populations. I explore these differences in more detail in the next section.

What Is Black Mobility?

Black mobility has a complex and conflicted relationship to the colonization of the Americas, being oppressed by the institutions of colonial society, struggling to free itself from these oppressive conditions, and also being shaped by institutional arrangements that were in the service of colonization. These conflicted relationships are reflected, in various ways—for example, in the exploits of the Black fur trappers of the eighteenth and nineteenth centuries and the tours of duty of the buffalo soldiers who were on the front lines of the "Indian wars" of the nineteenth and early twentieth centuries.[28] They are also reflected in the many and varied uses of enslaved blacks as traveling assistants for their owners[29] and the sojourns of precariously employed free blacks, some of whom opted to work as merchant sailors or join the "African colonization" projects that were organized and funded by U.S. elites.[30]

It is also well known that enslaved Blacks often formed alliances with American Indians and that many escaped slaves preferred to live and die with these people than flee to Canada or to the non-slaveholding states of the United States. One of the more remarkable examples of these stories is that of Joseph Godfrey. Joseph was the son of a free White man (French Canadian by nationality and birth) and an enslaved Black woman.[31] He was raised a slave, according to the laws of the day, in which slave status was determined by matrilineal descent.[32]

Joseph's life was marked by cruel ironies. He was enslaved in Minnesota, a state that was legally regarded as a "free state."[33] His mother, who was sold to another master when Joseph was five, ended up securing her freedom with the help of the same lawyer who filed the *Dred Scott* case, but Joseph lived out the rest of his childhood in slavery.[34] He also spent several years serving as a personal assistant and errand boy to Henry Sibley, a wealthy White fur trapper who eventually became the first governor of Minnesota.[35] When he reached his twenties, Joseph fled the Sibley household because of how cruelly he was treated, and made his way to Dakota territory, where he married and started a family with a Dakota woman.[36]

Years later, when the U.S.-Dakota War of 1862 broke out, Joseph decided to join sides with the Dakota warriors. According to one account, Joseph was ambivalent about this decision: "Godfrey's options were to leave his family to seek refuge among the army whose officers had enslaved his mother, or to stay with the Dakotas who had given him refuge. His life was imperiled no matter which way he turned: he remained with the Dakota and reluctantly accompanied the war party to Milford."[37]

Joseph was called Atokte, or "Many Kills," by the Dakota for his prowess in battle.[38] But when he was captured by U.S. troops, Joseph denied killing anyone and there were no white eye witnesses who could corroborate the honorary name he had been granted by the Dakota.[39] To avoid execution, Joseph ended up testifying against the Dakota warriors whom he had fought alongside.[40] It so happens that Joseph's boyhood master, George Sibley, was the commanding general at Joseph's trial. Sibley insisted on Joseph's execution but the military judges recommended clemency.[41] Joseph was granted clemency and eventually received a full pardon from Abraham Lincoln, but only after serving three years of a prison sentence along with close friends and relatives of some of the Dakota warriors who had been executed because of his testimony.[42] Not surprisingly, Joseph had enemies on all sides and the Dakota had more reason to hate him than did the whites. Joseph's testimony against eleven of the Dakota warriors in his war band aided the court in reaching a verdict that resulted in the largest mass execution in U.S. history, which included his own father-in-law.[43]

Many of the white soldiers who were present at Joseph's trial wanted to see him killed, and Dakota warriors made attempts on his life after he was released from prison.[44] Even so, Joseph decided to spend the rest of his life in Nebraska on the Santee Sioux Reservation, where he married two Dakota women and lived for several more decades as a "peaceable and industrious man."[45] Joseph died of natural causes at the age of seventy-four and it is reported that he has well over a hundred descendants living today, all of whom identify as American Indian.[46]

Joseph's story is not heroic, but his pathos and even his treachery were not simply a consequence of his personal choices. They also reveal something about the predicament of blackness in its relationship to White society and Indigenous people. In many ways, Joseph was more like the White settlers than the Dakota warriors. Even so, he decided to live out the rest of his life in Dakota-Sioux territory, choosing to associate with a people he had betrayed rather than return to a society that had granted him a presidential pardon. The following excerpt from Deleuze and Guattari provides some insight into the sensibility informing his decisions:

> The warrior is in the position of betraying everything, even the function of the military, or of understanding nothing. It happens that historians, both bourgeois and Soviet, will follow this negative tradition and explain how Genghis Khan understood nothing: he "didn't understand" the phenomenon of the city. An easy thing to say. The problem is that the exteriority of the war machine in relation to the State apparatus is everywhere apparent but remains difficult to conceptualize. It is not enough to affirm that the war machine is external to the apparatus. It is necessary to reach a point of conceiving the war

machine as itself, a pure form of exteriority, whereas the State apparatus constitutes the form of interiority we habitually take as a model, or according to which we are in the habit of thinking.[47]

Deleuze and Guattari use the contrast between the war machine and the state to describe a radical difference. The term *war machine* is unfortunate because it invites a confusion that Deleuze and Guatarri are constantly warning against. They insist that the war machine is not the same thing as the military arm of the state and that it does not actually pursue war as an end itself.[48] This thing that they call "the war machine" is defined, primarily, by a kind of mobility, which Deleuze and Guattari distinguish from that of the state-form. The state-form organizes space into categories that are derived from the symbolic order it uses to establish its cultural and political monopoly over the society it governs.[49] Movement is translated into measurable distances between fixed points in space that are integrated within a hierarchical organization; it's comparable to what Bartram was doing with his travel logs.

The war machine, in contrast, is defined by a quality of speed, and by trajectories of escape and retreat, that decompose the fixity of the territory into a sea of forces and flows. Deleuze and Guattari also liken the war machine to the force of the hunted animal, and they make a point of emphasizing that this is a very different thing than the relationship of the hunter to the animal. This is the point at which their discussion of the war machine becomes more relevant for a theory of Black mobility.

If we take the fugitive slave as a starting point, it becomes easier to see how Deleuze and Guattari arrive at their critique of the state-form. The very same social relations that generate stability and security for some also require the oppression and radical exclusion of others. The former can be described by an orderly movement across the space of the social, whereas the latter is better described as a flight from society; and this flight is to no place in particular. There are practical destinations, of course—the safe house, the "free state," or the Indian reservation—but the overarching aim is to avoid capture and to break with society in a way that makes it possible to cultivate new relationships that are conducive to a freer life. And because there is always a possibility of recapture—Fugitive Slave laws, for example, authorized the return of escaped slaves no matter where they were found—the condition of flight is permanent. No matter how normal and settled the new life appears to be, the fundamental relationship between the fugitive and the social order they have fled remains the same. There is always a possibility that tendrils of power, emanating from this order, will find a way to expose the "free life" as a charade and return the fugitive to bondage, which is why one can never trust the stability of things. All social relations must be viewed with an eye for the escape routes they can afford, should one's worst fears come to light.

One of the things that Deleuze and Guattari have accomplished with their meditations on the war machine is to write a theory of power into mobility. They identify three lines or modalities: the sedentary type, the migrant, and the nomadic.[50] Under this typology, the modern relationship to mobility that I described at the beginning of this chapter is turned on its head. The sedentary type is epitomized by the modern citizen, who is "static" not because they never travel but because their subjectivity derives from the state-form, which is invested in stasis—the production and regulation of territory and social structure as a principle of organization.

The immigrant's relationship to the state is more precarious, because they may not be granted a secure legal status; they can be deported or integrated as disposable undocumented workers. But the distinction between the legal migrant and the unauthorized migrant is still a product of the policy discourse of the state, and their mobility is also conceptualized and regulated through the lens of this policy discourse.

Nomadic mobility, on the other hand, follows very different coordinates. Whereas the state-form imposes a categorical matrix of its own invention on the land, the nomad moves in sympathy with the land, by deciphering qualities and patterns that are intrinsic to it. Because these qualities cannot be standardized, they are not useful to the state; they obstruct its universalist ambitions and its desire to subsume the natural and social world under its discursive categories. The nomad has more humble ambitions, which are merely to eat, love, and fight another day. Regardless of whether the terrain is social or natural, benign or treacherous, the nomad attempts to understand it on its own terms and be carried along by its flows and forces.

It is important to emphasize, however, that nomadism is a transient orientation rather than an identity. Although we are in the habit of identifying certain populations as "nomadic," Deleuze and Guatarri use the term to describe a quality that is latent to all things. The important question to ask is not whether this or that thing is nomadic but whether it has crossed a threshold into nomadism and how long the nomadic phase will last. People can also be possessed, for a period of time, by the spirit of nomadism, and then enter into a more sedentary existence. Deleuze and Guattari recount a Bantu myth that describes this process:

Nkongolo, an indigenous emperor and administrator of public works, a man of the public and a man of the police, gives his half-sisters to the hunter Mbidi, who assists him, and then leaves. Mbidi's son, a man of secrecy, joins up with his father, only to return from the outside with that inconceivable thing, an army. He kills Nkongolo, and pro-

ceeds to build a new State. . . . "Between" the magical-despotic State
and the juridical State containing a military institution, we see the
flash of the war machine, arriving from without.[51]

Joseph Godfrey is not so different from the mythical figures of Mbidi and his
son. Mbidi, the hunter-nomad, wages war against Nkongolo's government,
but Mbidi's desire to build a new state also requires him to give up his nomadic life and become "a man of the public," like the emperor he toppled.
Similarly, but less dramatically, Joseph transitions from a nomadic way of life
to a more sedentary existence. He begins his life in chains, then takes to a life
of a fugitive. He settles down, for a while, on Dakota territory, but is forced
to choose sides in the U.S.-Dakota War, and decides, perhaps begrudgingly,
to throw in his lot with a Dakota war band. The role Joseph plays in the conflict is shrouded in ambiguity; the evasive testimony he provides to the military tribunal, for example, evokes the tactics of the battlefield. But his eva-
siveness serves its purpose. Joseph escapes execution and ends his days living
what would appear to be the epitome of a sedentary life, that of a prosperous
farmer who is married and has children. It is also quite possible that Joseph's
relationship to the U.S. state, as a pardoned "free man," granted him a measure of status and privilege that allowed him to live a life on the Santee Reservation that was more comfortable than anything he could have realized in
U.S. society.

The main point is that Joseph did not spend his entire life as a fugitive-
nomad. Expanding on this point, it would be a gross overstatement to say that
all Black people are, necessarily, nomadic all of the time. To channel Ralph
Ellison, it would be better to say that blackness is a predicament that predis-
poses people to a nomadic pattern of movement.[52]

This tendency to give oneself over to a line of flight, like a hunted animal,
can also be understood as a sociostructural transformation that is catalyzed
by a change in consciousness. The schemas that make people into "persons,"
fixing them to a particular structure of social relations, are replaced by a sche-
matic of flight that is premised on a radical disillusionment with the ontological security of this structure. The structure is too weak; it cannot protect
you. Or maybe it is malicious and it wants to cannibalize you. Either way, the
schematics that normalize one's place in the structure are replaced by an
orientation that enables a different kind of movement, away and out of this
structure. Deleuze and Guattari's writing on nomadism describes a similar
experience, but in a curiously abstract way. They use Bantu myths and examples of Black radical posturing to describe a nomadism that, in their view,
is not specific to the Black condition itself. Consequently, they write at a distance from blackness and even, arguably, at a distance from nomadism itself.
This distance comes across when they describe the nomad as one who "cap-

tures the force of the hunted animal, and enters into an entirely new relation to man."[53]

The nomad may enter into this sympathetic relationship with the animal, but there is still something rather instrumental about the idea that the force of this animal can be captured and appropriated by the nomad. The nomad who "captures" this force is still distinct from the animal. Deleuze and Guattari's use of the word *capture* is also telling because, elsewhere in their writing, they associate this word with the state-form (described as an apparatus of capture).[54] This choice of words suggests that the nomad stands in relation to the hunted animal in the way the state stands in relation to the nomad. Even so, the positionality of the nomad vis-à-vis the hunted animal is not discussed. It also bears emphasizing that Deleuze and Guattari describe an experience that can be conveyed only from the perspective of the nomad, not from the perspective of the hunted animal whose force is "captured" by the nomad.

Similarly, when Deleuze and Guattari insist on the necessity of "becoming minoritarian" and "becoming Woman" (along with other kinds of transgressive becomings), they offer no reflections on their own race, class, or gender positionality in relation to these becomings.[55] They also repeat the Black Panthers' exhortation that "even black people must become Black," and Faulkner's insistence on "becoming Black" as the only way to avoid becoming a fascist.[56] In these passages, blackness is treated as a vehicle for transgressive politics—a means of resistance or escape—but these discussions are not accompanied by an analysis of antiblack racism or of the black/nonblack binary.

Deleuze and Guattari understand that these transgressive becomings do not produce the same effects in all people who become enmeshed in them. Even so, their writing on this subject is surprisingly reminiscent of the Hegelian master-slave dialectic, in which the "becoming woman" of the woman or the "becoming Jew" of the Jewish person sets an entire field of social relations in flight—providing an escape route for the man and the non-Jew, who can "become Jewish" and "become woman" in their own way.[57] They do not consider how these processes can fortify the very same majoritarian/minoritarian power relations they appear to be transgressing. For example, consider the many ways that Black culture has been appropriated by nonblacks in a way that converts their transgressive force into relatively mundane acts of consumption—acts that bolster the mainstream culture industry and that take shape alongside worsening patterns of race-class stratification.[58]

This is not to say that the transgressive becomings described by Deleuze and Guattari are of no consequence. But it is also necessary to underscore a point that they never directly address, which is that the Black experience of blackness and the nonblack appropriation of the "force" of Black fugitivity are two very different things. If you treat these things as somehow commen-

surate or as necessarily mutual, you are denying the salience of the black/
nonblack binary that anchors antiblack racism, bleeding the (Black) fugitive
experience of the very force that Deleuze and Guattari attribute to it.

Black Nomadism: The Endless Line of Flight

When it comes to blackness, Deleuze violates one of his own axioms, which
is that there is much more to gain from formulating problems than from de-
signing solutions.[59] A good problem is open-ended and can inspire the production of an endless variety of solutions. Solutions, on the other hand, tend
toward finality; they close off a line of inquiry. This is why it is especially significant that Deleuze and Guattari's writing on blackness has a prescriptive
quality. Black politics and culture are offered up to the reader as a "solution"
for a way of life that will lead toward a stultified authoritarianism if it is not
interrupted in some way. But exactly *whose* problem is being solved by these
nomadic readings of Black resistance?

I cannot provide a thorough answer to this question in the space of this
chapter. But it bears noting that Deleuze and Guattari had a more complicated relationship to the modern state than did the nomad of their written
work. For most of his professional life, Deleuze was a tenured professor at a
state university.[60] Guattari was more directly involved than Deleuze in social
movement activity, though much of this activity involved creating radical
psychotherapy and research collectives that were connected to universities,
unions, and professional organizations.[61] Their nomadism could be described
as an intervention that was partly enabled by and erupted from within the
very same institutions that constitute the state-form. This is not a damning
criticism, and in some ways it is consistent with Deleuze's understanding of
the way that change happens.[62] It can also be described as a variety of nonblack nomadism—or rather, a nomadism that erupts from a structural location that is typically legitimized and embodied as "nonblack."

Another important point of contrast for a Black nomadism is the territorial politics of Indigenous populations. The significance of the Indigenous-
American Indian experience is underscored by Frank Wilderson's theory of
the modern racial hierarchy, which is relationally structured through the categories of blackness, indigeneity, and whiteness.[63] For Wilderson, the "sedentary" and "immigrant" lines discussed by Deleuze and Guattari can be understood as iterations of the white (or nonblack by default) racial category.
Deleuze and Guattari's nomadism, on the other hand, can apply in different
ways to the Indigenous and black categories, which is why it is necessary to
consider the distinguishing features of both.

The territorial politics of Indigenous populations has an investment in
a sovereignty that predates the arrival of the European colonizer. But this

politics makes a marked departure from the mobility and aspirations of the immigrant, which affirms the sovereignty of the modern nation-state. The Indigenous claim on the land introduces a cartography that disrupts the geopolitical configuration of the modern state. It questions the authority by which the settler lays claim to the land, and it pronounces a moral judgment on the native-born citizen. This sensibility can also be described as a transgressive reterritorialization.

According to Deleuze and Guattari, all entities fluctuate between moments of deterritorialization and reterritorialization.[64] These moments can be understood as centrifugal and centripetal tendencies: a dispersion followed by a reconsolidation. The state-form has used these movements to consolidate and extend its geopolitical configuration. The nomad also reterritorializes, but in a very different way. The distinction between the one and the many collapses. One belongs by virtue of a nonpersonal identification with a tribal entity that creates a sense of place out of its own collective desire.[65] The tribe does not lay claim to the land so much as it resists other sovereign ambitions that would disrupt its relationship to the land. Nevertheless, there is still the impetus to reterritorialize, to claim a space that can be occupied by the tribe, no more matter how temporarily, in a way that befits its nomadic sensibilities.

The territorial politics of Indigenous populations resonates with both of these kinds of reterritorialization. It tends in a nomadic direction, insofar as it opposes the ideologies of settlement (aka settler colonialism) that normalize the histories of conquest that have produced the modern nation-state. But it imitates the logic of the state when its territorial ambitions are translated into a geopolitical language and mode of governance that would make it legible to the interstate system. In either case, this drive to reclaim territory accentuates the difference between a Black relationship to the land and an Indigenous one.

Jared Sexton picks up on this difference when he cautions Indigenous rights activists against trying to get Black people to identify with their African Indigenous past as a starting point for a joint struggle against settler colonialism.[66] For Sexton, these political desires do not take natal alienation seriously enough as an axiological feature of the Black condition.[67]

Sexton insists that, especially for the descendants of African people who were enslaved in the Americas, the identification with an Indigenous past can occur only at a highly abstract level.[68] It is not the same kind of identification as that of American Indian populations and it cannot play the same role, as an anchoring point for a politics of group identity. According to Sexton, this is why natal alienation has to be brought front and center if we want to properly diagnose the Black condition. It also bears emphasizing that natal alienation does not simply describe an empirical experience of displacement. It describes a location in a social ontology that situates black people as necessarily placeless, as people who have been sundered from a land that had no "history" to begin with.

The important point is that blackness is inextricably bound up with the ruptures that produce this radically depersonalized placeless condition. Whereas an Indigenous nomadism can anchor itself in a pre-Columbian memory of itself, the analysis of blackness has to contend with a problem that is irreducibly modern. The desire to jump over this problem, to an identification with an Indigenous past, participates in the same error that Deleuze and Guattari commit when they describe "becoming Black" as something "we all must do." In both cases, a "solution" is advanced that evades an analysis of problems that are singular to the Black condition.

The remedy proposed by Sexton runs in the opposite direction. Instead of affirming a Black Indigenous identity that sidesteps the analysis of natal alienation, the problem of natal alienation needs to be rendered more clearly and used as a starting point for rethinking the troubled relationship between blackness and territory. Sexton goes onto argue that if you want to create a new politics that is prepared to deal with the black condition, you have to dismantle the concept of sovereignty. Borrowing the words of Nahum Chandler, he proposes that "the field of Black Studies consists of 'tracking the figure of the *unsovereign*'" [italics in the original].[69] I also want to emphasize that this call for a politics of the unsovereign is not an invitation to a postmodern celebration of placelessness or a postnational multiculturalism (that would still be antiblack).[70] Instead, it requires you to face up to the web of power relations that requires territorial alienation as a precondition for the creation of the fungible black other.

This situation can be summed up in the following way: If there is a Black nomadism, it has to be understood as a line of flight that cannot reterritorialize and that resists the urge to reterritorialize. This kind of nomadism is not well described as a freedom of movement. It deterritorializes as a means of escape, and it cannot reterritorialize without becoming ensnared by the forces that set it to flight in the first place. So, Black mobility is confined to the deterritorialized side of a spectrum that is defined, on its other end, by all of the things that make it possible for a people to claim a territory. But both poles of the spectrum are problematic, in the same way that the immigrant/citizen binary is problematic.

The solution is not to champion the virtues of an interminable flux over territory, or to champion the immigrant over the citizen, but to call into question the field of social relations that pervades both sides of the continuum in which these "polar opposites" are situated. The question is not whether one should claim a territory. It is more important to raise questions about who is authorized to claim a territory, and under what conditions, and then explore what the answer to these questions says about the metanarratives and metaphysical assumptions that define the social field.[71] But as Sexton's analysis suggests, once you start to seriously explore these questions about who can claim territory (rather than insisting on sovereignty as a universal right), you are on the way to a politics, and a way of living, that does not require exclusive territorial claims as a way of anchoring itself.

It also bears emphasizing that nomadism is not a solution to any of these questions, any more than Black mobility is a flight to anywhere in particular. Nomadism is just an orientation toward mobility and territory that grants people a space to work on these questions with a measure of distance from forces that would completely inhibit their exploration. For Deleuze and Guattari, and most nonblack populations, it is possible to imagine a nomadism that can explore these questions as it treads water, between moments of deterritorialization and reterritorialization. But if you are going to use this sensibility to engage problems that are singular to the Black condition, you have to contend with the vicissitudes of an endless line of flight.

Closing Thoughts

I have ended this chapter with a discussion that uses Deleuze and Guattari's writing on nomadism to conceptualize some aspects of Black mobility, and also to interrogate some of the silences in their writing from the vantage point of the Black condition. I want to emphasize that I find nomadism useful as a way of describing features of Black mobility, but not as a prescription for the problems that Black mobility is being used to overcome. Nomadism can be understood as a means of escape that bears the imprint of the oppressive machinations from which it is fleeing.

Black people have been subjected to many kinds of controls that produce an oppressive confinement. But if you use the forced migration of the transatlantic slave trade as a starting point for understanding (anti)blackness, it becomes more apparent that black oppression begins with a series of traumatic displacements that prevent Black people from experiencing time and occupying space on their own terms. The end result is not confinement so much as a forced hypermobility that is a ghostly parallel of the privileged mobilities of the modern world.

I want to emphasize that I am not proposing that this kind of mobility has been experienced the same way by all people who are racialized as black. It is also possible for Black people to be swept up by other kinds of mobilities that are experienced by nonblack populations. But even after these qualifications are made, it is still possible to describe a kind of mobility that is singular to the troubled relationship between blackness and the modern world.

I have tried to show how the mobility resulting from this troubled relationship is different from that of the citizen, the immigrant, and the indigene. This is largely because Black experience does not lend itself to neat distinctions between agents and victims of colonization. Black people have occupied both roles, as victims and agents, being displaced people who were subject to a brutal system of forced migration and who were also used as instruments of the colonial order. The story of Joseph Godfrey provides one example of this predicament, which can trigger a fugitive line of flight that was not legible to White society or to the people of Indigenous nations.

Joseph's story also illustrates how Black mobility can take shape as an experience of fugitivity that leads to the unravelling of a personal subjectivity. His experience did not allow for a coherent narrative about the trials and abuses he suffered, that could be told from a recognizable "perspective," because he was confronting a regimen of power that was premised on the elimination of such a perspective. He lived a life of secrecies and tactical evasions. The role he actually played in the U.S.-Dakota War will probably never be known, but Joseph survived, precisely because he was successful in obfuscating the matter, and because he was able to assimilate, successfully enough, to the performance expectations of the Dakota peoples and the U.S. social order as the situation required.

For Joseph, as for many other fugitive slaves, (anti)blackness took the form of an unnamed predicament rather than a starting point for a shared identity or historical memory. Instead of being a kind of social experience, black experience marks the limit point of the social: a portal into things that cannot be articulated without calling into question the anchoring narratives of the social order. This is also why Black mobility should not be understood, simply, as the movement of bodies that have been racialized as black. Mobility is blackened when it is triggered by a confrontation with machinations of power that are singular to the Black condition.

These mobilities are usually motivated by a desire to escape to a freer place, but they are better understood as a flight from society itself in which the escape route becomes a means of creating a rupture with a given structure of social relations. The destination is not a particular cartographic location but a new quality of social relations. The line of flight becomes the crucible for this transformative process and not just a means to an end. Fugitives reinvent themselves and their relationships to others while they are in flight, and these changes become an enduring feature of the fugitive's consciousness even after return to a more sedentary life.

Deleuze and Guattari would probably insist that the transformative process I have just described is endemic to all forms of nomadism. I have tried to describe features of this process that are singular to the Black condition and that unsettle the mobility and subjectivity of the modern migrant.

NOTES

1. There are many possible points of reference, but I am referring to the singular and intimate relationship between blackness and subhuman qualities. See Saidiya Harman, *Scenes of Subjection: Terror, Slavery, and Self-Making in Nineteenth-Century America* (New York: Oxford University Press, 1997); Orlando Patterson, *Slavery and Social Death: A Comparative Study* (Cambridge, MA: Harvard University Press, 1982); Frank Wilderson III, *Afropessimism* (New York: Liveright Publishing, 2020).

2. This kind of analysis is primarily focused on the socialization of white, heterosexual masculine identities. See Cheri Jo Pascoe, "'Dude, you're a fag': Adolescent Masculinity and the Fag Discourse," *Sexualities* 8, no. 3 (2005): 329–346; Michael Kimmel and Matthew Mahler, "Adolescent Masculinity, Homophobia, and Violence: Random School Shootings, 1982–2001," *American Behavioral Scientist* 46, no. 10 (2003): 1439–1458.

3. For an overview and metacritique of the feminist critique of Fanon, see Luis Galanes Valldejuli, "Malinchismo and Misogyny in Fanon's *Black Skin, White Masks*: Reading Fanon from the Hispanic Caribbean," *Karib* 2, no. 1 (2015), https://doi.org/10.16993/karib.32. It bears noting that Fanon's writing has also been used, in more approving ways, by feminist scholars. See Jaco Hamman, "The Reproduction of the Hypermasculine Male: Select Subaltern Views," *Pastoral Psychology* 66, no. 6 (2017): 799–818.

4. For a more thorough treatment of racialization, gender, and sexual normality, see Hartman, *Scenes of Subjection*; Ladelle McWhorter, *Racism and Sexual Oppression in Anglo-America* (Bloomington: Indiana University Press, 2009); and Dorothy Roberts, *Killing the Black Body: Race, Reproduction and the Meaning of Liberty* (New York: Vintage, 1999).

5. For varied examples of these narratives, see Lawrence Fuchs, *American Kaleidoscope: Race, Ethnicity, and the Civic Culture* (Middletown, CT: Wesleyan University Press, 2011); Peter Salins, *Assimilation, American Style* (New York: Basic Books, 1997); and the perspectives on early-twentieth-century liberal assimilation theory recounted in *Incorporating Diversity: Rethinking Assimilation in a Multicultural Age*, ed. Peter Kivisto (Boulder, CO: Paradigm Publishers, 2005).

6. For a seminal example, see Robert Park, "Human Migration and the Marginal Man," *The American Journal of Sociology* 33, no. 3 (1928): 881–893.

7. The earliest European usage of the term *native* has been traced to 1450, referring to "one who is born in bondage," and from the 1530s onward as a reference to a person who has "always lived in a place." From the 1650s onward, these ideas about nativity, which had been applied to subdominant populations in Europe, became more closely associated with non-European Indigenous cultures that were encountered in the context of colonization (https://www.etymonline.com/word/native, accessed April 26, 2022). See also the discussion in Philip Kretsedemas, *The Immigration Crucible* (New York: Columbia University Press, 2012), 118–119.

8. See, Park, "Human Migrations and the Marginal Man."

9. For one account, see Jan Richard Heier, "Accounting for the Business of Suffering: A Study of the Antebellum Richmond, Virginia, Slave Trade," *Abacus* 46, no. 1 (2010): 60–83.

10. See n. 6.

11. See Philip Kretsedemas, *Black Interdictions* (Lanham, MD: Lexington Press, 2022), 29–56.

12. Calvin Warren, *Ontological Terror* (Durham, NC: Duke University Press, 2018).

13. See Ann Marie Beals and Ciann Wilson, "Mixed-Blood: Indigenous-Black Identity in Colonial Canada," *AlterNative: An International Journal of Indigenous Peoples* 16,

no. 1 (2020): 29–37; William Loren Katz, *Black Indians: A Hidden Heritage* (New York: Athenaeum Books, 1986).

14. Also discussed in the introductory chapter. See Roland Betancourt, "Anti-Blackness and Transphobia Are Older Than We Thought," *Washington Post*, June 16, 2021, https://www.washingtonpost.com/outlook/2021/06/16/anti-blackness-transphobia-are-older-than-we-thought/; Margaret R. Greer, Walter D. Mignolo, and Maureen Quilligan, eds., *Rereading the Black Legend: The Discourses of Religious and Racial Difference in the Renaissance Empires* (Chicago: University of Chicago Press, 2008).

15. William Bartram, *Travels through North & South Carolina, Georgia, East and West Florida, the Cherokee Country, Etc.* (Philadelphia: James & Johnson, 1791), accessed April 26, 2022, https://docsouth.unc.edu/nc/bartram/summary.html.

16. See the account of Bartram's interests and training in Judith Magee, *The Art and Science of William Bartram* (University Park, PA: Pennsylvania State University Press, 2007).

17. Bartram, *Travels*, 114.

18. For an account of Linneaus's influence that is situated in light of American colonial racial ideologies, see McWhorter, *Racial and Sexual Oppression in Anglo-America*, 66, 79, 80–82.

19. Bartram, *Travels*, 114.

20. For one account, see Edward Cashin, *William Bartram and the American Revolution on the Southern Frontier* (Columbia: University of South Carolina Press, 2000).

21. Henry Bibb, *Narrative of the Life and Adventures of Henry Bibb, An American Slave, Written by Himself* (self-publ., 1849), accessed April 26, 2022, https://docsouth.unc.edu/neh/bibb/bibb.html.

22. Bibb, *Narrative of the Life and Adventures*, xi.

23. Bibb, *Narrative of the Life and Adventures*, 46.

24. Bibb, *Narrative of the Life and Adventures*, 50–52.

25. For a thorough academic treatment, see Arthur Lovejoy, *The Great Chain of Being a Study of the History of an Idea: The William James Lectures Delivered at Harvard University, 1933* (Cambridge, MA: Harvard University Press, 1964).

26. Bartram was an American-born subject of the English crown who became a U.S. citizen after the British Crown ceded to the demands of the American revolutionaries in 1783. Although Bartram adjusted to a U.S.-citizen status later in life, he did not migrate to the United States or undergo the naturalization and acculturation processes that were typical for immigrants of that era. Cashin, *William Bartram and the American Revolution*.

27. Robert E. Park, "Racial Assimilation in Secondary Groups with Particular Reference to the Negro," *The American Journal of Sociology* 19, no. 5 (1914): 606–623 at 610.

28. Brian Shellum, *Black Officer in a Buffalo Soldier Regiment: The Military Career of Charles Young* (Lincoln: University of Nebraska Press, 2010); Eric Weber, "Bonga, George (ca. 1802–1874)," MNopedia, October 29, 2012, accessed April 27, 2022, https://www.mnopedia.org/person/bonga-george-ca-1802-1874.

29. For several accounts, see William Brown, *Narrative of William W. Brown, a Fugitive Slave. Written by Himself* (Boston: The Anti-Slavery Office, 1847), accessed April 27, 2022, https://docsouth.unc.edu/neh/brown47/summary.html.

30. Julius Scott, *The Common Wind* (New York: Verso, 2018); Warren, *Ontological Terror*; Fred Kaplan, *Lincoln and the Abolitionists* (New York: HarperCollins, 2017).

31. Sherick Francois, "Godfrey, Joseph (ca.1830–1909)," MNopedia, October 29, 2012, accessed April 27, 2022, https://www.mnopedia.org/person/godfrey-joseph-ca1830-1909.

32. Frank Sweet, *Legal History of the Color Line: The Rise and Triumph of the One-Drop Rule* (Palm Coast, FL: Backintyme Publishing, 2005).

33. Walt Bachman, "Slavery and Freedom on the Minnesota Territory Frontier: The Strange Saga of Joseph Godfrey," Black Past, August 31, 2013, accessed April 27, 2022, https://www.blackpast.org/african-american-history/slavery-and-freedom-minnesota-territory-frontier-strange-saga-joseph-godfrey/.

34. Bachman, "Slavery and Freedom on the Minnesota Territory Frontier."

35. Bachman, "Slavery and Freedom on the Minnesota Territory Frontier."

36. Bachman, "Slavery and Freedom on the Minnesota Territory Frontier."

37. Bachman, "Slavery and Freedom on the Minnesota Territory Frontier."

38. David Schleper, "David Godfrey," Facebook, May 22, 2020, accessed April 27, 2022, https://www.facebook.com/shakopeeheritage/photos/joseph-godfrey1830-1909compiled-and-written-by-david-r-schleper-shakopee-heritag/2630637420513760.

39. Schleper, "David Godfrey."

40. Bachman, "Slavery and Freedom on the Minnesota Territory Frontier."

41. Bachman, "Slavery and Freedom on the Minnesota Territory Frontier."

42. Bachman, "Slavery and Freedom on the Minnesota Territory Frontier"; Schleper, "David Godfrey."

43. Schleper, "David Godfrey."

44. Bachman, "Slavery and Freedom on the Minnesota Territory Frontier."

45. Bachman, "Slavery and Freedom on the Minnesota Territory Frontier."

46. Bachman, "Slavery and Freedom on the Minnesota Territory Frontier."

47. Gilles Deleuze and Félix Guattari, *A Thousand Plateaus: Capitalism and Schizophrenia* (Minneapolis: University of Minnesota Press, 1987), 354.

48. Deleuze and Guattari, *A Thousand Plateaus,* 352–353, 416–418.

49. Deleuze and Guattari, *A Thousand Plateaus,* 204, 284–285, 384–385.

50. Deleuze and Guattari, *A Thousand Plateaus,* 222–223, 227–228.

51. Deleuze and Guattari, *A Thousand Plateaus,* 353–354.

52. Ellison did not embrace the term *nomadic,* but he did insist that Black experience, especially in the United States, was characterized by patterns of movement that are singular to this experience. In every instance, the pattern of movement is expressed through an act of physical migration that is undertaken to escape an oppressive matrix of social relations. In Ellison's time, this phenomenon was epitomized by the mass migrations of black people from the American south to Northern urban centers in the early twentieth century (aka the Great Migration). As discussed in Ronald Judy, *(Dis)Forming the American Canon* (Minneapolis: University of Minnesota Press, 1993), 50–53; and Kretsedemas, *Black Interdictions,* 31.

53. Deleuze and Guattari, *A Thousand Plateaus,* 396.

54. Deleuze and Guattari, *A Thousand Plateaus,* 424–472.

55. Deleuze and Guattari, *A Thousand Plateaus,* 134, 242–243, 248, 268, 291–292.

56. Deleuze and Guattari, *A Thousand Plateaus,* 291–292.

57. For an updated reading of the master-slave dialectic that acknowledges some of its appropriations by poststructuralist theorists and the formative influence it has had on Western thought, see Nancy Harding, "Reading Leadership through Hegel's Master/Slave Dialectic: Towards a Theory of the Powerlessness of the Powerful," *Leadership* 104, no. 4 (2014): 391–411.

58. For an introductory discussion, see Kristen Broady, Curtis Todd, and William Darity, "Passing and the Costs and Benefits of Appropriating Blackness," *The Review of Black Political Economy* 45, no. 2 (2018): 104–122.

59. For an introduction to Deleuze's thinking on this matter, see John Brady, "Deleuze on Problems, Singularities, and Events," *Epoche: Philosophy Monthly* 34 (2020), accessed April 28, 2022, https://epochemagazine.org/34/deleuze-on-problems-singularities-and -events/.

60. Deleuze spent most of his academic teaching career (1969–1987) at the Paris 8 campus of the University Vincennes-Saint-Denis. Paris 8 was an experimental campus that had been created in response to the issues and demands raised by radical student movements and especially by the uprising of May 1968. D. Smith, "Gilles Deleuze," *Stanford Encyclopedia of Philosophy*, https://plato.stanford.edu/entries/deleuze/.

61. Richard Wolin, "Pierre-Félix Guattari," *Encyclopedia Brittanica*, updated April 26, 2022, https://www.britannica.com/biography/Pierre-Felix-Guattari.

62. Deleuze and Guattari never embraced Darwinism, but they intervened on Darwinian theory with their writing on the rhizome as a template for thinking about a kind of evolutionism that allows more room for ruptures and nonlinear developmental pathways (in which the most decisive adaptation can erupt from "the middle" of a process, rather than from the most highly developed "end point"). Deleuze and Guattari, *A Thousand Plateaus*, 3–25.

63. Frank Wilderson III, *Red, White & Black* (Durham, NC: Duke University Press, 2010).

64. Deleuze and Guattari, *A Thousand Plateaus*, 86–89. See also Gilles Deleuze and Félix Guattari, *What Is Philosophy?* (New York: Columbia University Press, 1994), 67–68, 86.

65. Their discussion of nomadic reterritorialization is exemplified by their concept of a "body without organs," which is the inspiration for my paraphrased summary of their thoughts on this matter. See Deleuze and Guattari, *A Thousand Plateaus*, 149–166.

66. Jared Sexton, "The *Vel* of Slavery: Tracking the Figure of the Unsovereign," *Critical Sociology* 42, no. 4–5 (2014): 583–597 at 587–589. Sexton also references Wilderson's *Red, White & Black*.

67. Sexton, "The *Vel* of Slavery," 593. The term *natal alienation* is not specifically used. Instead, Sexton writes of the "uprooting of the natal," which is, nonetheless, a reference to natal alienation being one of the criteria that Orlando Patterson uses, in *Slavery and Social Death*, to describe the conditions that are singular to the predicament of the black slave.

68. Sexton, "The *Vel* of Slavery," 588–589.

69. Sexton, "The *Vel* of Slavery," 593, citing Nahum Chandler, *X—The Problem of the Negro as a Problem for Thought* (New York: Fordham University Press, 2014), 163.

70. For two perspectives on this problem, see Marta Araujo, "Challenging Narratives on Diversity and Immigration in Portugal: The (De)Politicization of Colonialism and Racism," in *Migrant Marginality: A Transnational Perspective*, ed. P. Kretsedemas, J. Capetillo-Ponce, and G. Jacobs (New York: Routledge, 2013), 27–46; Mandisi Majavu, "The Whiteness Regimes of Multiculturalism: The African Male Experience in Australia," *Journal of Asian and African Studies* 53, no. 2 (2018): 187–200.

71. My reference to antiblack racism as a metanarrative and metaphysics borrows from the work of many scholars who have explained how antiblack racism is informed by a cosmology and evolutionary teleology that overcodes all aspects of state and society. See P. Khalil Saucier and Tryon P. Woods, eds., *Conceptual Aphasia in Black: Displacing Racial Formation* (Lanham, MD: Lexington Books, 2016); Warren, *Ontological Terror*; and Wilderson, *Afropessimism*.

3

Not Just about Being Haitian, [but] Being Black in America

*Race, Gender, and Blackness within the Haitian
Diaspora in Miami's "Little Haiti"*

Jamella N. Gow

When Category 5 Hurricane Matthew hit the island nation of Haiti on October 7, 2016, many people who watched the news were quick to donate to large organizations on the ground, such as the Red Cross. As with Hurricane Katrina, news media repeatedly portrayed impoverished Black[1] people standing bereft in the middle of ruined homes in ways that revealed the devastation of the natural disaster but also served to reaffirm common assumptions, born out of European colonialism, about Blacks as incapable of self-governance or political stability. In this case, popular media, bolstered by long-standing tropes of racialized paternalism and conventional discourses on development, reiterated racialized depictions of Haitian people as alien and uncivilized Black bodies who required foreign aid and supervision.[2] While it is true that multiple catastrophic disasters—in addition to poor economic conditions, minimal infrastructure, government corruption, and more recently, heightened violence—have forced waves of Haitian people to flee their country, such depictions are far from the reality of their lives or capabilities.

This chapter works to shed light on the migratory experience, cultural adjustment, and continued involvement with the home country by Haitian nationals living in "Little Haiti," a neighborhood of Miami that is home to one of the largest concentrations of Haitian immigrants in the United States.[3] I aim to understand these migrants' patterns of mobility, transitions, sense of identity, and level of involvement in broader movements to stimulate progress and political, economic, and social change for communities in the United States and in Haiti. Further, I seek to situate such processes within global anti-Blackness, colonial histories of resistance, and the important context of Black diaspora that all shape the experiences of Haitian nationals and their navigation of race, gender, and Blackness. Family networks and organized community groups provide the kind of agency and clarity that allows members of the Haitian diaspora to thrive in a foreign land, despite challenges posed by racial and class-based discrimination, language barriers, and other exclusionary practices, while continuing to contribute to their home country. These complex systems of migration also expose how Haitians experience various forms of inclusion and exclusion that challenge traditional notions of nation, citizenship, and social formation.

Situating Haitian Migrants within Global Perspectives of Anti-Blackness

Haiti and Haitians cannot be understood outside of the country's positionality as a Black nation of Black migrants. The framing of Haiti as a Black country has both revolutionary and anti-Black origins. Haiti holds the title of the "first Black republic."[4] Haiti's revolution (1791–1804) is an important flashpoint in the larger history of what Paul Gilroy has defined as the "black Atlantic,"[5] with the symbol of the transatlantic passage of slave ships as a point of connection across diverse Black communities living in the New World. Haiti's revolutionary success represented for many Black communities, pre- and postabolition, a shared anticolonial pride that has reverberated across generations. Black communities across the Black Atlantic saw Haiti as both an example of resistance and a point of common cause in the diaspora.[6]

In response to such a powerful challenge to imperialism and white colonialism, scholars have diminished Haiti's place in the history of revolutions of that period, including the American Revolution (1775–1783) and the French Revolution (1787–1799). Even as Haitian leaders like François-Dominique Toussaint Louverture applied the very words of his fellow French revolutionaries vying for freedom from another kind of slavery, history has insisted on seeing Haiti's triumph through an anti-Black lens that sought to silence the country's struggle. For example, Haitian scholar Michel-Rolph Trouillot asserts,

> The Haitian Revolution was the ultimate test of the universalist pretensions of both the French and the American revolutions. And they both failed. *In 1791, there is no public debate on the record, in France, in England, or in the United States on the right of black slaves to*

achieve self-determination, and the right to do so by way of armed re-
sistance.[7]

White silence on Black resistance further downplayed the revolutionary origins of the Haitian nation-building, and consequential depictions of the event
were reinterpreted through the lens of anti-Black primitivism, which in many
ways pervades depictions of Haiti today.

Further, Haiti's treatment by outside nations in its subsequent years also
reflects a continuation of that silencing and more direct colonial treatment
by other means. In many ways, the treatment of Haiti by Western powers after
its revolution served as a response to Haiti's pro-Black radical stance with a
clear, rejoinder of anti-Black sentiment and colonialism by another name:
occupation, embargos, and poor international relations, all of which siphoned
economic and political power from Haiti just as it began to develop as a nation. For example, Western powers sought "reparations" for Haiti's resistance.
Soon after becoming a new republic, the United States, also a progeny of revolution, placed an embargo on Haiti in 1806. In 1825, France accepted Haiti's sovereignty on condition of receiving 150 million francs in reparations
over a period of five years. Germany, Great Britain, and the United States also
sought reparations for their part in the conflict and, as a result, "repayment
of these loans consumed approximately 80 percent of the national revenue
by the end of the nineteenth century."[8]

In 1915, the U.S. military would initiate its first occupation of Haiti, lasting until 1934. During its occupation, U.S. bankers took control of Haiti's
national bank, consolidated its debt, and invested in its own businesses on
the island—even amending the Haitian constitution to allow foreigners to
own local land. Tropes of anti-Black primitivism were utilized yet again to
justify this occupation. As Stephanie Batiste writes, "Haiti's civil strife, political disorganization, and poverty proved the inherent inferiority and sav-
agery of the Haitian people to mainstream America."[9] In addition, U.S. occupation and support of later dictators in Haiti further contributed to the
political and economic instability of the island. However, none of this history is visible with the oft-repeated phrase attributed to Haiti: "poorest nation in the Western Hemisphere." In fact, the erasure of such history—of
resistance and retribution—is intentional, as it normalizes anti-Black policy
and reifies tropes of Black disarray.

Thus, the experience of Haitian migrants and the depiction of their homeland in the media must be understood through the lens of anti-Blackness.
The experience of Black migrants is also crucial to understanding race in
global perspective. As the following scholars note, anti-Black policies shape
the ways in which racially nonwhite migrants have become stratified in the
global racial hierarchy. Achille Mbembe, for example, describes this process

as the "becoming Black of the world" in which the condition of Blackness, emerging from the transatlantic slave trade, has come to encompass more increasingly vulnerable populations.[10] He describes this condition as "depredation, dispossession of all power of self-determination, and, most of all, dispossession of the future and of time, the two matrices of the possible."[11] One can argue that Haiti's history and development have been shaped and continue to be shaped by this condition of Blackness, where the nation and its migrants can be understood as a global category of Black precarity.

Further, migrants from Black nations such as Haiti have been rendered Black in Mbembe's conceptualization by virtue of anti-Black immigration policies from Western countries such that "Western lawmakers' denial of access to the privilege of immigration to phenotypically 'black' persons from 'black' nations functions as systemic and global anti-blackness."[12] For example, immigration policies toward Black migrants, as Vilna Bashi argued, have created seeming contradictions of recruitment/refusal in that Black labor has been desirable for migrant labor schemes in the West while Black citizenry (or its possibility) has remained a threat:

> Contradictory public policy [which] . . . has great disdain for black immigration yet also makes available opportunities to recruit temporary black labour establishes an ambivalence in immigration policy around blacks. This ambivalence, however, is tempered by fear of a permanent addition to the black population.[13]

Haiti and Haitians have functioned as a visible example of these kinds of policies to a global racial regime of anti-Blackness. For example, Haitian migrants remain highly visible in U.S. media as Black migrants from a Black nation whose homeland has deep historical ties to the United States and its neocolonial policies—policies that relied upon anti-Black rhetoric. Further, on repeated occasions U.S. national discourses have rendered Haitian migrants as racialized, Black threats to national borders, including the most recent crisis at Del Rio and elsewhere on the U.S.-Mexico border. As early as 1994, President Bill Clinton described Haitian refugees, fleeing to Florida in rickety boats to escape political instability in the country, as a potential "threat to stability in our region and control of our borders."[14] This manufactured threat was then used to justify the military invasion and occupation of Haiti that same year.

Diasporic Transnationalism in Black Perspective

Nevertheless, in the face of these negative portrayals and military actions that have impacted Haiti when in crisis, the global Haitian diaspora has not only consistently responded to natural disasters in Haiti with donations and advocacy but also mobilized to counter negative images of Haiti, both past and present, and influence national and global policies.[15] These practices have strengthened the visible presence of the Haitian migrant community in the United States.[16] Although it has called itself a diaspora, or a group held together by shared cultural or religious ties to a physical or imagined homeland, the Haitian community abroad also remains transnationally connected to family members and hometowns on the island that rely on their remittances, gifts, correspondence, and networks in order to bring future migrants to the United States.[17] In these ways, the Haitian community may exist at a middle ground between transnationalism (which emphasizes the connections between migrants and their home country) and diaspora (which emphasizes the connections among migrants in their new countries) through a form of what Khachig Tölölyan calls "diasporic transnationalism": members strengthen the local bonds among the Haitian diaspora through maintaining real and imagined ties to the island country.[18] Tölölyan observes that diasporic transnationalism has become the means by which Armenian, Indian, and Jewish Americans in his example create deep ties to their place of residence while remaining to varying degrees connected to their homelands, both real and imagined.[19]

At the same time, practices of diasporic transnationalism must be nuanced by the Black experience, particularly the practice of reclaiming negative racializations of Blackness by rooting identity in diaspora:

> Racialized peoples, particularly those who are diasporic (that is, scattered and away from their homelands), use ethnicity to formulate an articulate racial resistance. . . . For example, migrants of African descent were racialized when they were labeled "black," having first been involuntarily transported as slaves. . . . While seen monolithically as racially "black," they struggle to be viewed as distinct peoples.[20]

Migrants are read through the lens of race and may seek to challenge that label; however, migrants descended from the transatlantic slave trade must contend with anti-Blackness. While diasporic transnationalism is not unique to Haiti, I argue that the Haitian community in Little Haiti constitutes an especially strong form of diasporic transnationalism informed by Haiti's struggle with decidedly anti-Black policies from the West. In the present, the Haitian migrant community and its leaders' identification with diaspora serve as a means of making Haitians more visible as a political force in the United States. Their diasporic transnationalism must thus be read as a response to their discrimination as Black and migrant alongside what can be seen as a long-standing transnational connection to Haiti due to the nation's history of migration and Black resistance. Haitian practices of diasporic transnationalism can be more deeply understood within the context of the Black Atlantic. In so doing, it is possible to also see Haitian diaspora as a form of anticolonial pride and a response to the reverberations of the slave trade and its aftermath in Haiti. Haitian diaspora can thus be seen as closely tied to diasporic Blackness. Haitian diasporic transnationalism, although it became more visible in the late twentieth century, stems from a long history of Haitian migration to the United States, which stretches back to when Haiti itself became a nation in 1804.[21]

Haitian migrants and Haitian Americans living in the United States experience marginalization not just stemming from immediate racial discrimination as Black people but also as representatives of Haiti, a nation whose existence has been shaped by U.S. histories of imperialism. However, they remain connected to and identify with a strong diasporic identity rooted in Haitian resistance and a transnational connection to the homeland in the present tense. The impacts of Haitians' experiences of racialization and marginalization as both Black and migrant in the United States as well as their practices of transnationalism can be understood in two ways. First, their experiences reveal how Black migrants become racially discriminated against through interpersonal as well as state-level and global anti-Black processes.[22] Second, as this study focuses on, Haitians resist such discrimination by taking refuge in transnational connections as well as in the Haitian Black diaspora and sometimes the Black diaspora in the United States.

As Black migrants, Haitians experience a unique form of discrimination. As migrants, they must reckon with U.S. immigration policies that have been created in the context of anti-immigrant and xenophobic sentiment that disadvantages migrants and especially those of color and with less economic capital. As Black in the United States, Haitians are also subject to discrimination and treatment as second-class citizens. The compounding of the two leads to their unique targeting as an ethnoracial group.

This chapter suggests that members of the Haitian diaspora living and working in the ethnic enclave of Little Haiti utilize diasporic transnationalism, in ways rooted in global-historical processes begun in the Black Atlantic and alongside unique forms of Haitian diasporic pride. In their everyday lives, they utilize practices of Haitian diasporic Blackness as a means of maintaining culture and as a method of resistance against marginalization locally and globally. These practices are informed specifically by their experiences as both Black and migrant in the United States and the ways such experiences are inflected by gender. Migrants arriving to the United States may face a variety of struggles as they settle into their new locations. Those who experience exclusion due to racial, ethnic, class, and citizenship status may turn to their ethnic communities not only for emotional and cultural support but also as a means of "practicing citizenship" and as a source of political strength.[23] As Engin Isin explains, "Citizenship is enacted through struggles for rights among various groups in their ongoing process of formation and reformation."[24] Practicing citizenship, thus, is a way to define and even redefine one's belonging within the nation or the diasporic community. Engaging in transnationalism and identifying as diaspora have been described by scholars such as Rogers Brubaker, Linda Basch, Nina Glick Schiller, and Cristina Szanton Blanc as practices that migrants can use to maintain cultural affinities with their homelands while adjusting to a new place.[25]

In this chapter, I focus on the experience of first- and second-generation Haitian community leaders and volunteers living and working in Little Haiti in order to investigate how socially active Haitian migrants use practices of transnationalism and diaspora both locally and transnationally. I argue that Haitian conceptions of diaspora and transnationalism are unique in that these practices are informed not only by formerly colonial processes that negatively depicted Haitians through anti-Black tropes but also by how Haitians have reimagined those tropes through Haitian diasporic pride. I explore how such practices encourage them to view their activist work and community engagement as part of a transnational, socially active citizenry tied to Haiti. For the people interviewed, diasporic transnationalism works in multiple ways. Living as part of the Haitian diaspora becomes a way to challenge their own notions of nation and place through diasporic transnationalism. Further, practicing diasporic transnationalism in Miami means grappling with both the impact of anti-Black racism individually and the ways their community either collaborated or clashed with the African American community. For women, especially, practicing diasporic transnationalism also meant navigating patriarchal norms in their families and culture; however, many emphasized that part of their diasporic transnational activism meant challenging and redefining gender roles within the Haitian diaspora.

Called a "bicultural" city, Miami is a key site for researching not only how migrants integrate into an increasingly diverse U.S. culture but also how they can claim a transnational identity and a diasporic community as political tools to try to influence issues on both the local and the global scale.[26] Accordingly, this study focuses on two key themes: how these Haitian community leaders and volunteers came to see themselves as "diasporic transnationals," and how preserving the Haitian community through cultural practices and volunteerism functions as the conduit by which they become politically engaged to support not only their fellow Haitian Americans living in the United States but also newer Haitian migrants and those still living in Haiti. Through eight in-depth interviews with Haitian and Haitian American volunteers and community leaders, I found that, for my informants, living in diaspora and practicing transnationalism can be manifested in numerous ways that work not only to solidify ethnic communities but also to challenge ideas of citizenship and nationality though race, Blackness, and gender.

Creating Haitian Black Diaspora in the United States

Haitians also have a long history of migration to the United States. Social scientists note three peak waves of Haitian migration to the United States: during the Haitian revolution and its aftermath (1791–1810), in the U.S. occupation of Haiti (1915–1934), and under the Duvalier and post-Duvalier regimes (1957–1994). During the revolution, as many colonial planters and their slaves fled to nations throughout the Caribbean, a small number of them went to the Southern United States—particularly Louisiana, where French planters and Haitian slaves contributed to the French Creole population. During the François Duvalier regime of the 1950s and 1960s, mostly middle-class and upper-class professionals fled to New York, where they formed political activist groups and community service organizations. These groups were closely related, as Haitians desired to integrate but remain politically active and cognizant of politics in Haiti.

This politically active community was notably documented in Basch, Glick Schiller, and Szanton Blanc's *Nations Unbound*,[27] which argued that Haitian migrants in the United States are one of several examples of ethnic communities that remained tied to the homeland and remained actively engaged as transmigrants. Their anthropological work set the stage for discussions of transnationalism. They introduced the idea of seeing nation-states with transnational immigrant populations as deterritorialized. As Glick Schiller and Fouron note in a later work,

> Persons who have emigrated and their descendants are defined as continuing to belong to the polity from which they originated. They are seen as having rights and responsibilities in that state even if they have adopted the language and culture of their new country and have become legal citizens in their new home.[28]

While Basch, Glick Schiller, and Szanton Blanc allocate part of the discussion in their book to Haitians in Miami, they refer to Alex Stepick, who provided key statistics on Haitians in Miami during the late 1980s and early 1990s, for their data on Haitians in Miami.

Tatiana Wah and François Pierre-Louis note that Haitians in New York, due to their status, are marginalized and politically aware. They have also focused on group formation across Haitian class differences in order to maintain solidarity: "Haitians in New York City form a triple minority group, marginalized linguistically, racially, and nationally. As a result, Haitian immigrants have learned to reshape their organizations' structures to include members of various classes and backgrounds to pursue their common interests."[29] That is, marginalization reinforced their unity as a transnational community in the United States.

However, it was not until after Aristide was overthrown in 1991 that Haitians in New York took on a specifically diasporic identity. Wah and Pierre-Louis note, "Haitians who wanted to return home realized that the political and economic conditions of Haiti would not allow them to do so."[30] Thus, they focused on "adopting U.S. citizenship, retiring, and putting their efforts into hometown associations."[31] Such work led to the forming of Haiti's tenth department, or *"Dizyèm Departman-an,"* whose U.S. office opened in 1994 "in the very center of the Brooklyn Haitian enclave in New York City."[32]

Thus, Haitians became known for their transnational and diasporic characteristics, what Michel Laguerre terms "diasporic citizenship . . . a set of practices that a person is engaged in, and a set of rights acquired or appropriated, that cross nation-state boundaries and that indicate membership in at least two nation-states."[33] He argues that this particular form of citizenship has allowed Haitians not only to recreate Haiti for their fellow Haitian compatriots abroad but also to use their citizenship in the United States to influence U.S. policy toward Haiti. Thus, diasporic citizenship implies a political responsibility to the homeland that exists outside of one's nation of residence. I extend Laguerre's concept further to point to the ways in which diasporic citizenship is uniquely diasporic and transnational and, I argue, is deeply inflected by Black identity and gender.

The experience of Haitians in Miami is particularly unique as it involves systematic marginalization of a population made up mostly of lower-class Haitians, as compared to their upper- and middle-class compatriots in New York. This wave of Haitian migrants was negatively racialized through the lens of anti-Blackness and contrasted with the more well-heeled migratory waves. As Stepick writes, "In contrast to previous flows to the United States, the boat people are primarily poor, rural, and black."[34] With these Haitians having suffered marginalization by being portrayed as boat people with AIDS, as well as by being falsely accused of spreading tuberculosis, Stepick asserts that there has been "a consistent U.S. policy designed to repress the flow of Haitian refugees to Miami."[35] Global Miami,[36] with its high competition for jobs among numerous ethnic groups, has pushed some Haitians into forming their own informal economy as a result of their discrimination in the workplace and in the media.[37]

In the 1970s, Haitians from New York began to move south to Miami. However, these upper-class Haitians could afford to live in the suburbs of

Miami and in Miami-Dade and Palm Beach Counties.[38] Those Haitians with capital from their previous employment, and with support from ethnic communities in Haiti, may have a transition experience in Miami different from those entering Miami as new migrants. Newly arrived Haitian migrant boat people "were defined, from the start, as a redundant labor force and were deprived the de facto protection provided by employers to established sources of immigrant labor."[39] This exclusion from the labor force has thus pushed this particular subgroup of Haitian migrants into the informal economy for survival.[40] This informal economy has given rise to close-knit diasporic communities in Little Haiti and makes this population crucial for delving further into the experience of the Haitian Black diaspora and its material basis.

Transnationalism and "Transmigrants"

Anthropologists Basch, Glick Schiller, and Szanton Blanc coined the term *transmigrant* and popularized transnationalism as a challenge to the traditional concept that migrants will, over time, assimilate or simply integrate into the culture and society of their host country.[41] Instead, their concept of transnationalism highlights the ways in which migrants straddle both their home country and their nation of settlement, such as through cultural practices, familial connections, and remittances. As transmigrants, Haitians utilize transnationalism through diverse practices that maintain cultural and material links among family members and communities who remain in Haiti while also helping to foster relationships between Haiti and migrants abroad. Most Haitians who migrate remain connected to the home country through direct state support and the familial and community networks that finance and encourage their travel. In return, they provide remittances and gifts, make return visits, and actively participate in or keep abreast of politics in the homeland. Haitian migrants' active engagement with politics and development in the homeland also illustrates the increasingly transnational nature of Caribbean states—a development shaped by neoliberalism[42] but rooted in earlier colonial history of dispersion via the transatlantic slave trade.[43] Many Caribbean governments, such as Haiti and Jamaica, have incorporated their migrant populations back into local politics and development by encouraging transnational practices that support the state economy through direct investment or even political participation through dual citizenship, voting in local elections, or lobbying for their homeland's interests in their country of residence.[44]

Thus, transnationalism not only manifests in individual practices but also becomes institutionalized at the level of the state, particularly with sending countries that benefit from exported labor and remittances. Though Haiti and other Caribbean countries benefit financially from migrants' labor and remittances, this transnationalism "from above" also has potentially negative implications since, as Alejandro Portes and others have noted, some nation-states have shifted to rely on remittances from the diaspora in lieu of the state supporting its local population.[45] In this way, globalization takes place not only "from above" and "below," a dichotomy that contrasts the transnational business class "above" with the migrant workers "below"; rather, through globalization, each arena is interwoven with the other, bringing "above" and "below" into a mutually dependent relationship.[46]

Diasporic Claims and Communities

While Haitian migrant communities have also used transnational political participation to criticize and challenge politics at home, they also vocally advocate on behalf of their diasporic communities in the United States. In so doing, they create a unique culture of resistance from outside their homelands. As my respondents shared, by calling themselves "diaspora," they claim shared historical origins rooted in anticolonial resistance and in political allegiances to Haiti, at the same time that they consider their current national residence as a permanent or semipermanent home.

The Haitians I spoke to who fled political violence, particularly during the regimes of François "Papa Doc" and Jean-Claude "Baby Doc" Duvalier from 1957 to 1986, came to see their migration as political since they, in turn, had begun to see themselves and be labeled as diaspora. As they shared, the Duvalier government had criticized Haitian migrants as diaspora who had abandoned the nation. However, Haitians who escaped to the United States and formed active political or ethnic communities claimed diaspora as a means of allegiance to the more populist, revolutionary image of Haiti and viewed their migration as a temporary exile that later became more permanent.[47] Migrants and those in Haiti whom they supported from afar came to see diaspora as a source of support, and soon the diaspora came to be infused with an ever-present responsibility to the Haitian nation.[48] These migrants reflect the transformation of "diaspora" from its origins in Jewish history to a more flexible claim to identity that encompasses multiple forms of voluntarily or involuntarily dispersed communities.[49] By claiming diaspora as a political identity, the Haitians I spoke to also reveal how diasporic communities can emerge out of practices of a collective "idiom, a stance, a claim" to diasporic identity.[50] Further, the unique experiences of Haitian nationals and diaspora in the United States reveal the ways in which Black Atlantic histories shape their diasporic practices as both globally Black and nationally Haitian.

Black Caribbean Migrants: Race, Ethnicity, and Gender in Diaspora

Thus, I contend that Haitians living as diaspora may retain a cultural nationalism that shapes their experiences as migrants abroad—especially in the United States, where their status as Black comes to significantly shape their experience. Because Haitians navigate the United States not only as migrants but also as racialized Blacks, I suggest, they experience concerns that are specific to immigrants, such as restricted access to citizenship and the threat of deportation, in addition to the gendered and classed racism that comes with living in the nation while Black. Thus, they exist at the juncture of race and ethnicity and experience differential forms of inclusion and exclusion by their networks, society, and the state. Within the context of the United States, both race and ethnicity are inextricable from racial stratification, such that "ethnicity has indicated a sort of belonging-in-progress, while race has indicated not really belonging at all."[51] Ethnicity functions alongside racial hierarchies in the United States such that racialized migrant groups can claim difference from racially oppressed groups by virtue of their cultural difference.[52]

I argue that Haitians, as racialized Black migrants, exist at the intersection of U.S. exclusion and inclusion, which can be understood as a more local extension of Mbembe's definition of *global Blackness*.[53] While their status as migrants appeals to the needs of the U.S. labor market, their status as Black also makes them subject to the discrimination that that categorization has meant for those racialized as such in this country. Migrants have been frequently racialized throughout the history of the United States based on labor needs, colonial histories, foreign policy, and trade agreements, sometimes with contradictory results.[54] Although valued for their flexible, low-wage labor, migrants also experience discrimination and increased vulnerability when politicians and the media, by encouraging a tightening of borders and increasing xenophobia, use them as scapegoats for economic woes caused by global capitalism.[55]

However, intersections of race and ethnicity must be seen within the context of gender. Racialized women's labor has become a significant source of surplus value in the globalized economy, not only in the global North where many migrant women take on traditionally feminine service work, but also in the global South where waged-labor under neoliberal restructuring has created a pool of flexible female workers primed to become future migrant laborers.[56] Women have increasingly joined the labor force as workers in free trade zones and as migrant workers abroad in the wake of shrinking social services under neoliberalism. In sum, the image of the global migrant has increasingly come to be embodied in the figure of the racialized woman from the global South.

Further, Black women have long been treated both as exploitable bodies for labor and as caretakers inside and outside the home. Angela Davis, for example, points out that the image of the home for the housewife has never been applied to U.S. Black women, who, as manual laborers as well as reproductive caretakers, have had to nurture not only families but also their communities in the face of systemic oppression in the United States.[57] As Grace Chang argues, the U.S. state and media recycled racist and sexist rhetoric surrounding African American women's work ethic and so-called rampant reproduction, to then stigmatize racialized migrant women and deny them access to social services such as welfare.[58] The lack of support produces a pool of migrant women funneled toward low-wage, flexible labor. Because of the globalization of capitalist production, there exists an increasingly global gendered, racialized, and classed division of labor as migrant women workers become part of a larger global pool of workers. Their recruitment depends in part on their flexibility as laborers and on stereotypes about their work ethic and skills based on race and gender.[59]

Black migrant women thus navigate both global and local processes of racism and sexism. Both immigrant policies and their relations with those inside and outside their communities reinforce racial and gendered tropes around their labor value, sexuality, and reproductive labor. The Haitian women I spoke to shared how their experiences were shaped by sexism and racism, and how this informed how they practiced diasporic transnationalism.

Although Haitians and other Afro-Caribbean migrants to the United States navigate a context in which they are doubly excluded as racialized migrant and Black—and at times triply, through the intersection of gender—the Haitian community leaders I spoke to in Little Haiti use such experiences to foster political activism and cultural cohesiveness. Cultural and political practices that not only raise awareness of marginalized ethnic groups in the receiving country but also help to build up community collectives can offer marginalized migrant populations a renewed sense of cultural identity. Such practices are important in locations that can appear simultaneously hostile and inviting: where migrants are welcomed for their labor but excluded for their racial, linguistic, and cultural Otherness. However, the example of Haitian diaspora is also unique in that those cultural and political practices are rooted deep within the larger context of both the reverberations from slavery and consequent displacement, as well as anti-Black policies leading up to the present that render Haiti as a Black nation. Thus, one must frame Haitian identity and pride within a larger negotiation with anti-Black policy and an unyielding resistance to negative racialization in the present and the traumas of enslavement in the past.

Those members of the Haitian diaspora with whom I spoke connected their admiration for Haiti's resistance as a nation born of successful liberation from slavery with their current activity as diaspora, contributing to Haiti's economic survival and political visibility in the global economy. Such practices on the part of these diasporic transnationals provide strong examples of the ways that culture and politics can merge: transnational practices become forms of resistance at the same time as they help sustain communities of diaspora. For those interviewed, cultural consciousness becomes solidified as marginalized communities rally together as part of a unique diaspora while transnational connections reinforce these connections and help maintain that cultural distinctiveness.

I suggest that these leaders in the Haitian community foster diaspora as a means of unity, not only out of a long history of dispersal based on waves of migration and escape from political persecution. They also foster diaspora through transnational political and cultural practices that, in turn, encourage the formation of a politicized diaspora rooted in an anticolonial Black identity originating in Haiti's formation as a nation. Transnationalism and diasporic activism go hand in hand for these members of the Haitian diaspora. Their transnational connections with Haiti don't just build communities both at home and abroad; these links also foster political activism as a way to resist individual forms of marginalization and encourage broader support of Haiti by countering anti-Black national policies in the United States in the present.

Researching Diasporic Transnational Practices in Little Haiti through Ethnographic Methods

For this project, I conducted ethnographic fieldwork and sought interview participants in Miami's Little Haiti to explore examples of transnational political practices in the Haitian diaspora. Little Haiti is a key site for studying Haitian migration and transnationalism. Of the many migrant groups in Miami, Haitians number 123,835, or 29.65 percent of the Miami population.[60] As of 2004, scholars and policymakers estimated that Little Haiti contained 40,000–55,000 Haitians,[61] while a five-year estimate from the American Community Survey placed this number at an average of 32,334 for the 2006–2011 period.[62] This difference in count may suggest either a gradual decline in population or, more likely, an undercount due, in part, to the precarity of migrant status in which persons of mixed or undocumented immigrant status may not be fully represented. Nevertheless, the Haitian population is constantly changing: on the one hand, more Haitians migrate to Miami from Haiti and Haitians in New York increasingly decide to join those Haitian communities established there, and on the other hand, varying immigration and asylum policies impact especially newer Haitian migrants' ability to stay.

Haitians living in Little Haiti, in the northern half of the vast city, consist mostly of the newly arrived.[63] As they become established, some eventually move to the surrounding suburbs.[64] Thus, the population of those who settle Little Haiti becomes a unique subset for understanding how migrant marginalization fuels the formation of diasporic communities. Little Haiti is a significant site for exploring transnationalism and diaspora, as this population uses the discourse of transnationalism and diaspora to build community in the face of marginalization.

I conducted eight in-depth interviews with politically active community leaders and volunteers at the Little Haiti Community Support Center (LHC-SC; a pseudonym) in Little Haiti who were able to speak on the role of political activism in creating and maintaining diaspora in Little Haiti and transnational connections to Haiti. Further, I observed and engaged with members of the community of Little Haiti. I also volunteered as an English as a Second Language instructor at the LHCSC, where I spoke informally with clients and other volunteers and met with many of my interviewees. While such a sample is small and thus not statistically reflective of the larger Haitian population in Florida, all but one informant (Nadia, who is a young adult volunteer) were well-known or vocal representatives of the Little Haiti community who serve as a "voice" in the neighborhood as well as maintain politically active ties in Haiti. Three were identified as "pioneers" of the Little Haiti activist community. Five of the interviewees were part of the migrant generation fleeing the dictatorship in the 1970s and 1980s and have remained committed to activism in Haiti and the United States. All eight lived, worked, or volunteered in Little Haiti and had done work on behalf of the LHCSC. Some, through their own organizations, contributed to the legal, financial, or cultural support of newly arrived migrants there. Thus, they had much to say about the community in Little Haiti and the goings-on of the region.

To focus on their experiences of activism, rather than strictly adhering to a prepared interview script, I first spoke briefly about my research and then asked informants to tell me a little bit about themselves. Further questions delved into how they identified themselves culturally or nationally as well as how they maintained and shared their culture. Questions were intentionally open-ended so that respondents could speak freely at length, and many did. Follow-up questions allowed me to request clarification on a topic or continue the conversation on a new topic. Thus, while I had a prepared set of questions, I merely used them to keep conversation going or to respond to experiences the interviewees shared with me. I obtained interviews through an informant who shared contact information for potential informants who were part of a larger network of Haitian activists in and around Little Haiti. Using these contacts and one referral by a family member who lived in the surrounding area, I interviewed four men and four women.

I found that transnational identity was important for all interviewees, as they perceived a certain obligation to fellow Haitian migrants and Haitian Americans in their community, although they interpreted this obligation in varying ways. At the same time, many also challenged this nation-centric paradigm by identifying themselves as diaspora. Their identification as diaspora and their transnational practices were also shaped by their navigations of anti-Black and anti-immigrant bias. Fostering diasporic transnationalism served to counter racism and reinforce cultural community. Further, women also shared their own experiences with gendered discrimination within the diaspora and discussed ways that they sought to change it. For some women, practices of diasporic transnationalism meant countering anti-Black and anti-migrant bias and also resisting patriarchal practices within their own communities. In all, diasporic transnationalism helped members of the Haitian diaspora not only to change the culture and politics of present Haiti but also to pass down radical political practices to the next generation.

Haitian Diasporic Transnationalism in Practice

Haitian Diaspora and Black Diasporic Transnationalism

While Haitian migrants navigate diasporic transnationalism as a means of survival, they must also contend with "multiple marginalities"[65] of anti-migrant, anti-Black, and gendered inequality. The Haitians I spoke with experienced anti-Blackness as personal and also as a means of strategic alliance—and sometimes tension—with other Black groups, especially African Americans whom they were pitted against when it came to gaining resources as a migrant community. To navigate these two processes—anti-Blackness and anti-immigrant marginalization—the Haitians I spoke to shared how claiming diaspora and practicing it through volunteerism bolstered the Haitian community and served as a challenge to discrimination. Further, Haitian and Haitian American women also shared the ways in which they navigated these forces along with sexism in the community. In all, respondents shared the ways in which they saw their rendition of Black diaspora as both dynamic and politically minded.

Navigating Blackness in the Diaspora

Interviewees James, Emmanuel, Sandra, and Nadia brought up their experiences or thoughts on the relations between the African American and Haitian communities in Miami, and how this reflected their identities as Black and ethnic in the United States. For example, interviewees pointed to the ways in which U.S. culture pitted African Americans against Haitians to accumulate various forms of capital from these marginalized populations. This is reflective of a larger history of racialized groups in the United States being pitted either against other marginalized groups or against a white majority.[66] In one instance, Emmanuel, a volunteer at the community center and a Haitian community leader, points to how the state redefined *Blackness* in a way that, as he argued, provided unequal advantages to different ethnic groups within Black-identified communities. He says, "When Haitians are figuring out the census form, they do not give you . . . an option to identity your ethnicity." He interpreted this lack of options as a way of disadvantaging certain groups at the expense of others: "They are trying to protect the African American community in terms of their numbers because the government grants are used to address poverty issues." For Emmanuel, such institutional discrepancies emphasize that *Blackness* is indeed an expansive and flexible term that at the same time can be used to cause divisions within communities. In this case claiming Blackness had material benefits, while ethnic difference may serve better in others. Emmanuel's experiences point to how Blackness can have both individual and institutional meanings, with serious implications for communities that are struggling to survive in the United States.

However, within these differences, Haitian community activists would point to those times when leaders in the African American community would collaborate with the leaders in the Haitian community, if only tenuously. As Emmanuel says, "Nothing has been handed to us in a fair way from immigration benefits to benefits in everything we have. The community had to fight, making protest after protest, making demand after demand, and also sometimes compromising with the African American community as well." Emmanuel's reflection here reveals how members of the overall Black Atlantic do not necessarily always have a consistent sense of unity and commonality; however, there are still opportunities for strategic collaboration. Different histories and experiences may cause these initial divides, but as can be seen in this case, relationships and bands of solidarity are formed, although at times provisionally.

Nadia, a second-generation Haitian in her early twenties, provides a different perspective that speaks to the reality of both the Black experience in the United States and the ways in which anti-Blackness impacts both Black migrant communities and African American communities. In our conversation, she described her experiences of negative stereotyping—of "not just about being Haitian, [but also] just being Black in America"—and later concludes that, as a result, "you need something to keep you grounded. You need something to have pride in, and I think that's why it's important to volunteer." For Nadia, negative stereotypes surrounding Haitians and African Americans are equally destructive, and for her, both groups need the support that comes with cultural grounding and diasporic activism. What would become important in this context is how such shifts in identity and possible unity around a common experience can later translate into political solidarity and shared social movements within the Black Atlantic.

Redefining Haitian Identity through Diasporic Transnationalism

As these interviewees shared, the Haitian community is challenged by both anti-Black and anti-migrant policies. Members of the Haitian diaspora experience negative racialization from both racist policies, which sought to divide African communities and downplay their specific needs as migrants. Amid these struggles, members of the Haitian diaspora shared that both Haitian pride and transnational and local volunteerism became a necessary means to counter such policies.

The nation of Haiti and its people have been repeatedly challenged by anti-Black processes that seek to diminish Haiti's accomplishments and thwart Haiti's development as a nation. Nevertheless, Haitian migrants and descendants I spoke to held complex claims to Haitian pride. Although cognizant of the inability to return to Haiti safely, each emphasized the importance of diasporic pride and transnational investment in the nation. Such actions served to counter not only experiences of racism toward Haiti as a nation but also experiences of anti-Black and anti-migrant marginalization in the United States.

For example, Emmanuel[67] related to me the mixed feelings he felt as part of the diaspora, especially his and others' active role in Haitian politics from afar. He says,

> Time has passed, and the country has changed, the people have changed, and the people going back ... many of them are disappointed and disillusioned. They come back to the diaspora because what they are hoping—*what they are wishing*—we could not realize it in Haiti. They were not ready yet for Haiti or Haiti was not ready yet for them.

Here, he points to the tensions he observed among diaspora members who, he felt, wanted to change their home country for the better but found that even with all their work, Haiti might not ever be the kind of nation many hoped it would become. What emerges here is Emmanuel's heightened sense of activism, since he feels a sense of responsibility for Haiti based on a transnational allegiance. Although Haiti as a country still exists, for Emmanuel and others in the diaspora, the country they desire to see through the work of their political activism from afar has not yet been realized. Accordingly, what once was a short-term migration becomes a long-term feeling of displacement from a country that still exists in place but is an unfulfilled memory or an idealized dream. Such a stance leads him to keep transnational ties but from a distance, until perhaps the country of his imagining can exist again.

However, despite Emmanuel's sense of complex disillusionment with the role of the Haitian diaspora and Haiti's future, several Haitians abroad argue for continued contact and connection with Haiti. Even those respondents who initially told me that they consider the United States their home, or that they do not acknowledge national affiliations, still emphasized a connection to Haiti directly or indirectly. Some use advocacy and philanthropy toward Haitians in the United States and in Haiti to stay connected to their original homeland or culture. They express their transnationalism in ways that go beyond remittances or other forms of informal networks. Some see their work in helping Haitians abroad as part of how they can help Haitians in the United States. Ultimately, many express some form of connection to Haiti through social activism or a simple desire to give back to their cultural community.

Jean, a woman organizer who has worked alongside the LHCSC to support the Haitian population, provided a more hybrid explanation of her transnationalism. Initially, when I interviewed her, she critiqued those who held closely to their Haitian culture and identity, and she offered her own definition of *identity* as a "merging" in which she picked the aspects of each culture she preferred and made them her own. At first, I was surprised by her reticence to fully embrace her Haitian side. She emphasized both aspects of her identity, U.S. American by citizenship and Haitian by blood, saying it would be "unfair" to see herself only as Haitian. As she says,

> I consider myself Haitian American. . . . I'm Haitian first of all by blood and the fact that I live here and reside here. . . . It would be pretty much unfair to say I consider myself Haitian and not Haitian American when I literally, on oath, said I'm becoming American, so I think it would be safe to say I'm a Haitian American proudly.

Unlike Emmanuel, who sees his identity as part of the diaspora and thus is invested heavily in the welfare of his home country, Jean feels that her obligation is to her new country. In some ways, her citizenship as a resident of the United States translates into a sense of responsibility that she needs to meet. She takes these obligations seriously, such that tensions emerge between her allegiances to Haiti, her country of birth, and the United States, to which she has sworn an oath confirming her citizenship. As a result, she focuses her energies mainly on her own work and how it will impact herself and her family.

Initially I thought, based on her prioritizing her immediate family, local community, and personal happenings, that she had no ties to Haiti. During our conversation, however, it came to light that she also maintained links to Haiti through Haiti-based organizations in which she is heavily invested. She repeatedly goes to Haiti, not for cultural or social reasons but simply to focus on her humanitarian work. As she says, "In Haiti, you go, and you do what you got to do. . . . At the end of the day, I know as long as you know what you're doing is from the heart and you're doing no harm, it's good." Thus, her connection to Haiti remains. Earlier in the interview, she reflected on the positives and negatives of working in the United States to reach Haitian migrants and the struggle of working within grant requirements and bureaucracy. For her, aiding Haitians works best when she can go directly to Haiti itself and help people there. While holding onto her identity as a U.S. citizen, Jean still takes the time to return to Haiti for the benefit of other Haitians outside her familial network who need support.

Jean and Emmanuel were born in Haiti and thus had a tangible history and connection with the country. However, transnationalism also exists across generations. A theme that emerged among a few of the older interviewees, many of whom had migrated in the 1970s and 1980s, was their concern with the generation of Haitians born in the United States who would decide to either stay within their community or branch out. These respondents hope that the younger generations will keep their Haitian culture alive and contribute to the growth of the Haitian diaspora and Little Haiti. Nadia, a Haitian American born in the United States, volunteered at the LHCSC to "engage with [her] community." Throughout the interview, she expressed her desire to learn more about her Haitian culture through service. She describes what many children of immigrants may feel: the desire to make their family's sacrifice worthwhile by being successful and giving back in some way. For her, this desire translates into service to her fellow Haitians. She says,

> I think, as a second generation, you see the sacrifices your parents make, and so as you're going through college, as you're going through your education, getting a job . . . there's a pressure to make it worth it: their experiences, their struggles to get you a better life. You want to make sure that, you know, you're successful to just give back to your community, and I think that's kind of what I want to do. I don't know how yet—still working on that. But I would definitely want to give back to the Haitian community, probably the Haitian American community.

Here, Nadia expresses her concerns as a second-generation child who desires her parents' approval, but she also connects this feeling to her cultural community in the United States. Perhaps this speaks to the role that assimilation and continued migration play: they may weaken connections to the homeland and close off transnational ties. Earlier in the interview, Nadia had talked about her trips to Haiti and about her desire to learn more about her culture. She pointed out, however, that as more and more members of her family move to the United States, such trips will likely diminish.

Sandra, a Haitian community leader and full-time worker at the LHC-SC, saw the work she does with Haitians abroad as closely tied to the work she does with Haitians living in the United States, and as part of a global framework. As she describes it, having a transnational or global perspective necessitates her involvement with Haiti. She says, "We don't work in silos, because we believe that in order to help people here, *we must*—we must intervene in Haiti." Sandra sees the LHCSC as facilitating such transnational connections through the implementation of programs that support Haitian economic and social development. Her vision is indeed global, and for her the LHCSC's goal is to tackle the roots of the problems in Haiti that lead to people crossing in boats to the United States. Like Emmanuel, who sees Haiti's problems as something he and the diaspora must grapple with, Sandra also contends that her work with the LHCSC must necessarily help those in Haiti.

Such a perspective is representative of other interviewees who, because of their status as Haitian refugees and members of a marginalized Black migrant group in Miami, have no choice but to be aware of their actions as both transnational and political. For the respondents who fled Haiti as political refugees, being part of the Haitian diaspora in Miami means that they must contend with the fact that they may never go home to the dream of Haiti that they strive for through their advocacy in the United States. While for Emmanuel this causes disillusionment or becomes a source of contention, others like Sandra see their placement in the United States as an opportunity to do the most good where they are. The people I spoke to saw their social advocacy as important to their connection to the Haitian community. Many saw that their work helped them understand both how tenuous migrant life has been for their fellow Haitians and how their own position in the United States facilitates their support of not just family members in Haiti but the nation itself.

Challenging and Reinventing Gender in the Haitian Diaspora

Haitian women I spoke to also challenged and redefined practices of diasporic transnationalism within the Haitian diaspora. Many, like Sandra, were key pillars of the Haitian diasporic community in Miami who sought to challenge what they described as patriarchal and sexist ideas that had been passed on to the U.S. community from Haitian culture. For the women I spoke to,

Black and gendered marginalization were a source of struggle and also a source of opportunity for change both within and outside the Haitian diasporic transnational community.

As Nadia and others show, gendered discrimination and sexism in Haitian was a source of critique for interviewees. In response, they emphasized their own work toward gender equity even as they supported Haiti and Haitian diaspora. For example, Nadia had much to say on how her ethnic and racial identities intersected with gender. Nadia found Haiti's culture of heteronormativity problematic and she felt the need to call out such beliefs in cultural spaces such as the church. She also joked about how her values clash with those of culturally traditional Haitian men, and how this would affect her marital decisions in the future. As she says,

> There's certain things the Haitian community believes [that], growing up in America, I just don't agree with. Like . . . LGBT rights. Haitians are extremely homophobic, and, growing up in America, I have a completely different viewpoint. So, when I'm down here, I go to a Haitian church, . . . there are some times where I'm just like: "You probably shouldn't say that." Or "I don't—I understand where you're coming from, but I grew up differently and I have different ways of thinking." . . . In terms of culture, I always make fun of Haitian men, and I say that I can't marry a Haitian man. I can marry a Haitian American man but not a Haitian man . . . simply because of the values they hold and how differently they treat women.

As Nadia notes, her own upbringing in the United States has allowed her to see other perspectives on gender and sexual norms. As a result, she feels empowered to critique such forms of discrimination within her community and even to make life choices based on her personal social stances. Her willingness to critique her culture shows her ability to not only go against tradition but also take steps in changing how her community's culture deals with certain social issues. Such a stance already places Nadia in a position as a social activist, since she is willing to change her community's practices through conversations with her cultural peers.

Many of the women I spoke to were eager to describe how they combated such sexism in their personal lives and their interactions with others. Some, such as Sandra, use the ways they express their culture in their family to not only combat sexism but also teach the next generation how to recognize and dismantle sexism. Such criticism and active work to undo sexism in their homes and personal lives illuminated an awareness of patriarchy as a system and the ways that integrating their own practices could contribute to changing both Haitian culture and Haitian society.

In another example, Jean shows how hybridizing identity works to re-shape culture. Using the space of the family, Jean actively combats sexism while she passes down cultural values to her children. She says,

> I mean, there's certain things I don't do. You know what I'm saying? So, to me, taking this from my culture, the way I was raised . . . and take that and bring that here . . . to me, a parent that does that should go to jail. But that's me, so that's why I said . . . I have both cultures.

In our conversation, she describes the clash between her set of values and those of her male family members. She also compares her experience to that of women in the United States by pointing out how Haitian women would not be allowed the same freedoms of education and social interactions as are found in the United States. Consequently, she aims to raise her family differently. In another part of our conversation, she says,

> Now I'm saying I would probably allow my daughter to go . . . [to] college and explore. I would probably allow my daughter to go to big grad and homecoming and prom and all that. My dad, he'll give you a good cuffing before that happens. I will probably allow my daughter to date, you know, to meet the boyfriend at sixteen and bring him home and we'll talk about it. My dad wouldn't do it. But see, that's different culture. And until this day, it still exists.

Here, she describes how her own daughter will be raised and allowed to have some of the freedoms she herself did not have. She contrasts this with her own Haitian upbringing in a male-led household. As she says, "My dad was so narrow-minded, he didn't see the big picture" and "My dad wouldn't allow it."

Throughout her recounting, Jean ties her personal practices at home to her identity as Haitian and American, and what aspects of her cultural identity she will pass to her daughter. Jean shows her willingness to challenge a society in which women are not given access to resources and advancement. Jean, who still claims her Haitian identity and supports the Haitian community in Haiti and the United States, shows that while she may claim her culture, she has the agency to hold onto the parts that she believes in and that can support her children.

Like Jean, Sandra also describes how she wants her children to be aware of sexism and be able to combat it. In describing her sons, she emphasizes how, as she says, she "raised them to be aware and respectful of everybody, of women, and to be open, you know. And my hope is that they will contribute, they will do their part to contribute to the peace that I envision." Sandra also uses her familial space to critique gender norms and instill such practices in her male children. Thus, such critiques of sexism are valuable not only in Sandra's own work with women at the LHCSC but also in her daily life. For Jean and Sandra, passing down such values to their children allows for the possibility of larger changes in both Haitian culture and society's stance on gender and patriarchy.

Sandra also extends her feminist perspective to her interactions with women in her community. She emphasizes how she uses her personal activities to strengthen the women with whom she works and interacts and their families as well. The arts function as one way for Sandra to express the experiences of women and thus empower them and their families. As she details,

> I also used poetry to empower women and their children—poetry that speaks of the conditions of women, the reality that women face, and that, investing in women, when we invest in women, you know, the family benefits and is happy.

Here, Sandra shows how her own cultural practices created venues for her to spread gendered awareness and better support for families. These concepts are important to Sandra. Indeed, when asked to define *activism*, Sandra points to women's rights as playing a key part. She says,

> We need safety for women. We need domestic violence to stop. We need domestic violence to be raised to the level of human rights because when the local government is unable or unwilling to protect women, it is a human rights violation. And this is what we call activism.

For Sandra, issues of gender are important not only in her family but also in her community and in her perspective as a social activist.

The efforts of Sandra and other women that have been highlighted here reflect the dynamism of diaspora and further extend the concept of diasporic transnationalism. They are an example of what Samantha Pinto describes as indicative of feminist Black Atlantic culture—a culture that "resist[s] narratives of black identity that emerge as masculine and nationalist but also . . . entrench a definitive culture and politics of African diaspora femininity."[68] The experiences of these women contribute new ways of practicing and reinventing diasporic transnationalism in the Black Atlantic.

Conclusion

As these interviews show, the Haitian migrants I spoke to in Little Haiti may navigate multiple social fields of race, Blackness, gender, and coloniality as they seek inclusion in the United States while supporting Haiti from afar. As culturally and nationally Haitian, some feel an obligation to support the Haitian nation to counter the long history of anti-Black policies that have crippled the nation and negatively racialized its people. Thus, they see advocacy and support of other Haitian migrants as part of that project. However, as racialized Black migrants in the United States, they have had to also contend with racial discrimination—which, for one respondent, fit alongside and informed her identity and activism. Further, as female respondents shared, not only do they contend with anti-Black racism and anti-Haitian discrimination, but they also work to change what they see as patriarchal institutions within their communities and families.

As migrants, however, the people I spoke to describe a Haitian diaspora whose members consider their main obligations to support Haiti and to alleviate global inequality, albeit in various ways. As they recount, within the Haitian diaspora there exists an ambivalent longing for the homeland, since transnational connections help maintain allegiances to Haiti. Nevertheless, living within the diaspora also works to shape identity into a more hybrid form incorporating the home country and the place of residence, particularly when one is doubly marginalized as Black and migrant. Studying diasporic transnationalism within the context of anti-Blackness may uncover these complex relationships and contradictions and demonstrate the ways that migratory movement, racialized marginalization within the country of residence, and the consequent reliance on transnational ties work to reshape cultures and, in turn, fashion modes of political awareness and activism within diasporic communities. To see oneself as part of the Black diaspora necessitates an active engagement with and reconceptualization of one's identity and political practices, especially as it comes to be interwoven with racial and gendered experiences.

Longing for the homeland of the past, or the vision one conceives of its future, can be assuaged by participating in forms of activism that promote cultural solidarity and the possibility of return. In these interviews, the intricacies of maintaining transnational connections while forging hybrid identities were explored through the lens of diasporic transnational practices. Further, these practices were informed by navigations of anti-Black and anti-migrant biases in the United States and their global contexts in the form of anti-Black racism against Haiti. For my respondents, Black diasporic transnational practices became one way of engaging with the established diasporic community in the face of anti-Black and anti-immigrant rhetoric, preserving the culture of diaspora activism for the next generations while reinventing it through a more feminist lens, and supporting those who are still living in the homeland that is being impacted by new forms of imperialism. Black diasporic transnational practices are thus one medium not only for building and maintaining transnational connections but also for constantly challenging one's own cultural identity and political beliefs.

The term *diaspora* is helpful as it points to this longing for home. Further, studying transnationalism within the context of diaspora demonstrates the ways that migratory movement, marginalization within the country of residence, and the consequent reliance on transnational ties work to reshape cultures and, in turn, fashion modes of political awareness and activism within communities. This work explores how transnationalism and diasporic consciousness work together in fostering political and cultural consciousness through new forms of diasporic transnationalism and the ways it is mediated by intersections of race and gender. Through the example of Haitian diaspora, one can find a critical, hybrid form of diaspora that provides new spaces for social activism within the Black Atlantic.

NOTES

1. Throughout the text, I intentionally capitalize the word *Black* to emphasize the cultural and political history of the term within the diaspora.

2. Jennifer Greenburg, "The 'Strong Arm' and the 'Friendly Hand': Military Humanitarianism in Post-Earthquake Haiti," *Journal of Haitian Studies* 19, no. 1 (2013): 95–122; Sibylle Fischer, "Haiti: Fantasies of Bare Life," *Small Axe* 11, no. 2 (2007): 1–15.

3. An earlier version of this work was published as Jamella N. Gow, "Race, Nation, or Community? Political Strategy and Identity-Making within the Transnational Haitian Diaspora in Miami's 'Little Haiti,'" *Journal of Haitian Studies* 27, no. 1: 135–156, https://doi.org/10.1353/jhs.2021.0005.

4. Flore Zéphir, *The Haitian Americans* (Westport, CT: Greenwood Press, 2004).

5. Paul Gilroy, *The Black Atlantic: Modernity and Double Consciousness* (Cambridge, MA: Harvard University Press, 1993).

6. See, for example, Gerald Horne, *Confronting Black Jacobins: The United States, the Haitian Revolution, and the Origins of the Dominican Republic* (New York: Monthly Review Press, 2015).

7. Michel-Rolph Trouillot, *Silencing the Past: Power and the Production of History* (Boston: Beacon Press, 1995), 88.

8. Zéphir, *The Haitian Americans*, 44.

9. Stephanie Leigh Batiste, *Darkening Mirrors: Imperial Representation in Depression-Era African American Performance* (Durham, NC: Duke University Press, 2011), 90.

10. Achille Mbembe, *Critique of Black Reason*, trans. Laurent Du Bois (Durham, NC: Duke University Press, 2017), 6.

11. Mbembe, *Critique of Black Reason*, 5–6.

12. Vilna Bashi, "Globalized Anti-Blackness: Transnationalizing Western Immigration Law, Policy, and Practice," *Ethnic and Racial Studies* 27, no. 4 (2004): 585.

13. Bashi, "Globalized Anti-Blackness," 585.

14. Sarah Gammage, "Exercising Exit, Voice and Loyalty: A Gender Perspective on Transnationalism in Haiti," *Development and Change* 35, no. 4 (2004): 749.

15. Michel S. Laguerre, *Diasporic Citizenship: Haitian Americans in Transnational America* (New York: St. Martin's Press, 1998).

16. Nina Glick Schiller and Georges Eugene Fouron, *Georges Woke Up Laughing: Long-Distance Nationalism and the Search for Home* (Durham, NC: Duke University Press, 2001).

17. Linda Basch, Nina Glick Schiller, and Christina Szanton Blanc, *Nations Unbound: Transnational Projects, Postcolonial Predicaments, and the Deterritorialized Nation-State* (New York: Gordon and Breach, 1994).

18. Khachig Tölölyan, "Beyond the Homeland: From Exilic Nationalism to Diasporic Transnationalism," in *The Call of the Homeland: Diaspora Nationalisms, Past and Present*, ed. Allon Gal, Athena S. Leoussi, and Anthony Smith (Leiden: Brill, 2010).

19. Tölölyan, "Beyond the Homeland."

20. Vilna Francine Bashi, *Survival of the Knitted: Immigrant Social Networks in a Stratified World* (Stanford, CA: Stanford University Press, 2007), 41.

21. Laguerre, *Diasporic Citizenship*.

22. Vilna Bashi Treitler, "Racialization and Its Paradigms: From Ireland to North America," *Current Sociology Monograph* 64, no. 2 (2016): 213–227.

23. Engin F. Isin, "Citizenship in Flux: The Figure of the Activist Citizen," *Subjectivity* 29, no. 1 (2009): 367–388.

24. Isin, "Citizenship in Flux," 383.

25. Rogers Brubaker, "The 'Diaspora' Diaspora," *Ethnic and Racial Studies* 28, no. 1 (2006): 1–19; Basch, Glick Schiller, and Szanton Blanc, *Nations Unbound*.

26. Alejandro Portes and Alex Stepick, *City on the Edge: The Transformation of Miami* (Berkeley: University of California Press, 1993), xi.

27. Basch, Glick Schiller, and Szanton Blanc, *Nations Unbound*.

28. Georges Fouron and Nina Glick Schiller, "Transnational Lives and National Identities: The Identity Politics of Haitian Immigrants," in *Transnationalism from Below*, ed. Luis Eduardo Guarnizo and Michael Peter Smith (New Brunswick, NJ: Transaction Publishers, 1998), 133.

29. Wah, Tatiana, and François Pierre-Louis, "Evolution of Haitian Immigrant Organizations and Community Development in New York City," *Journal of Haitian Studies* 10, no. 1 (2004): 160.

30. Wah, Tatiana, and François Pierre-Louis, "Evolution of Haitian Immigrant Organizations," 154.

31. Wah, Tatiana, and François Pierre-Louis, "Evolution of Haitian Immigrant Organizations."

32. Basch, Glick Schiller, and Szanton Blanc, *Nations Unbound*, 146; Wah and Pierre-Louis, "Evolution of Haitian Immigrant Organizations," 154.

33. Laguerre, *Diasporic Citizenship*, 190.

34. Alex Stepick, "The Haitian Exodus: Flight from Terror and Poverty," in *The Caribbean Exodus*, ed. Barry B. Levine (New York: Praeger, 1987), 137.

35. Alex Stepick, "The Refugees Nobody Wants: Haitians in Miami," in *Miami Now! Immigration, Ethnicity, and Social Change*, ed. Guillermo J. Grenier and Alex Stepick III (Gainesville: University Press of Florida, 1992), 57.

36. Portes, Alejandro, and Ariel C. Armony, *The Global Edge: Miami in the Twenty-First Century* (Oakland: University of California Press, 2018).

37. Alex Stepick, "Miami's Two Informal Sectors," in *The Informal Economy: Studies in Advanced and Less Developed Countries*, ed. Alejandro Portes, Manuel Castells, and Lauren A. Benton (Baltimore: Johns Hopkins University Press, 1989).

38. Alex Stepick, *Pride Against Prejudice* (Needham, MA: Allyn and Bacon, 1998).

39. Alex Stepick and Alejandro Portes, "Flight into Despair: A Profile of Recent Haitian Refugees in South Florida," *The International Migration Review* 20, no. 2 (1986): 347.

40. Stepick, "Miami's Two Informal Sectors," 126.

41. Basch, Glick Schiller, and Szanton Blanc, *Nations Unbound*, 7.

42. D. Alissa Trotz and Beverley Mullings, "Transnational Migration, the State, and Development: Reflecting on the 'Diaspora Option,'" *Small Axe* 41 (2013): 155–171.

43. Harry Goulbourne and John Solomos, "The Caribbean Diaspora: Some Introductory Remarks," *Ethnic and Racial Studies* 27, no. 4 (2010): 535.

44. Basch, Glick Schiller, and Szanton Blanc, *Nations Unbound*; Glick Schiller and Fouron, *Georges Woke Up Laughing*; Deborah Thomas, "Blackness across Borders: Jamaican Diasporas and New Politics of Citizenship," *Identities: Global Studies in Culture and Power* 14, nos. 1–2 (2007): 111–133; Steven Vervotec, "The Political Importance of Diasporas" (working paper no. 15, Centre on Migration, Policy and Society, University of Oxford, 2005).

45. Douglas Massey, "International Migration at the Dawn of the Twenty-First Century: The Role of the State," *Population Council* 25, no. 2 (1999): 303–322; Luis E. Guarnizo and Michael P. Smith, "The Locations of Transnationalism," in *Transnationalism from Below*, ed. Luis E. Guarnizo and Michael P. Smith (New Brunswick, NJ: Transaction Publishers, 1998); Alejandro Portes, "Migration and Development: Reconciling Opposite Views," in *How Immigrants Impact Their Homelands*, ed. Susan Eva Eckstein and Adil Najam (Durham, NC: Duke University Press, 2013).

46. Guarnizo and Smith, "The Locations of Transnationalism."

47. Wah and Pierre-Louis, "Evolution of Haitian Immigrant Organizations."

48. Glick Schiller and Fouron, *Georges Woke Up Laughing*.

49. William Safran, "Diasporas in Modern Societies: Myths of Homeland and Return," *Diaspora: A Journal of Transnational Studies* 1, no. 1 (1991): 83–99; Robin Cohen, *Global Diasporas: An Introduction*, 2nd ed. (New York: Routledge, 2008).

50. Roger Brubaker, "The 'Diaspora' Diaspora."

51. Stephen Cornell and Douglas Hartmann, "Conceptual Confusions and Divides: Race, Ethnicity, and the Study of Immigration," in *Not Just Black and White: Historical and Contemporary Perspectives on Immigration, Race, and Ethnicity in the United States*, ed. Nancy Foner and George M. Frederickson (New York: Russell Sage Foundation, 2004).

52. Vilna Bashi Treitler, *The Ethnic Project: Transforming Racial Fiction into Ethnic Factions* (Stanford, CA: Stanford University Press, 2013).

53. Mbembe, *Critique of Black Reason*.

54. Mae M. Ngai, *Impossible Subjects: Illegal Aliens and the Making of Modern America* (Princeton, NJ: Princeton University Press, 2014).

55. William I. Robinson, *Global Capitalism and the Crisis of Humanity* (New York: Cambridge University Press, 2014).

56. Grace Chang, *Disposable Domestics: Immigrant Women Workers in the Global Economy*, 2nd ed. (Chicago: Haymarket Press, 2016); Rhacel Salazar Parreñas, *Servants of Globalization: Women, Migration, and Domestic Work*, 2nd ed. (Stanford, CA: Stanford University Press, 2015).

57. Angela Davis, *Women, Race, and Class* (New York: Random House, 1983).

58. Chang, *Disposable Domestics*.

59. Chang, *Disposable Domestics*; Parreñas, *Servants of Globalization*; Robyn Magalit Rodriguez, *Migrants for Export: How the Philippine State Brokers Labor to the World* (Minneapolis: University of Minnesota Press, 2010).

60. All statistics taken from U.S. Census Bureau, *State and County QuickFacts* (last updated December 4, 2014) and U.S. Census Bureau, *American Community Survey* (2013).

61. Miami-Dade Portal, "Little Haiti Targeted Urban Area," Miami-Dade County, 2011, http://www.miamidade.gov/business/library/maps/little-haiti-tua.pdf.

62. This point is drawn from an observation made by a respondent.

63. Stepick, *Pride against Prejudice*, 6.

64. This point is drawn from an observation made by a respondent.

65. James Diego Vigil, "Urban Violence and Street Gangs," *Annual Review of Anthropology* 32 (2003): 225–242.

66. Johanna Brenner and Robert Brenner, "Reagan, the Right and the Working Class," *Verso Blogs*, November 15, 2016, https://www.versobooks.com/blogs/2939-reagan-the-right-and-the-working-class.

67. Pseudonyms used throughout for interviewees.

68. Samantha Pinto, *Difficult Diasporas: The Transnational Feminist Aesthetic of the Black Atlantic* (New York: New York University Press, 2013), 9.

4

Migration and Lived Experiences of Antiblack Racism

The Case of African Immigrants in Queensland, Australia

Hyacinth Udah

Australia is a country of immigrants—a home for many migrants and refugees from across the globe. Aside from the First Nations people—the Aboriginal and Torres Strait Islander peoples—everyone who lives in Australia is a migrant or a descendant of people who came to Australia from other continents. While Africans[1] in Australia might be formally citizens, antiblack racism remains a significant problem, impacting their lives in Queensland and wider Australian society today. The legacies of colonization, white Australia, antiblack racial thinking, and discursive strategies of Othering continue to affect the social, economic, and political life and well-being of contemporary black and minority populations. In this chapter, therefore, I explore the nature and character of antiblack racism in Australia by interrogating its connections with historical racism, slavery, colonialization, and the legacy of white Australia. Drawing on data from a study conducted in Queensland, Australia, I focus and reflect primarily on the experiences of African immigrants in Queensland that has a white Australian[2] majority. The chapter serves to refigure antiblackness as a relevant category in the migration discourse and African racialized experience. It seeks to contribute to an improved understanding of the significance of race, racism, and Othering practices, not only in the incorporation of black Africans but also in the identification and integration of other visible ethnically and racially marked minority populations in white-dominated societies. I begin the chapter with a brief historical review of immigration and African migration to Australia. I then discuss and clarify precisely what I mean by antiblack racism in order to develop a theoretical understanding as well as to illuminate how antiblack racial thinking and Othering practices remain important dimensions for experiences of marginalization, exclusion, and disadvantage. I also examine the African condition and highlight the complex intersections of past racial ideologies and stereotypes that racialize and shape present race relations, beliefs, and imaginations of blackness and black identities. I conclude the chapter with a call for a major rethinking of strategies for addressing and tackling antiblack racism today, and for building a more racially just and socially inclusive society.

Immigration to Australia

For immigrants, Australia is one of the most culturally diverse and most desirable destination countries in the world. It has an estimated population of over twenty-five million, and is made up of six states and two territories.[3] As in other immigrant-receiving and settler-developed countries, such as Canada and the United States, immigrants to Australia are an integral part of the society. Australia is one of the few countries in the world with a planned immigration program. Immigration has not only been central to Australia's nation-building strategy but also, together with the First Nations people, has contributed to its major demographic changes and transformation.

From once being the most "homogenous" British white society, Australia has become, today, a more populous, diverse, multiethnic, multiracial, and multicultural contemporary society. Mass immigration after the Second World War transformed it from an insular, Britain-oriented society to a more multicultural society. Before the British arrived in 1788 to set up their penal colony, the First Nations people had lived in Australia for over sixty-five thousand years.[4] Between 1788 and 1868, about 162,000 convicts came to Australia. In the early years of European settlement, free workers, more than the number of convicts, emigrated from various parts of Britain and Ireland as young, single men seeking work and fortune. During the gold rush era (1851–1860), about fifty thousand people arrived in Australia each year. The Chinese were the largest non-British group arrivals. In response to the aspirations for an all-white Australia, including the fear and antagonism felt toward cheap colored labor, the Immigration Restriction Act—the White Australia policy—was introduced during Australia's federation on January 1, 1901, favoring white immigration.

The White Australia policy—a racist and legal policy—was designed, especially, to prohibit legal immigration from Asia and Africa and to secure a white Australia, preserving the purity of Australia's British heritage and building a population that was overwhelmingly white, British, and homogenous. For a seventy-three-year period, until immigration reform in 1973, almost all legal immigrants to Australia were white. The implementation of the White Australia policy was explicitly exclusionary and discriminatory.[5] It erected a color bar and restricted colored immigration. With its introduction, immigrants were either selected or excluded based on their race, ethnicity, skin color, culture, religion, or language. Also with its introduction, nonwhites were discouraged from settling in Australia; they could enter only on a temporary basis under a strict permit.[6] Throughout the first half of the twentieth century, during the Act's implementation, Australia's population growth was based mainly around "white" settlers.

Before the 1970s, most immigrants to Australia came predominantly from Europe or the U.K. Exceptions were made in the 1960s for a small number of educated and professional Asians to settle in Australia. During the early 1970s, Chilean, Cypriot, Lebanese, and Timorese people were admitted on humanitarian grounds. There was a significant intake of refugees from Laos, Cambodia, and Vietnam in the late 1970s and early 1980s. The removal of race as a factor for immigration in 1973, by the Whitlam Labor government, led to the eradication of the White Australia policy, allowing for colored and African migration to Australia. The phasing out of the policy has led to Australian major cities and regional towns becoming more diversified and cosmopolitan in character, which has brought about a great degree of cultural, religious, linguistic, and ethnic diversity.[7]

The 2016 census results published by the Australian Bureau of Statistics (ABS) indicate that Australians come from nearly two hundred countries, speak more than three hundred languages other than English at home, practice over one hundred religions, and represent more than three hundred ethnic ancestries.[8] Nearly 49 percent of Australia's population are born overseas or have one or both parents born overseas. Although a very diverse group, Africans—the migrant and refugee groups[9]—add an important chapter to the history of immigration to Australia.

African Migration to Australia

There is a long history of migration between Africa and Australia. While African immigration was restricted during the White Australia policy, some people of African descent came to Australia via the First Fleet, which brought the first British colonists and convicts in the late 1700s. In recent years, many Africans have migrated to Australia for various reasons. Some migrate to build and establish new lives and to get better education and employment. Some come to escape war, violence, and persecution. The abolition of the White Australia policy has allowed for voluntary African migration. Today, the number of Africans has increased in both absolute and relative terms. In the period from 1861 to 2011, the total African-born population in Australia increased from 1,590 to 337,825. Before World War II and 1976, white South Africans and Egyptians of Greek, Italian, and Maltese origin largely dominated the African migration to Australia. In the mid-1960s and early 1970s, under the Special Commonwealth African Assistance Plan, a small number of (black) African students, from Commonwealth African countries, arrived in Australia. Immigration to Australia from Africa reached a peak between 1996 and 2005, with the admission of large numbers of African refugees and displaced persons on humanitarian grounds from Central, East, and West Africa. Since then, more Africans from sub-Saharan Africa and Sudan have arrived in Australia.

Based on the 2021 census, Africans make up 1.7 percent of Australia's total population—over four hundred and thirty thousand Australian residents identify as Africa-born or as having at least one African-born parent.[10] In terms of distribution by state and territory, in 2021 Victoria had the largest number of people of African descent (125,505) followed by New South Wales (116,993), Western Australia (75,603), Queensland (74,329), South Australia (22,974), the Australian Capital Territory (7,502), Tasmania (4,004), and the Northern Territory (3,288). In 2021, the city of Melbourne (82,189) was home to the larger number of sub-Saharan Africans (white South Africans and Zimbabweans included), followed by Sydney (60,424). Perth (59,733) came third and was followed by Brisbane (39,353), Adelaide (15,878), Canberra (5,516), Hobart (2,008), and Darwin (1,940).

Currently, the Sudanese are the fastest-growing African community group in Australia, partly because they were given priority in the early 2000s and admitted on humanitarian grounds.[11] Although still a small group, Africans have become firmly part of Australian society and account for an increasing proportion of its total population. They come from nearly all countries on the African continent, representing a diverse range of cultures, religions, and language groups. Many of these Africans have come to Australia, leaving behind familial and familiar environments, to make a new life and give new hope to their dreams and aspirations. These African settler arrivals were comprised of people who bring additional skills and talent to Australia. While some have prospered, research indicates that persistent, subtle, and sometimes blatant antiblack racism, racial discrimination, xenophobia, and related intolerance continue to undermine many Africans' hopes for a better future in Australia.[12]

Racism and Antiblackness

Today, racism takes many forms. As an ideology of racial domination, racism is the belief in the superiority of one race over another race that is seen as inferior. For the purposes of this chapter, *racism* is defined as a system of advantage based on race. While race is a complete social construct with no biological basis, the idea of race has been a dominant means by which people are classified and their apparent differences explained. While for the most part, racism may be no more and may be outlawed, the application and use of race in racialization[13] continue to have real impacts on the experience of people racialized through enslavement and colonialization as blacks.

Racial slavery and colonialization contributed to shaping ideas of blackness that continue to impact the lives of Africans to the present day. During slavery, Africans were property of white owners—exploited, oppressed, denigrated, and dehumanized. They were not considered persons, nor worthy of treatment as full persons; rather, they were disposable as the owners wished. With no legal restrictions, their white owners could sell, whip, brand, rape, harm, or even kill them.[14] As Moon-Kie Jung explains, "The life of the enslaved is radically uncertain, radically subject to forces beyond their control. They have no legitimate standing in the social world. They have no legitimate claims to power or resources, including their very own selves."[15] They lack what Anthony Giddens calls *ontological security*—"Confidence or trust that the natural and social worlds are as they appear to be, including the basic existential parameters of self and social identity."[16] While slavery has stopped, one important legacy of slavery is the close connection between blackness and inferiority in the popular imagination.

What follows after enslavement of Africans is the production of whiteness and the degradation and dehumanization of black people as lacking intellectual capacities, and as morally inferior—the seeds and foundations of antiblackness. The attribution of intellectual and moral inferiority meant that black people were seen as intellectually inferior and inherently dangerous. Through slavery and discursive antiblack rhetorical strategies, the black subject has emerged as the unthought.[17] Through racist beliefs and antiblack rhetoric, forged during slavery, the black body, black subject's human being continues to be put permanently in question, leading to skewed life chances, fewer rights, limited access to health and education, incarceration, impoverishment, and inequality.[18] While slavery targeted the black body in the fifteenth and sixteenth centuries, the justice system targets the black body of the twentieth and twenty-first centuries. The legacies of slavery continue; they are seen in the different forms of antiblackness discourses and antiblack immigrants' sentiments that position Africans in lower or subordinate positions. This has led not only to white people being deputized in the face of black people but also to blackness becoming the site of absolute dereliction and generating no categories for respect.[19]

Coined by Akua Benjamin, Director of the School of Social Work at Ryerson University in Toronto, *antiblack racism* is a specific form of racism and racial practice targeted at Africans. It is rooted in the history of enslavement and colonialization of Africans. The legacies of slavery and colonialism continue to influence antiblack racism. In many contexts, blackness is treated as a proxy for criminality, and black people are seen as inferior, dangerous, and suspicious. Based largely on skin color, blackness—or to be precise, antiblack racism—highlights the unique nature of systemic racism on Africans. Antiblack racism is not limited to white-on-black racism; it also includes the relationship that nonblacks and nonwhites have to blacks.[20] Antiblack racism is embedded in everyday life and is recognized in individual acts of discrimination, including the policies, laws (local, state, and federal), social norms, and practices rooted in institutions and structural systems such as education, health, economy, and justice that mirror and reinforce racist beliefs, attitudes, prejudice, stereotypes, discrimination, or hatred directed at Africans,[21] denying them rights and full recognition as equal citizens and persons in society. It is a serious and insidious problem for many Africans.

Antiblack Racism and White Australia

Racism is a fact of life in Australia. While it differs depending on location,[22] racism is systemic, pervasive, and productive. While the influx of successive waves of migrants and refugees has changed Australia's demographic, racism was deeply embedded in Australia's immigration policies and practices until at least the 1970s. Two forms of racism still coexist in Australia—"old racism" of denigration, dehumanization, and discrimination based on the belief in the inherent superiority of one race over others (inferior races) and "new racism" based on perceived differences such as national origin or ethnic or cultural differences.[23] Being *numerological*—based on fear of migrant influx (too many Asians, too many Muslims, too many Africans)—and *existential*—based on disgust at difference and a belief in the superiority of white people,[24] racism has a long-standing, foundational persistence in Australia. Whiteness, particularly, is an important factor in understanding the persistence of old racist beliefs that continues to influence modern Australian society and its policies, laws, and politics. Whiteness is understood here as a category of privilege that puts whites at an advantage in the Australian context, while differentially oppressing, disadvantaging, or otherwise neglecting racial groups viewed as inferior. This privilege, white privilege, operates as an unseen or invisible package of unearned assets that white Australians cash in on every day, at the same time that they remain oblivious to the advantages that they gain from it.[25]

White Australia can be traced back to the late 1850s during the gold rush era. Driven by racial prejudice, xenophobia, and fear of foreign invasion, Australians promoted racist ideologies of white superiority and supremacy, favored British immigration, and demanded that "colored races" be kept out of Australia during the White Australia policy. The demand to keep "colored races" away is said to be dialectically linked with an emerging sense of an imagined community of Australians, at that time a collectivity that signified whiteness. The demand for a white Australia and the fear of being swamped by massive Asian immigration led to the federation of Australian colonies in 1901 and the enactment of the infamous Immigration Restriction Act of 1901—the White Australia policy, which provided the legal means to restrict colored immigration and remove colored people already in Australia. For scholars, James Forrest and Kevin Dunn, the policy represents a blunt *form of sociobiology* in which some "races" are deemed inferior and should be kept apart.[26] During the implementation of the White Australia policy, race was employed to exclude or set apart racialized groups deemed different and inferior. As Victoria Mence and her colleagues suggest, the preference for white immigration was deeply embedded in widely held views during the era that were based on racial theory and domination, white superiority and supremacy, antiblackness, eugenics, polygenesis, and social Darwinism, including the fear of Australia (seen as an outpost of the British) being swamped by its Asian neighbors.[27]

The discursive and material construction of white Australia came at an enormous cost to the Aboriginal and Torres Strait Islander peoples (Indigenous Australians). Their treatment was the closest Australia got to formal apartheid—a sad chapter in Australia's history. The Aboriginal and Torres Strait Islander peoples, who are the first inhabitants, were defined by racial discourses. Based on their skin color and heritage, they were racialized, viewed as black people,[28] subjected to xenophobic hostility, and confined to marginal spaces.[29] Virtually all racial slurs and antiblackness practices were directed at them. Being dark-skinned, they were less-valued; were denied the right to citizenship, voice, and representation,[30] and ultimately were pushed to the edge of economic, cultural, political, and social extinction. Also, the increasing presence of Chinese immigrants during the gold rush era was far from welcome—they were feared and thought of as having the potency to threaten and pollute Australia's superior white race. They were also accused of immorality and were seen as undermining "fair go" principles, particularly related to employment and working conditions of Australians. Similarly, the South Sea Islanders, known as Kanakas,[31] who were recruited to work in Queensland's sugar cane fields between 1863 and 1904, were treated terribly and were defined by racial discourses as being racially inferior. Thus, being perceived as inferior, the South Sea Islanders were segregated from mainstream society, exploited as cheap labor, and discarded when no longer needed.[32]

With the White Australia policy, Australia emphasized its whiteness and built itself, to a large extent, on a deep and abiding belief in racial domination and white superiority and supremacy, demarcating and defining whites as biologically and culturally superior. The process of dismantling the policy was gradual. It began following the end of World War II with the admission of refugees and displaced persons from Eastern Europe. To fill immigration targets, and driven by the pragmatic slogan "populate or perish," Australia also admitted many Italian and Greek migrants from Southern Europe. Attitudes toward these immigrants were heavily influenced by racial prejudice and superiority—they were considered to be nonwhites and non-British. Being the first non-British immigrant groups to arrive in large numbers, they suffered racism and economic deprivation. They were also stereotyped as socially incompatible, discriminated against in the labor market, and called contemptuous names such as "reffos," "wogs," "dagos," and "Balts."

Since the abolition of the White Australia policy in 1973 and its replacement with the 1975 Racial Discrimination Act,[33] which made race-based immigration selection criteria illegal, many immigrants have come to Australia—in large numbers—from different backgrounds and countries in the world. Attitudes toward immigrants now range from generally tolerant to generally intolerant. While racist attitudes and nonracist attitudes still coexist, the sociobiological form of old racism, seen during the years of the White Australia policy, is by no means a popular ideology in contemporary Australia. As Forrest and Dunn explain, "The key ideological bases of racism, and exclusive nationalism now draw from so-called 'new racism' or 'cultural racism,' based on the perceived incompatibility and 'insurmountability of cultural differences."[34] While this new ideology of racism is expressed primarily, though not exclusively, on the grounds of ethnicity, social cohesion, and national unity, antiblack racism continues to be transformed and revived in Australia. It continues, also, to influence Australia's policies and politics. White Australia is still an important factor in understanding antiblackness. It pushes blackness to the margins in Australia.

Antiblack Racial Thinking, Othering, and Australian National Identity

Australia is a nation that has been built socially, economically, and culturally by its First Nations people, by its early British and European settlers, and by subsequent waves of migration.[35] With many Australian governments and politicians pursuing progressive agendas and abolishing discriminatory immigration policies, there has been rapid growth in the number of racially and ethnically marked migrants and refugees—including Africans, who are among the new and emerging communities in Australia. However, the role of racialized blackness cannot be underestimated. Antiblack racism remains an important dimension of prejudice and discrimination directed at Africans in Australia. White Australians still see the black body through the medium of historically structured forms of knowledge that regard it as inferior and as an evil or an object of suspicion to be avoided or disciplined. As Frantz Fanon observes, not only must the black man be black; he must be black in relation to the white man.[36] The life of the African in Australia is still racialized, imperiled, and devalued based on racial stereotypes of the past. As Virginia Mapedzahama and Kwamena Kwansah-Aidoo argue, blackness is "not only that which defines whiteness but is also inferiorized by it."[37] The black body in Australia is often constructed as a problematic difference to whiteness: an inferiority and an Other. Rooted in the history of slavery, colonialization, and white Australia, Africans in Australia continue to endure racial oppression from actions by the police, politicians, and private citizens. While their citizenship is put permanently in question, they are not by default accepted. While their need for belonging is always under assault, their blackness is othered and associated with inferiority, incompetency, criminality, disruption, and violence, which has a negative impact on their perception, acceptance, and inclusion in the wider society. Within this chapter, therefore, I introduce the notion of Othering and the idea of Australian national identity—Whiteness—to examine antiblack racism against Africans and to explore how they inform, together with colonial legacies of white Australia, contemporary antiblack racial thinking, influencing how Australians define and see Africans as black (with all the racial tropes that blackness embodies).

First, as an imposed state of difference, *Othering* relies on binary dualistic thinking, making divisions into two opposing categories such as "I" and "You," "We" and "Them," "Self" and "Other." Othering practices, which mark and name those perceived as fundamentally different from Self, derive from hierarchical "us" and "them" thinking. Here, "them" is seen through negative stereotypes and narratives that can reinforce and reproduce positions of domination, marginalization, and subordination. It is a process of seeing oneself positively and seeing an Other negatively, as undesirable and lesser. Through the process of Othering, one group or individual is empowered with a positive identity and the Other becomes subjected, dehumanized, denied of voice, and seen as less worthy of dignity, love, respect, and any entitlement to human rights, which has consequences for how the Other is welcomed, valued, included, or excluded. Thus, inherent in Othering practices is dichotomy: there must be the Other (inferior) for the Self (superior) to exist, and vice versa. As a process, Othering suggests something fundamental about the nature of group-based exclusion and expressions of prejudice. It encompasses not only the many expressions of prejudice and negative stereotypes based on group identities, but also provides a clarifying frame that reveals a generalized set of common processes, structures, and conditions that propagate and legitimize group-based exclusion, marginality, and persistent inequality and disadvantage.

Historically, the process of Othering has been used to marginalize, disempower, oppress, subordinate, exploit, and colonize groups that are constructed through discourses of race as racially, intellectually, and morally inferior. Considered sociologically, Othering is about the dominant majority group, which is powerful, producing the Other as subordinate and establishing a manipulative discourse that makes the Other pathological and morally inferior.[38] Othering practices are made real during discourses[39] and regimes of meaning. Discourses, as defined by Amina Mama, are historically constructed regimes of knowledge that include common-sense assumptions and taken-for-granted ideas, belief systems and myths that groups of people share and through which they understand each other.[40] In other words, discourses refer to the ways of constituting knowledge as well as the social practices, forms of subjectivity, and power relations inherent in such knowledge and the relations between them. Discourses position people socially, culturally, and politically in relation to each other.

Discourses (and discursive practices) shape how the Other is viewed, read, represented, constructed, and even treated. There are two major forms of racist discourses involving the Other: being about the Other, and being directed at the Other.[41] The first form (being about the Other) is usually acted out in groups, between members of the dominant group, in a negative portrayal, and often in combination with a positive representation. The second form (being directed at the Other) is expressed by members of the dominant group, for example, in the use of derogatory slurs and insults in verbal interactions with dominated ethnic visible minority group members. Though these discourses tend to be subtle or indirect, they constitute a threat to the well-being and quality of life of those who are perceived as different—as the Other. Thus, the "Other" is created in discourses.

Despite support for a policy of multiculturalism, and despite the immigration of people from diverse backgrounds, Australia is still a predominantly white society, where whiteness is normalized and has been used in policy, politics, legislation, and practice over visible and ethnically marked people, including African migrants and refugees. Being founded on and firmly grounded in white Australia, the existing metadiscourses of Otherness in Australia still give primacy to whiteness,[42] at the direct expense of members of ethnically and racially marked minority people. At the heart of the metadiscourses of Otherness in Australia are a set of pervasive ideologies that valorize whiteness as the norm, from which Others are constructed, defined, scrutinized, and controlled. Using Foucauldian ideas about power and knowledge, Millsom Henry-Waring asserts that these metadiscourses of Otherness act as hegemonic carriers of ideology and power within which ideas about difference and diversity are created and refuse to be dismantled.[43] They shape attitudes, beliefs, and actions and uphold the systems of privilege and/or disadvantage that have characterized the Australian society for a very long time.

In many cases, contemporary Australian social landscape still reflects white Australia and *nationalist practices based on group identities*. As Ghassan Hage argues, there is still the existence of a shared white-nation fantasy among some Australians who are worried over the presence of "Third World–looking" people in Australia.[44] While the white-nation fantasy continues to shape the dialectics of inclusion and exclusion of members of minority groups, the hoary folk myths and stereotypes about members of minority groups are continually refurbished and confidently peddled as facts. For example, the vitriolic attacks and racist violence—against Arabs, against Muslims and Islamic identity, and against Africans, including other migrants and refugees, by some politicians, groups, and individuals—are some of the nationalist practices based on group identities and conception of the "ethnic/racial Other" as a mere object within Australia. Another example of colonial legacies of white Australia is in the recurring tropes for immigration to Australia, which suggest a movement by white Australia to stop the boats and to impose selective and tougher immigration controls and a national security crackdown. Australia's selective points-based immigration policy, and by extension other institutionalized barriers to employment and education, seems to be based on what Saskia Bonjour and Jan Duyvendak describe as the racialization of certain categories of migrants into irretrievably "unassimilable Others" who must be kept out.[45]

In addition, Pauline Hanson and other Australians who criticize immigration and attack the influx of foreigners continue to perpetuate whiteness, antiblackness, and racism against African migrants. For example, in 1996, Pauline Hanson, the One Nation founder, claimed that Australia was in danger of being "swamped by Asians." In her speech to the Senate in 2016, she said, "Now we are in danger of being swamped by Muslims, who bear a culture and ideology that is incompatible with our own" way of life and culture. Hanson has also called for a ban on burqas, the abolition of multiculturalism, and the deportation of African youths accused of crimes. Hanson's radical and racist views continue to attract support across Australia, including among some Australian politicians. Amid the debate over crime and other issues, Australian politicians Kevin Andrews, Peter Dutton, and Tony Abbott (a former Australian prime minister) have questioned all African immigration, seeing these immigrants as people who are difficult to assimilate, integrate, and fit into Australian society. Similarly, lamenting the racial and cultural conquest of Australian identity, former Queensland senator Fraser Anning called for a return to a European Christian immigration system and for certain migrants to be kept out. Anning's views, like those of Hanson, follow what Hage calls the "discourse of Anglo decline," which either passively mourns the loss of Anglo or Anglo-Celtic Australians' privileged position or actively calls for resistance against increased immigration.

The immigrant population of modern Australia has become highly diversified, with a yearly increase in arrivals of migrants and refugees of diverse cultural, linguistic, religious, ethnic, and racial backgrounds. But the discursive and specific construction of identity has followed, and continues to follow, binary divides and a history of settlement that has *othered* and considered as *ethnic* the identities of many members of minority groups, migrants, and their descendants, including the identity of Australia's First Nations people. In public discourses, words like *difference, race*, and *minority* are still used to refer to the Aboriginal and Torres Strait Islander peoples and many ethnically and racially marked people. While Australians of Anglo-Celtic heritage, who occupy a privileged and dominant position, are considered to be normative, seen as unmarked, identified as Australians, and viewed as governors of the nation, many Indigenous Australians, Arab Australians, Asian Australians, Muslim Australians, African Australians, and other non-white migrants, in contemporary diversity discourses in Australia, are conventionally constructed and positioned as the "Other" in relation to the Australian normative "Self" in the space of objectified Otherness. They are perceived as passive objects to be governed, moved, or removed according to a white national will. For Forrest and Dunn, this reflects "an Anglo (or Anglo-Celtic) view on nationalism"—"a hallmark of the 'new racism': an assimilationist or ethnocultural view of Australian society which is different from the 'civic nation' ideal envisaged by multiculturalism."[46]

Though Australia's race relations have significantly improved, the structures of white supremacy have not entirely disappeared. Even though White Australia is officially abolished, the current political moment demonstrates the rise of white nationalism. Despite the rhetoric and policy of multiculturalism, blackness[47] is the ontological referent point for whiteness that informs the White Australia policy and the definition of Australian national identity. Whiteness is not only central to Australian identity but also a crucial category in the reception of any group in Australia. It is an essential component of being Australian, conferring dominance and privilege. Also, it plays an important part in determining one's inclusion, acceptance, and access to certain resources. In modern Australia, whiteness is still valorized as the norm, and as the governing identity that shapes the national imaginary of who does, and does not, belong in Australia. In effect, whiteness has created the unequal power relations that persist to this day, and that are even reproduced in everyday racial thinking and Othering practices. As an effect of racialization, whiteness is "real," material, and lived in Australia. It is the absent center against which Africans and other migrants are positioned and perceived only as inferior, marginal, undesirable, uncivilized, ugly, deviant, or points of deviation.[48]

Even though most of the racialized migrants entering Australia are Asians, blackness plays a centrally important role in the ideas of racial Otherness that inform migration discourses, irrespective of "who" is migrating. Without a doubt, antiblackness is most relevant in terms of who is allowed to enter into Australia and who is prohibited from doing so.[49] Antiblackness still plays a role in anti-Aboriginal and immigrant sentiments that single out not only Aboriginals but also black Africans in Australia. For example, an issue that is alive and well today is the living discrimination against dark-skinned Aboriginals.[50] Since the arrival of Europeans, Aboriginal Australians have experienced hardships ranging from the denial of rights of Australian citizenship, including the right to vote and be counted, to the forced removal of their children, resulting in what are now described as the Stolen Generations.[51] Aboriginal and Torres Strait Islander Australians still experience high levels of poverty, racism, and unemployment; lower educational achievements; and higher rates of incarceration. The structural and historical oppression of Aboriginals in Australia has created among them a mistrust of Australia's government policies and interventions.[52] Not surprisingly, many Indigenous Australians use the category "black" to highlight their experiences as a result of institutional racism, and in contrast to white Australia, which creates and sustains their subjugation and lower socioeconomic status.[53] Similarly, due to their relationship to white Australia, the experience of black Africans, though different from that of Indigenous Australians, is an experience of Australian blackness.[54]

Indeed, the colonial legacies of white Australia play major roles in systemic antiblack racism. This is not just a matter of Africans being marginalized and excluded from economic opportunities but the fact that whiteness presumes blackness, conceptually, as its archetypal Other (in terms of the social Darwinian/biopolitical imaginary that informed past racial typologies and ideologies of denigration and dehumanization). For many Africans, their blackness is associated with intellectual and moral inferiority, which continues to reinforce, revive, and perpetuate antiblackness. Like other racialized societies, the Australian mainstream news media together with some political leaders, groups, and individuals continue to valorize white bodies as natural, normal, and standard, and embody the plague of criminality, deviance, violence, immorality, and corruption in the black body.[55]

The legacy of white Australia perpetuates antiblackness and attacks the very identities of Africans. For example, images and beliefs that characterize

Africans in terms of real or attributed differences are still used to represent them in mainstream media, policies, and political speeches. Fluctuating between the emphasis on difference, on the one hand, and supremacist derogation—stressing their intellectual, moral, and biological inferiority—on the other hand, such images, beliefs, and evaluations influence public opinion about Africans, and continue to inform antiblackness and sustain antiblack racist thinking and practices.

Understanding African Lived Experience— Research Design and Methodology

In 2016, I conducted a qualitative study in South East Queensland,[56] Australia, to learn more and understand the everyday lived experiences of Africans. In particular, I wanted to examine how Africans define their identity and their personal and socioeconomic well-being in white-majority Australia, focusing on the role of racialized identity constructions and the mediating effects of skin color on their experiences and overall outcomes. As a black immigrant negotiating identity and belonging in Australia, my motivations for the study came from my personal experiences and my passion for social justice. The qualitative study allowed me to examine in detail and capture a richer depth of information from participants' lived experiences with antiblack racism.[57] The remarkable feature of the participants ($N = 30$) is the diversity of their culture, religion, values, languages, heritage, and national backgrounds.[58] Of these participants, seventeen came as refugees through Australia's humanitarian program and thirteen came as temporary migrants (six arrived on a student visa and seven on a skilled migration visa). I selected the participants purposefully and got their informed consent for participation. I assured them of privacy and confidentiality and encouraged voluntary participation. I collected data through individual face-to-face semistructured interviews. The interviews gave me an opportunity to gain a rich understanding of participants' experiences, views, perspectives, and perceptions. I conducted most interviews in the English language. The interviews each lasted for sixty minutes, during which I probed participants' responses while encouraging them to provide more details and clarification. The interview questions covered issues around participants' settlement experiences, personal and socioeconomic conditions, life satisfaction and well-being, employment, and sense of belonging. The interviews were audio-recorded with participants' consent and were analyzed using thematic analysis—to identify, interpret, and report common thematic elements across the participants' transcribed interview data. The transcribed interview data were coded using

NVivo. The coding process helped to identify and produce a concise matrix of key emerging themes.

While some Australians believe that racial discrimination is over and no longer has a significant impact on people's lives, I found, on the contrary, that many Africans are affected by systemic antiblack racism. Against the predominant narrative of progress, I found that African lives are still racialized, denigrated, and devalued. Building on critical race theory (CRT) and everyday racism to inform my analysis of racism against Africans in Australia, I argue that Africans still experience antiblack racism, leading to their socioeconomic disadvantage.

CRT begins with these basic tenets: that race is socially constructed; that racism is ordinary, natural, everyday, and pervasive; and that racism advances white privilege and advantage. For CRT scholars, issues of race and racism, including antiblackness, in society must be paid attention to and challenged. To address antiblack racism and ameliorate African disadvantage and differential outcomes, CRT scholars call for recognizing, valuing, listening to, and championing the voices of African (minority) people.[59] Following CRT, I argue that racial domination, discrimination, exploitation, and oppression still exist in Australia. Also, I recognize race as central to the lived experiences of Africans in Australia. Therefore, placing the relationship between race and skin color (blackness) and the normalization of whiteness at the center of my analysis, I account for specific forms of antiblack racism against Africans in Australia.

Similarly, everyday racism identifies as theoretically relevant the lived experiences with antiblack racism. As a process, everyday racism is routinely created, and reinforced, through everyday practices. It is manifested in attitudes (prejudice) and actions (discrimination). Within Philomena Essed's conceptualization, everyday racism exists not as a single event but as a complex of cumulative racist and discursive practices that are systemic, recurrent, repetitive, and familiar in everyday life and that become part of what is seen as "normal" by the dominant group.[60] Everyday racism is manifested in smaller and larger everyday violations of the civil rights and dignity of minority people in continual ethnic jokes; ridicule; patronizing behaviors, including assumptions of lack of competence and civility; associations with criminality; and other attempts to humiliate and intimidate them. Using the notion of everyday racism, I qualify the implications of centralizing experiential knowledge in understanding and identifying converging forms of everyday antiblack racism. In this chapter, I consider as theoretically relevant and meaningful, whether overt or subtle, the African everyday lived experiences with antiblack racism. While everyday antiblack racism is often ignored, over time it can have damaging effects on Africans who are racialized and subjected to it on a daily basis.

Antiblack Racism and African Disadvantage in Australia: Case Study

Despite all significant developments—end of white Australia, support for a policy of multiculturalism, and introduction of antidiscriminatory legislation—antiblack racial discrimination remains a significant problem, impacting the lives of Africans in Australia and beyond. It is a daily and pervasive fact of life for many Africans. An important defining characteristic of Africans in Australia is their blackness, which plays a vital role in their incorporation, identification, and integration in Australia. Given their blackness—based on their skin color—they are distinct and highly visible in terms of difference from the predominantly white Australian majority. While the daily dynamics of color and race expose the limits of Australian citizenship in absorbing difference, the discursive constructions of African black identity in everyday language and social relations work to construct their lived reality of being, becoming, and being positioned as a racialized subject "Other," leading to their subordination, oppression, marginalization, exclusion, and disadvantage.

Consistent with the existing literature, participant accounts confirm that antiblack racism has yet to be eliminated. Many participants believe that being black is a problematic marker. Being black, twenty-eight out of the thirty participants feel marginalized by their skin color. These participants feel that expressions of prejudice and discrimination based on their skin color, language, religion, and culture were central in their experiences of discrimination. The account of Celine, a warm and energetic female participant, is a good illustration. Born in Congo, Celine arrived in Australia with her family in 1987. Coming to Australia as a black teenager has been a challenge for her. She says, "I still recall days when I went to bed crying myself to sleep because people bullied me at school, called me names because I look different to them."

The above data indicate that Celine was traumatized and made to feel different, disheartened, saddened, rejected, unsafe, excluded, and even disdained and scorned. While the incidents may seem petty, cumulatively the bullying and derogatory name-calling that Celine experienced at school constitute a stream of lived experiences that communicate denigration and a lack of social respect. If a person is constantly perceived or treated differently, as the problematic Other, they are more likely to experience a great deal of mental, emotional, or physical strain or tension. Also, research shows that these kinds of experiences can have a significant impact on morale, mental health, and self-esteem.[61] For those who are perceived unidimensionally, who are seen stereotypically, and who are defined and delimited by mental sets that may not bear much relation to existing reality, the consequences are often alienation, isolation, marginalization, decreased opportunities, internalized oppression, and exclusion. Thus, for Africans like Celine, antiblack racism can impact not only their sense of belonging but also their health, self-esteem, interpersonal relationships, performance, well-being, and integration outcomes.

Blacks are subjected to derogatory stereotyping that is built on slavery, on legacies of colonization, and on racial ideologies of degradation and dehumanization of blacks as intellectually and morally inferior. Africans continue to be stereotyped as inferior, dangerous, uncivilized, and less competent. Thus, by default they often are not accepted. For example another participant, Damian, in describing his experience of being black, says this:

You are not by default accepted. For you to be accepted, you have to prove it. . . . You really have to do twice as much to be seen as half as good. It is definitely an impression or perception of the society that you don't have anything to offer. . . . So whatever you put on the table gets scrutinised twice. Your suitability for any sort of project or anything is in my opinion questioned more thoroughly than [that of] anybody else.

Damian, originally from Ghana, immigrated to Australia in 2008 from New Zealand. Damian's statement just above reveals something interesting about the African experience, which is one of stereotypes, marginalization, exclusion, disadvantage, barriers, missed opportunities, and frustration. As Damian suggests, by default Africans are not accepted in the normal fabric of institutional life but are treated as the Other. To be accepted, they have to work twice as hard as whites. As racialized discourses construct categories of whiteness and blackness, within these discourses African migrants are categorized and positioned as deficient, an approach that leads to scapegoating, discrimination, and hatred of Africans. As Barbara, a female participant, states,

I didn't think that it was the case. I got up believing that it is a country of fair go, ample opportunity, you know. It is not a country that looks at the color of your skin, your religion, you know, all those things. These are things, issues that people have left their countries of origin to escape from, not to be just subjected here to the same thing. So, when they start judging you, you realize oh, I am black.

Born in South Sudan, Barbara migrated to Australia in 2001 (at the age of 12) with her family as refugees. For Barbara, black Africans are assumed to be inferior and poor. In addition, Barbara feels sad that the South Sudanese people are labeled as "violent," "gangs," "drunkards," "good for nothing," and "alcoholics" and as people who are difficult to assimilate and integrate into Australia. Barbara's comment is reminiscent of some Australian politicians' attack on all African immigration. For many participants, their experiences of racism could not be detached from their blackness. These participants believe that existing stereotypes of blacks, based on fantasies and ideas of black qua inferior, still shape how people define and relate to Africans.

Helen, for one, talks about how her skin color impacted the way people saw and defined her, and accordingly stereotyped her. In 2009, Helen came to Australia from Nigeria as an international student. She contends that skin color should not be used for discrimination. According to Helen, "People see you because of the way you are, and they don't know who you are, they just stereotyped you. Probably because of your color or the way you look." Thus, for many participants, their skin color—their blackness, to be precise—shapes how they are viewed and the degree to which they are accepted, determining their inclusion, their participation, and their access to certain resources. According to one participant, Kevin, it is a constant struggle to survive as a black person. As Kevin explains, "Black man in this country means struggle, continue to struggle."

Born in South Sudan, Kevin spent most of his teenage years in Uganda. In 2005, he migrated to Australia with his mother and three siblings on humanitarian grounds. Given the existing stereotypical projections and ideas of black qua inferior that manifest not only on an individual level but also on a systemic level, Kevin feels that people will misjudge and underestimate his skills, knowledge, and competencies. To counter such underestimations and realize his dream, he believes in working twice as hard. According to Kevin,

For me, as an African, to realize my dream here, I believe I should work twice as hard. We are disadvantaged in a certain way. What they think of us is completely what we are not. You know when you have people think of you as inferior; people think of you as incapable before you even speak, that is a challenge in itself. You have to try and prove otherwise.

Three points can be highlighted from Kevin's data extract above. First, Kevin recognizes the everyday, unending pressures, conscious and unconscious, to work twice as hard in order to be recognized. However, working twice as hard can take a toll that is felt mentally, socially, and economically. For example, the lived reality of working twice as hard can be one of exhaustion and burnout. Second, Kevin understands that for Africans, life would be a constant struggle filled with proving one's capability and skills because of the existing racist discourses, biases, and prejudices that many people carry. For Kevin, his skin color is associated with inferiority. Third, Kevin feels that the preference will always go to a white Australian when it comes to getting skilled, upper-level office jobs. According to Kevin, "When you are seen as a black man there is a certain expectation of who you are."

By expectation, Kevin suggests that Africans are underestimated and are seen only in terms of their specific black identity, without any thought being given to their capacities as individuals, which can be a huge problem. For Kevin, the expectation of an African is to be in the cleaning, age care, and disability sectors, or to work on a farm, or to do factory jobs. This expectation can impede upward social mobility. Not surprisingly, for several participants like Kevin, being black is a handicap and comes with many labels. For example, in discussing his experience as a nurse, one participant from Liberia named Jason, who immigrated to Australia in 2007 as a skilled migrant, says, "With your skin color, some may feel that you will not be able to do certain things." Similarly, Margaret from Zimbabwe, one of the female participants who migrated as a skilled migrant in 2004, points out, "In the work environment, someone might think you don't know much because of where you have come from or because of your color." Another participant from South Sudan, Thomas, who arrived in 2004 as a refugee, adds, "If you are black, without knowing you they just categorize you as inferior."

Participants' data demonstrate the unfortunate reality of being black and African: that is, being underestimated by those who seek to dehumanize or other them. Existing stereotypical perceptions about the color "black" continues to sustain a wrong impression about Africans' intellectual capability. Some people will always look down on them, regardless of their educational status and performance. In a way, participants' accounts reveal something about everyday antiblack racism and the vital role that blackness plays in the racialization of Africans in Australia, leading to their experiences of socioeconomic disadvantage. Many participants recall how they were discriminated against and underestimated as less competent. These participants believe that some people perceived of them as incapable based on their skin color. For example, according to Barbara,

Even when you are successful and you are good at things, some will try to underestimate you because for some people, it is not okay for a black person to know more than them.

For Barbara, antiblack racism is a real problem, an issue that is alive and well, making life hard for Africans. As she adds, "I just want to say, it is a real issue. It is an issue that some people want to deny and some people are not open about it."

Everyday antiblack racism, whether subtle or covert, is damaging to the lives of people who experience it on a regular basis. Research shows a strong link between daily experiences of racism and psychological distress, including chronic adverse effects on mental and physical health due to the stress and other negative emotions that accompany the racism.[62] Indeed, everyday negative discourses of the African Other as inferior, incapable, and dangerous—one of the mechanisms of antiblack racism—continue to blight the lives of Africans, denying them opportunities to thrive, feel they belong, and participate in Australia.[63] Moreover, their awareness of how other people stereotype and perceive them can place them at risk for internalizing the stereotypes, leading to loss of self-esteem and self-confidence, including a decline in morale. For example, when reporting about his experiences with antiblack racism, Josh says,

> It has not been easy, and it is not easy. This is a society that is white. It is a white-driven society. Everything is white. When you come in, the perceived theory of color, that there is a color called "black," you are a total stranger, and nobody thinks you have something in your brain.

Josh comes from the Democratic Republic of the Congo (DRC). He relocated to Australia in 2009 after fleeing political persecution in the DRC. He believes that Australia is still a white nation, where racially and ethnically marked migrants are objects to be governed and constrained within a system built on whiteness. With the country being white-driven, he contends, racism is a normal part of how the Australian society functions. For Josh, it will take a while for Africans to be part of the system, because they are still constructed as strangers, as not belonging, and are viewed as less in the imagined Australian nation. In fact, the continuity of specific patterns of racialized Othering of Africans in the Australian public discourse partly explains the persistence of antiblackness.

Discussion: Towards a More Racially Just and Socially Inclusive Society

Antiblackness is part and parcel of white Australia and its afterlife. To understand antiblack racism against Africans, it is important, therefore, to examine the ways in which it is linked to historically variable forms of racial oppression, and to the legacies of African enslavement, colonialization, and white Australia. While the current Australian immigration program allows immigration of people from diverse backgrounds, the normalization of whiteness still upholds antiblack racist practices and the systems of inequality that have characterized Australian society for a very long time.[64] As participants' data indicate, antiblack racism is one of the critical complexities of racial oppression in Australia and needs to be part of our understanding of the African experience. It operates in many places and locations, in gestures, conversations, rejections, neglects, workplaces, job applications, and streets and through all social relations that are also race relations—involving racial thinking and practices.

The peculiar experiences of participants suggest that they do not fully participate in society. As contemporary blacks and minority populations in white Australian majority, they are racialized, disempowered, and disenfranchised. As their blackness embodies that which is inferiorized, feared, loathed, and despised, they are cast as inferiors, as less competent, and as a problem group. Comparing the present to the time of white Australia, as a nation, Australia has made progress in terms of racial justice, but has also retrogressed. The big difference as compared with the White Australia era is that today black Africans and other racially and ethnically marked people can come to Australia. No policy prevents them from migrating. However, as participants' experiences suggest, black Africans are not by default accepted as members of society. They bear the brunt of discrimination, resulting from antiblack prejudice and negative representations of their black identity. Hence, there is a need to understand, confront, and challenge institutional and systemic antiblack racism.

In 2020, antiblack racist practices continue to manifest and camouflage in nationalist, religious, and personal views,[65] and sometimes, in the so-called right to free speech, including structures and institutions that differentially oppress and disadvantage Africans. Of course, part of what it means to conceive human beings as agents is to conceive them as empowered members by their access to resources of one kind or another. In the case of Africans in Australia, participants' accounts indicate that they constitute one of the most disadvantaged groups. Blackness shapes how they are seen and included. As a social group, they are less likely to feel, belong, and receive equitable treatment. While street crimes are blamed on their communities, the label "African gangs" is discursively employed to demonize and criminalize African youths. Being constructed and perceived as disruptive and violent, African youths are unfairly targeted and scrutinized by police and other law enforcement agencies.

Contemporary antiblack racism in Australia continues to portray Africans as criminogenic, and as a backward people who are incapable of joining

Western societies as efficient and productive members. Being identified as the unfamiliar Other, many participants have a perception that they are constructed as the unwelcome, problematic black Other and are structurally positioned in opposition to normality and all its signifiers, including demonstrations of civility, respectability, and obedience. As participants' data reveal, prevailing antiblackness narratives and discourses that associate blackness with criminality, incapability, and violence continue to undermine Africans' hopes for a better future in Australia. On many levels, antiblack racism affects all facets of African lives. Thus, the African experience with antiblack racism calls for the acknowledgment of the reality of antiblackness in Australia.

As a society, Australia takes great pride in being multicultural, democratic, egalitarian, and inclusive, but it constantly racializes and marginalizes the different black Other. One important feature of antiblack racism in Australia, as participants' data indicate, is that it involves, and can be seen in, discursive strategies of Othering and practices that support specific forms of discrimination against Africans—through unwitting prejudice, stereotypes, and seemingly subtle covert acts—namely, those social cognitions and social acts and processes that are recurrent and familiar in everyday life and become part of what is seen as normal, but that directly or indirectly contribute to marginalization, exclusion, and disadvantage. While there is no easy way to confront and eliminate antiblack racial thinking and practices, individuals and community agencies can do something by understanding and challenging their beliefs and assumptions across everything they do.

Not only does antiblack racism affect the socioeconomic outcomes of Africans; it impacts their human rights. As participants' data indicate, it also traumatizes them. In Australia, which is an increasingly diverse and multicultural democratic society, addressing antiblack racism and committing to meaningful sustained change requires major rethinking of strategies and support from all levels of government, institutions, community agencies, and individuals. This entails prioritizing actions to eliminate antiblackness discourses and to eliminate the impacts of the historical legacies of white Australia, slavery, and colonialization on the contemporary racialization of Africans, through policy and education. Every effort, therefore, should be made by the government and the citizens to become aware of what Africans, who have been grappling with antiblackness, think and feel about a range of issues affecting them. This awareness creates opportunities for a change of action and attitude. As Udah explains, "Things can be completely different if we step outside of our old attitudes and practices, recognize the uniqueness of each person, avoid stereotyping and leave behind assumptions based on a person's race, ethnicity, language, or religion, and transform our conceptions of Self and Other. When we see each other as individuals, as part of us, we uphold all the things we have in common rather than what divides us."[66]

Indeed, antiblackness discourses cannot deliver the kind of cultural change needed to build and achieve a more integrated, just, and socially inclusive society. This is because antiblackness discourses not only oppress but also limit life opportunities, pushing blacks to the margins of the society. Thus, participants' experience of antiblack racism calls for a deep understanding of how such racism is embedded in the country's constitution, social structures, systems, and institutions, and how it continues to be enacted in policies and laws, producing racial, social, and cultural inequality and differential outcomes. Understanding the historical roots of antiblackness and its connections with white Australia and legacies of slavery and colonialization can shift the conversation from normalizing whiteness to helping Africans and other ethnically and racially marked people to feel included and to belong. Therefore, there is a need for an unwavering commitment, not only to tolerate and respect difference but also to ensure that everyone has available the conditions necessary to achieve or realize their full potential within Australia's structures and institutions. This calls for building a society based on justice, inclusion, belonging, and equal opportunity, where all are embraced and can share in the wealth of the country.

Conclusion

This chapter has explored antiblack racism in Australia. Though Australia's race relations have significantly improved, antiblack racism remains a significant problem. While its existential effects on Africans remain inadequately understood, the salience of antiblackness has a considerable impact on the racialized "black" African Other. The discursive constructions of Africans in everyday language and social relations work to construct their lived reality of being, becoming, and being positioned as a racialized subject, leading to marginalization, exclusion, and disadvantage. Given the global significance of issues around race, ethnicity, identity, difference, and living across cultural diversity, antiblackness is relevant in contemporary migration and minority discourses. The chapter hopes, therefore, to renew public interest and broaden discussion on antiblack racism and its effects on the experiences of Africans and black diaspora in Australia and beyond.

NOTES

1. The word *African* refers to people of African descent, both male and female, who are dark-skinned, socially constructed, and, often, racialized as black. *Black*, in this context, is used as a reference term for their skin color. These Africans include those who have migrated as refugees and asylum seekers, and those who have come as students and as highly educated professionals such as doctors, accountants, lecturers, teachers, nurses, and engineers.

2. The term "white Australian" is more satisfactory than the oft-used concept of "Anglo Australian," because the categories "Anglo" and "Anglo-Celtic" are far from being a dominant mode of self-categorization by the dominant white Australians or by people who share the racial category "white," whether at a conscious level or an unconscious level.

3. Australian Bureau of Statistics, "National, State and Territory Population," accessed October 1, 2021, https://www.abs.gov.au/statistics/people/population/national-state-and-territory-population/latest-release.

4. Chris Clarkson et al., "Human Occupation of Australia by 65,000 Years," *Nature* 547 (2017): 306–310.

5. Hyacinth Udah, "'Not by Default Accepted': The African Experience of Othering and Being Othered in Australia," *Journal of Asian and African Studies* 53, no. 3 (2018): 384–400.

6. Hyacinth Udah and Parlo Singh, "'It Still Matters': The Role of Skin Colour in the Everyday Life and Realities of Black African Migrants and Refugees in Australia," *Australasian Review of African Studies* 39, no. 2 (2018): 19–47.

7. Peter McDonald and Andrew Markus, "It Is All About the Numbers of Immigrants: Population and Politics in Australia and New Zealand," in *Global Political Demography*, ed. Achim Goerres and Pieter Vanhuysse (Melbourne: Palgrave Macmillan, 2021), 275–301.

8. The ten most common ancestries are English (36.1%), Australian (33.5%), Irish (11.0%), Scottish (9.3%), Chinese (5.6%), Italian (4.6%), German (4.5%), Indian (2.8%), Greek (1.8%), and Dutch (1.6%). In 2016, Australia added two new ancestries: Pitcairn and Yezidi. See Australian Bureau of Statistics, "Census of Population and Housing: Australia Revealed, 2016," last updated March 21, 2023, https://www.abs.gov.au/ausstats/abs@.nsf/Latestproducts/2024.0Main%20Features22016.

9. There are two types of migrants: proactive and reactive. Proactive migrants are usually driven by economic and education factors or the promise of a better life, while reactive migrants are driven by war or persecution, violence, famine, political instability, conflict, or natural disaster. Reactive migrants can be seen as refugees. To qualify as a refugee, one must have a "well-founded fear of being persecuted for reasons of race, religion, nationality, membership of a particular social group or political opinion, is outside the country of his nationality and is unable or, owing to such fear, is unwilling, to avail himself of the protection of that country; or to return there, for fear of persecution" (See United Nations High Commissioner for Refugees (UNHCR) 2011, Art. 1A(2)).

10. Australian Bureau of Statistics, "Census of Population and Housing: Reflecting Australia—Stories from the Census, 2016," accessed March 10, 2022, https://www.abs.gov.au/ausstats/abs@.nsf/mf/2071.0.

11. Krystle Gatt, "Sudanese Refugees in Victoria: An Analysis of their Treatment by the Australian Government," *International Journal of Comparative and Applied Criminal Justice* 35, no. 3 (2011): 207–219.

12. Mandisi Majavu, "The 'African Gangs' Narrative: Associating Blackness with Criminality and Other Antiblack Racist Tropes in Australia," *African and Black Diaspora: An International Journal* 13, no. 1 (2020): 27–39.

13. *Racialization* refers to the set of historical practices, cultural norms, and institutional arrangements that reflect and help to create and maintain race-based outcomes in society.

14. Frank B. Wilderson III, "The Prison Slave as Hegemony's (Silent) Scandal," *Social Justice*, 30, no 2 (2003): 18–27.

15. Moon-Kie Jung, "The Enslaved, the Worker, and Du Bois's Black Reconstruction: Toward an Underdiscipline of Antisociology," *Sociology of Race and Ethnicity* 5, no. 2 (2019): 157–168.

16. Anthony Giddens, *The Constitution of Society* (Berkeley: University of California Press, 1984), 375.

17. Wilderson, "The Prison," 18–27.

18. Jung, "The Enslaved," 157–168.

19. Wilderson, "The Prison," 18–27.

20. Jared Sexton, "People-of-Color-Blindness: Notes on the Afterlife of Slavery," *Social Text* 28, no. 2/103 (2010): 31–56.

21. Virginia Mapedzahama and Kwamena Kwansah-Aidoo, "Blackness as Burden? The Lived Experience of Black Africans in Australia," *SAGE Open* (2017): 1–13.

22. James Forrest and Kevin Dunn, "Racism and Intolerance in Eastern Australia: A Geographic Perspective," *Australian Geographer* 37, no 2 (2006): 167–186.

23. Forrest and Dunn, "Racism and Intolerance," 167–186.

24. Ghassan Hage, *White Nation: Fantasies of White Supremacy in a Multicultural Society* (Tokyo: Heibonsha Publishers, 2012).

25. Peggy McIntosh, "White Privilege and Male Privilege: A Personal Account of Coming to See Correspondences through Work in Women's Studies," in *Race, Class and Gender: An Anthology*, ed. Margaret L. Andersen and Patricia Hill (Wadsworth, 1998), 94–105.

26. Forrest and Dunn, "Racism and Intolerance," 167–186.

27. Victoria Mence, Simone Gangell, and Ryan Tebb, *A History of the Department of Immigration: Managing Migration to Australia* (Canberra: Communication and Media Branch, Department of Immigration and Border Protection, 2015).

28. In white-dominated countries, the word *black* is, generally, used to refer to Africans or people of African descent or diaspora. In Australia, however, Aboriginals are regarded as "blacks" in dominant narratives—being black Australian is being Aboriginal. While non-Indigenous blacks are constantly described as migrants or people from culturally and linguistically diverse (CALD) backgrounds, Africans in Australia have a distinct racial identity—racialized as black.

29. Tracey Banivanua Mar and Penelope Edmonds, *Making Settler Colonial Space: Perspectives on Race, Place and Identity* (New York: Palgrave Macmillan, 2010).

30. The Aboriginal and Torres Strait Islander peoples gained the right to citizenship in 1967. They were recognized and counted as Australian citizens after the federal referendum held on May 27, 1967. The 1967 referendum altered the Australian constitution. More than 90 percent of Australian voters chose to allow Aboriginal and Torres Strait Islander peoples to be counted in the census and subject to Commonwealth laws. However, the 1967 referendum did not give Aboriginal and Torres Strait Islander peoples the right to vote. The right had been legislated for Australian federal elections in 1962. Queensland was the last state to give Indigenous Australians the right to vote, in 1965.

31. *Kanakas* is a derogatory term often used to describe South Sea Islanders. "Sugar slaves" was another term used to describe them.

32. Tracey Banivanua-Mar, "Belonging to Country: Racialising Space and Resistance on Queensland's Transnational Margins, 1880–1900," *Australian Historical Studies* 43, no. 2 (2012): 174–190.

33. Australia's Racial Discrimination Act came into existence in 1975 with the purpose of providing a platform for policies and legislation that aim to eliminate racial discrimination and make race-based selection criteria illegal in Australia.

34. Forrest and Dunn, "Racism and Intolerance," 169.

35. Australian Human Rights Commission, *African Australians: Human Rights and Social Inclusion Issues Project* (Sydney: Australian Human Rights Commission, 2010).

36. Frantz Fanon, *Black Skin, White Masks* (London: Pluto Press, 2008), 82–83.

37. Mapedzahama and Kwansah-Aidoo, "Blackness as Burden," 1.

38. Individuals can be categorized or labeled as an Other according to perceived differences, which may be based on race, on how they look (skin color), speak (accent), dress (ethnic cloth), and worship (religion); or on their sexuality, gender, disability, or ideological self-differences. Being the Other is consciousness of being different. If one is the Other, one will inevitably be perceived unidimensionally, seen stereotypically, and defined and delimited by mental sets that may not bear much relation to existing realities. By talking about individuals or groups as the Other, people magnify and enforce projections of apparent difference from themselves.

39. Often, those defined as the Other are constantly marked and classified based on the recollection of memories and ideologies of the dominant group buried deep in society, culture, and history. This involves the use of language, which becomes discourses. *Discourses* are more than ways of thinking and producing meaning. They are institutionalized and taken-for-granted ways of understanding relationships, activities, and meanings about the way the world works. Discourses can foster Othering by directing people's relationships—both with themselves and with others—as well as influencing what people take to be true, right, or inevitable.

40. Amina Mama, *Beyond the Masks: Race, Gender, and Subjectivity* (London: Routledge, 1995), 98.

41. Camilla Hällgren, "Working Harder to Be the Same: Everyday Racism among Young Men and Women in Sweden," *Race Ethnicity and Education* 8, no. 3 (2005): 319–342.

42. As a product of history, whiteness makes race privilege relevant. According to Ruth Frankenberg (*White Women, Race Matters: The Social Construction of Whiteness* [Minneapolis: University of Minnesota Press, 1993], 1), whiteness has three linked dimensions: (a) a location of structural advantage, of race privilege; (b) a "standpoint," a place from which white people look at themselves, at others, and at society; and (c) a set of cultural practices that are usually unmarked and unnamed.

43. Millsom S. Henry-Waring, *Multiculturalism and Visible Migrants and Refugees: Exploring the Yawning Gap between Rhetoric and Policy in Australia* (Melbourne: University of Melbourne, 2008).

44. Hage, *White Nation: Fantasies*, 1.

45. Saskia Bonjour and Jan Willem Duyvendak, "The 'Migrant with Poor Prospects': Racialized Intersections of Class and Culture in Dutch Civic Integration Debates," *Ethnic and Racial Studies* 41, no. 5 (2018): 882–900.

46. Forrest and Dunn, "Racism and Intolerance," 167.

47. Blackness has become a social construct persistently distorted and conceived of as an opposition to whiteness.

48. Sara Ahmed, "A Phenomenology of Whiteness," *Feminist Theory* 8, no. 2 (2007): 149–168.

49. Val Colic-Peisker and Farida Tilbury, "Being Black in Australia: A Case Study of Intergroup Relations," *Race & Class* 49, no. 4 (2008): 38–56.

50. Alison Markwick et al., "Experiences of Racism among Aboriginal and Torres Strait Islander Adults Living in the Australian State of Victoria: A Cross-Sectional Population-based Study," *BMC Public Health* 19, no. 1 (2019): 1–14.

51. Carole Zufferey, "'Not Knowing that I Do Not Know and Not Wanting to Know': Reflections of a White Australian Social Worker," *International Social Work* 56, no. 5 (2012): 659–673.

52. Zufferey, "Not Knowing," 663.

53. Markwick et al., "Experiences of Racism," 2.

54. Natasha Guantai, "'Are There Black People in Australia?'" *Overland*, March 10, 2015, accessed April 16, 2022, https://overland.org.au/2015/03/are-there-black-people-in-australia/

55. Connie Wun, "Unaccounted Foundations: Black Girls, Antiblack Racism, and Punishment in Schools," *Critical Sociology* 42, no. 4–5 (2016): 737–750.

56. South East Queensland (SEQ) stretches from the Gold Coast in the south to Noosa in the north and extends inland to include the Toowoomba urban area in the west. SEQ was chosen for this study for at least three reasons. First, it is culturally and ethnically diverse and is home to people from different parts of the world. Second, it has a significant presence of black African immigrants. Third, it is where social interactions occur and where both skilled and unskilled job prospects are very high.

57. Hyacinth Udah, "Understanding African Immigrant Experiences in South East Queensland" (unpublished Ph.D. diss., Griffith University [Brisbane], 2016).

58. Participants, consisting of ten females and twenty males between the ages of twenty-two and sixty-seven years, who had lived in Australia for more than three years and self-identified as black Africans, were selected because of their level of education as well as their English proficiency. A third of the participants hold a bachelor's degree and two have a doctorate degree. They came from Ghana, Liberia, Nigeria, and Sierra Leone in West Africa; Tanzania and Uganda in East Africa; Congo and Rwanda in Central Africa; Eritrea, Somalia, Sudan, and South Sudan in Northeast Africa; and Botswana and Zimbabwe in Southern Africa.

59. Kimberlé Crenshaw, "Twenty Years of Critical Race Theory: Looking Back to Move Forward," *Connecticut Law Review* 43, no. 5 (2011): 1253–1353.

60. Philomena Essed, "Everyday Racism," in *Encyclopedia of Race and Racism*, ed. John Hartwell Moore (Detroit, MI: Macmillan Reference USA/Thomson-Gale, 2008), 447–449.

61. Monnica Williams, Daniel Rosen, and Jonathan Kanter, eds., *Eliminating Race-Based Mental Health Disparities: Promoting Equity and Culturally Responsive Care across Settings* (Oakland, CA: Context Press, 2019), 79–97.

62. David Williams, "Stress and the Mental Health of Populations of Color: Advancing Our Understanding of Race-Related Stressors," *Journal of Health and Social Behavior* 59, no. 4 (2018): 466–485.

63. Udah, "'Not by Default Accepted,'" 384–400.

64. Hyacinth Udah, "Searching for a Place to Belong in a Time of Othering," *Social Sciences* 8, no. 11 (2019): 297.

65. Majavu, "The 'African Gangs,'" 27–39.

66. Udah, "Searching," 15.

5

Afropessimistic Justice in *New York v. Strauss-Kahn* and Chimamanda Ngozi Adichie's *Americanah*

MAYA HISLOP

W hen the disparity between the #MeToo movement and hashtag, begun by the white actress Alyssa Milano in 2017, and the Me Too movement, begun by the black activist Tarana Burke in 2006, is examined through a critical race lens, the Internet seems to have served as a relatively positive force. It was the Internet that helped connect survivors to one another, while also making apparent how the needs of some survivors, namely black women, were being neglected in the name of gender solidarity.[1] Of course, as Safiya Noble asserts, the Internet was built by straight white men, and therefore it inherently reinforces structures of oppression. In addition, social media platforms and other websites deliver some of the most virulent strains of racism, misogyny, homophobia, and xenophobia, and are therefore not often seen as a valuable resource for those who are most vulnerable to hateful comments and death threats.[2] There is evidence, however, to suggest that black immigrant women, literary and real, are using digital platforms to supplement and/or replace legal justice for sexually violent crimes committed against them. Two contemporary cases bring the issues of migration, blackness, justice, and sexual violence to the fore in new and exciting ways: *New York v. Strauss-Kahn*, a high-profile case of the sexual violation of an immigrant woman of color, and *Americanah*, Chimamanda Ngozi Adichie's novel about a young immigrant woman of color who is the victim of a sexual assault. Both *New York v. Strauss-Kahn* and *Americanah* demonstrate how digital platforms may carry out justice for black femme-presenting immigrant survivors of rape and sexual violence. In this chapter, I investigate the ways in which technology supports as well as harms the women creating their own justice systems. I also examine Afropessimistic justice from the perspective of black feminist studies whose connection to an immigrant/postcolonial framework, or lack thereof, has implications for black-femme-made justice projects as a whole. We have seen, time and time again, the ways in which immigration policy and antiblack violence intersect, most recently evinced by the abhorrent treatment and expulsion of Haitian refugees at the U.S.-Mexico border. It is vital to put this intersection in conversation with sexual violence and Afropessimism, especially given the ways that the two cases under discussion here present doom, failure, self-harm, and destruction as valuable alternatives to "justice."

A Brief Introduction to Nafissatou Diallo and Ifemelu

On May 14, 2011, the French politician Dominique Strauss-Kahn attacked Nafissatou Diallo, a 32-year-old Guinean maid who entered his room at the Sofitel Hotel to clean it. A grand jury quickly indicted Strauss-Kahn, charging him with so many counts of assault that he faced up to seventy-three years in prison. Only a few months later, however, Manhattan District Attorney Clarence A. Vance officially dismissed the case upon determining that Diallo would not be a reliable witness. In five interviews with the DA, Diallo admitted to lying to the grand jury about details of the Strauss-Kahn assault, as well as admitting to other lies about assaults from her past. When considered in context, many of these statements are, in fact, not so much lies as they are the survival strategies of a black, immigrant woman. Many immigrants hoping to achieve residency or a path to citizenship through the U.S. immigration system are keenly aware that it is an inherently unfair system. The unfairness often expresses itself through class: the more educated you are, the more money you have, the more assimilable you seem, the more pathways to citizenship there are for you. Of course, all forms of immigration have their obstacles, but I pay special attention to the process of obtaining asylum, which Nafissatou Diallo did years before her assault. As more immigrants pass through this system, more of them become aware of its classism, thus learning that it is a system that can and must be manipulated. What the district attorney may have classified as "lies" were, to Diallo, survival strategies.

Diallo manipulated the immigration system so that she could escape intimate violence in her home country of Guinea. The lie most central to Vance's "motion to dismiss" is Diallo's statement that she was gang-raped by a group of soldiers in Guinea, an act of violence that was precipitated by her then-husband's involvement with political dissidents.[3] In one interview, Diallo told the DA's office that she put the story of this rape on her application for asylum, which was filed at least seven years prior. In a subsequent interview, however, Diallo claimed that this story was untrue. And in additional interviews Diallo stated that she was raped not by soldiers but by a group of men when she was closing the restaurant where she worked in Conakry, Guinea. It makes sense that Diallo shifted her attackers from a group of civilian men to a group of soldiers. Claiming the latter allowed her to qualify for asylum, whereas the former did not. One of the categories that qualifies a candidate for asylum is to identify oneself as a victim of "political violence." Diallo, allegedly, argued that she needed to repatriate herself in another country because she feared that these soldiers would return.[4] Due to the asylum system's prioritization of political violence over "nonpolitical" violence, Diallo felt compelled to lie. One of the spaces in which Diallo tells the true story is her *ABC News* interview.

The *ABC News* interview is at the center of this analysis because it is evidence of one kind of technology that immigrant women of color use to supplement and/or replace legal justice. The novel *Americanah*, by Chimamanda Ngozi Adichie, explores another kind of technology: the black blog. The Nigerian protagonist of *Americanah,* Ifemelu, begins a blog long after she has a traumatic sexual experience as an indirect result of her immigrant status. I argue that, like Diallo's use of the televised interview, the blog is a direct response to Ifemelu's emotional assault. Unlike Diallo, Ifemelu does not use her blog as a strategy for garnering public support around her case for legal justice. Instead, the protagonist uses her blog to control time, create community, and express feelings around the issues of race and immigration. Ifemelu's blog is titled *Raceteenth or Various Observations About American Blacks (Those Formerly Known as Negroes) by a Non-American Black*. She uses *Raceteenth* to express ideas about race and identity in the United States from the perspective of someone born elsewhere. Though Ifemelu never discusses her assault in the blog, it is less through the content and more through the production process that Ifemelu is able to enact a form of healing. Ifemelu owns a blog over which she has total control, she can decide which commenters she will engage with, which users she will dispense with and/or block. However, Adichie refuses to let this assertion of control as a form of freedom go unquestioned, as is made clear when Ifemelu shuts the blog down not long before permanently relocating to Lagos, Nigeria, in the last quarter of the novel.

Nafissatou Diallo and the Pros and Cons of Television

Nafissatou Diallo chooses two public platforms to tell her side of the story of her assault: the nightly televised news interview and the press conference. I focus on the interview because it is in a longer form and offers far more detail. It is also significant that the interview is the first media platform Diallo chooses. Diallo's interview with Robin Roberts of *Good Morning America* airs on ABC on July 25, 2011. Prior to her interview with Robin Roberts, Diallo maintained her anonymity. Though her name was known to anyone following the case in local newspapers, to the grand jury who indicted Strauss-Kahn, and to the various official handlers of the case, Diallo's face was not known and she made no public statements.[5] In fact, the only reason that Diallo feels compelled to, as she says in the interview, "show herself" was to combat the lies that are being spread about her in the media. The number one news outlet that was spreading lies about Diallo was the *New York Post*. And these were not just any lies. The *Post* made multiple baseless claims that Diallo was a prostitute.[6] The first issue of the newspaper to make this claim about Diallo was the July 2nd issue, which followed immediately after a letter was leaked to the press from the New York DA to Strauss-Kahn's lawyers expressing their doubt about their case (see Figure 5.1).

The DA's letter and the subsequent motion to dismiss filed on August 22, 2011, explain that this doubt was not general, but was, in fact, a very specific doubt that they had about Diallo's unreliability as a witness. I cite the motion to dismiss as the smoking gun. Once the prosecution admitted that they found fault with Diallo, the *Post* responded with the most extreme, racist, sexist accusation. By Diallo's account, the accusation of being a sex worker propelled her into television, a space where she could speak for herself and tell her side of the story to a national audience. So how might we understand Diallo's identity as a black immigrant woman who has been sexually violated in the space of justice-seeking through public media? And what do black feminist and immigration studies discourses tell us about the history of such justice-seeking for black "disrespectable" bodies and voices?

Diallo and her defense team chose the televised news interview. There are two very important elements of television that Diallo uses to her advantage and that also, I argue, work against her: visual and sonic. The visual and sonic aspects of Diallo's *ABC News* interview act as both openings through which and boundaries against which immigrant women of color who experience sexual violence can tell their stories. Early on in the interview, Roberts asks Diallo why she has decided to come forward now, and Diallo responds, "I never want to be in public. Now, I have to be in public. I have to show myself. I have to tell the truth. . . . I hear people call me many names."[7] On the surface, Diallo is lamenting the fact that she must expose herself to the public and is explaining that she is doing so only as a means of protecting herself from the "many names" that "people" are calling her. In this brief moment, however, Diallo makes a subtextual connection between the visual and misogynoirist myths around black female sexuality. When Diallo says, "I have to show myself," she implies that her visage (how she is dressed, what kind of makeup she is wearing, the styling of her hair) functions as a part of the evidence, part of the proof she can use to demonstrate that her status as an innocent victim is more real than the misogynoirist lie that she is a hooker and therefore complicit in her assault (see Figure 5.1).

Her body, and particularly her hair and dress, speak volumes. Diallo wears a peach-colored, half-sleeve-length cardigan over a white, scoop-neck peasant top. Her hair is straightened and pressed into a neat, shoulder-length bob, and she wears little to no makeup. Not pictured are the long, black, wide-legged slacks and sensible shoes that Diallo wears in another scene from the edited interview. Diallo uses dress, hairstyling, and makeup to supplement her counternarrative as an innocent victim of assault rather than a rumored prostitute. What is perhaps most significant is that the format of the televised news interview allows for visuals to be one of the aspects that the interviewee and/or her allies manipulate to their advantage.

Visuals are an especially useful weapon for immigrant women of color, as they can use dress, hairstyling, and makeup as the building blocks of a counternarrative. Diallo builds a narrative that runs counter to the narrative that her body (its race, gender, and national origin) communicates for her. Many black feminist scholars have alluded to the myriad ways that black women continue to endure the legacy of enslavement. But there is a parallel in bell hooks's statement from her landmark text *Ain't I a Woman*, because she places television at the center of such contemporary subliminal messaging: "One has only to look at American television twenty-four hours a day for an entire week to learn the way in which black women are perceived in American society—the predominant image is that of the "fallen" woman, the whore, the slut, the prostitute."[8] Of course, a visual medium would be the culprit in perpetuating stereotypes about black women as always sexually accessible, but Diallo reveals the usefulness of television as a means of presenting counternarratives to those misogynoirist labels. The *Post* narrative projects misogynoirist stereotypes onto Diallo: the sexualities of black women have been criminalized in one way or another for centuries, but the label of "prostitute" has proven especially salient in the contexts of post-Reconstruction and twentieth-century America.[9] To combat myths around their hypersexuality and to prove their worthiness as citizens, black free women used conservative dress and hairstyling in the 1880s if not earlier. In her book *Righteous Discontent*, Evelyn Brooks Higginbotham terms this realm of accommodationist strategizing "the politics of respectability" in specific reference to black churchwomen of the late nineteenth and early twentieth centuries.[10] This visual strategizing, however, is a mobile theoretical frame for understanding Diallo's *ABC News* interview because of how her dress attempts to communicate that she is aligned with white, middle-class values: her body is modestly covered, she wears muted colors, the clothing is simple and does not appear to be overly expensive. Where Higginbotham's frame begins to stretch is when we consider that Diallo is using these strategies to combat not only the myths that her black and femme body speak but also the myths that her identity as an immigrant speak, with and/or without her knowledge. Diallo is not only an immigrant but also a refugee, which means that she is in a particular class of immigrants. There are ways that class and dress intersect that make the visual element of television a disadvantageous medium for a survivor of sexual violence who is attempting to get justice for that assault.

The edited version of Diallo's interview with *ABC News* was published on YouTube on July 25, 2011. The YouTube comment space is a common storage space for some of the worst hate speech on the Internet, but in this case the comments offer additional evidence of the ways that Diallo's image is being received/perceived. Any negative responses that focus on how Diallo looks or criticize her appearance are strong indications that one of the negative aspects of the television interview is that it exposes the survivor's image to ridicule. Diallo's intention was to set the record straight, so to speak, about a racist and sexist rumor that she is a hooker. However, Diallo ran the risk of exposing herself to even more damaging rumors, as the YouTube comments under her aired interview with Robin Roberts evince. Commenters repeat all kinds of conspiracy theories about Diallo, but the majority believe that she is falsely accusing Strauss-Kahn to get money, even though the civil case had not yet been filed. Very few of the comments say anything about Diallo's appearance, which is very unusual for YouTube, especially comments on a video featuring a woman, which is almost always a shockingly crude slew of insults on that woman's appearance.[11] What's more surprising is that there is little to no overt racism in the comments, though there is a great deal of misogyny. The few comments on Diallo's appearance do not translate into the demise of her case, and therefore it does not seem that the visual is an enormous limitation of television for the immigrant woman of color seeking justice for her sexual violation. In fact, what these comments show is that black women are already exposed and hypervisible even before they "show themselves" as Diallo does.

The tool of audio in the televised news interview is just as powerful as the visual for immigrant women of color, if not more powerful. The average viewer likely sees Diallo as a black woman or a woman of ambiguous racial/ ethnic origins. Sonically, however, Diallo comes across as an immigrant woman of color because she speaks with quite heavily accented English.[12] Diallo's first language is Fulani, a dialect spoken across twenty African countries, including her original home of Guinea. Diallo's accented English works both for and against her efforts to write a counternarrative, to portray herself as a sympathetic victim of sexual violence rather than the lying prostitute from the *Post*. There is no reality to these narratives. No one actually sounds and/

or looks like a liar any more than one actually sounds and/or looks like an innocent. However, visuals and sonics function together in the televised news interview format to paint interviewees with the broadest of brushes. Her accent slots her into the stock categories that television can easily communicate: immigrant, maid, victim, etc. The segment that *ABC News* aired on Diallo and her case is less than four minutes long, a limited amount of time to transmit the most basic facts of her case while telling the story from a particular perspective. Even in this limited time, the sonics of Diallo's voice speak vibrantly to her perspective as an immigrant woman of color. In the unedited interview, Diallo is hyperconscious of her accent from the very outset when she responds to Roberts asking her why she chose to come forward now: "I decide to come—Sorry, my English you know is difficult for me. I don't speak that much, but I'm gonna try."[13] Diallo's apology to Roberts (and, presumably, the viewer) about her perceived lack of facility with the English language is a moment in which she is both agent and subject of the mainstream narrative about her and the self-made counternarrative by and about her. The sonics of her voice in this moment begin quite soft and shy, yet they end with a tone of effort and determination when she says, "I'm gonna try." Throughout the interview, Diallo slides along this spectrum in terms of vocal and tonal registers. The softness and demureness act as affirmations of her counternarrative as she comes across as the innocent victim of an act of sexual violence perpetrated by a man who is much more powerful and more wealthy than she. When she speaks at a higher, softer pitch, she sounds somewhat frightened, shy, and sad. However, the sonics of "victim" can also betray Diallo's counternarrative, sliding back into affirming the *Post*'s narrative of Diallo as a liar and a criminal, which raises serious questions around citizenship and the American myth of the "good immigrant."

The critical texts *Impossible Subjects*, by Mae M. Ngai, and *Immigrant Acts*, by Lisa Lowe, touch on this need that immigrants have to mold themselves— in response to a long history of fluctuating U.S. immigration policies—into subjects that look like, sound like, and/or behave like those deserving of citizenship. In short, Ngai and Lowe establish the trope of the "good immigrant."[14] Ngai and Lowe are also adamant to point out that this image of deservingness has always been racialized. Supreme court cases such as *Ozawa v. United States* (1922) and *United States v. Thind* (1923) are good examples of how the trope of "good immigrant" as white immigrant came to life. Due to a law that only those of white or Aryan descent could be citizens, two Asian men, a Japanese man and an Indian Sikh man, respectively, attempted to petition the government for citizenship on the grounds that they were white. In these cases, whiteness became coterminous with a person who can be easily molded into a good citizen—that is, a good immigrant. Though both Thind and Ozawa make the case for their whiteness on ancestral and/or phenotypical grounds, they also raise their character traits and/or patriotism as the grounds upon which they can be made into citizens and are therefore good immigrants. Thind uses his time served in the U.S. army during World War I, and Ozawa leans heavily on his "industriousness" as qualifying him as a man who will fit seamlessly into the American citizenry.[15]

Despite the lack of official immigration policies that cordon off American citizenry from the racialized other, like Ozawa and Thind, Diallo leans on certain aspects of her character to portray herself as "good": hard worker, mother, someone who loves her job, who pays her taxes, and who is not deserving of ill treatment. Though Diallo uses "universal" deracialized phrasing here, all of these aspects are implicitly racial and gendered. When examined through the lens of misogynoir, the final characteristic, "not deserving of ill treatment," is especially fraught given the centuries during which the mistreatment of black women in the United States has been not only perfectly legal but also a source of white enrichment. The other, more universal markers of "goodness" that Diallo attempts to use to arm herself from "bad immigrant" narratives are worthy of attention as well.[16] The self-narrative that Diallo builds around "hard worker," however, is also wrapped up in a self-narrative as "uneducated." The sonics of her voice put her into the camps of both "good" immigrant and "bad" immigrant. Early on in the interview, Diallo declares, "I'm so glad to have this job especially without education."[17] This statement shows that Diallo is a "good immigrant," one who is grateful for the gift of employment that the United States has bestowed upon her. But her lack of education can easily cause her to slip into the territory of "bad immigrant," as a statement she makes later on in the interview, about reporting the assault to her supervisor, implies: "I don't know what to do, I feel so . . . but I was so afraid to lose my job. I don't know the law, I don't know if someone do this to you, what do you have to do? I don't know nothing about that in that job I don't know because I never had that happen there."[18] By declaring the things that she does not know, Diallo fits into the "good" and "bad" categories simultaneously. Her lack of knowledge makes her a "good immigrant" figure, one who is not granted as much time and access to knowledge and/or education but perseveres despite these obstacles. However, Diallo's insistence and her repetition of the phrase "I don't know" also put her at risk of being perceived as a "bad immigrant," one who is not taking advantage of all of the resources the United States provides (such as education) and is therefore not suitable to be a part of the country. The phrase "I don't know the law" puts Diallo in an especially risky position to be victim-blamed. She could be perceived as someone whose lack of knowledge about the country in which she lives is her own fault, someone whose assault is her own fault.

Diallo's voice both emphasizes and contradicts this reading of her statement, because she says "I don't know the law" with a great deal of force, pausing a beat before moving on to explain what else she does not know. This forcefulness qualifies her as a part of a strong American woman archetype, one who will not passively accept her victimization but will stand up in defiance of it. However, her blackness and her gender can easily convert strength into anger, determination into bitchiness. As Andrew Taslitz writes about black women in the courtroom, they are caught in a "Catch-22": if they are too outspoken and strong-willed the jury will read them as angry black women, but if they are too meek and passive the jury will read them as uneducated failures, deserving of their misfortunes.[19] There is no way for Diallo to use her voice to satisfy all of the various spoken and unspoken requirements around her identity, and therefore the limits of the televised news interview are also the same as the openings and/or liberative spaces that immigrant women of color create for themselves in the medium. She is attempting to use the platform as a mode through which to express her story of the crime committed against her. The visual and sonic aspects are extremely important for Diallo and other immigrant women of color in the ways that they allow those women to have more tools at their disposal with which to combat misogynoirist myths about them. However, those same elements of the television format can backfire, placing immigrant women of color back into the very "bad immigrant" archetype that they are trying to avoid. It is important to remember that, if Diallo's goal for "showing herself" on television was actually to get a criminal conviction of her assailant, her strategy failed.

In *Americanah*, the protagonist Ifemelu uses an entirely different platform than Diallo from which to indirectly express her thoughts and feelings around her experience of sexual assault. Though Ifemelu is not assaulted according to the legal definitions of "sexual assault," she still undergoes a trauma, and her subsequent creation of a blog is an attempt to, indirectly, work through that trauma. What, then, are the advantages and disadvantages of the black blog space as the author of *Americanah*, Chimamanda Ngozi Adichie, lays them out?

Ifemelu, the Black Blog, and Control

Soon after her 1993 arrival from Nigeria to the United States to attend college, Ifemelu falls on very hard financial times.[20] The sexual encounter that occurs as a result of this financial difficulty makes it impossible to separate Ifemelu's financial difficulty from her identity as a black female immigrant. The international student visa, also known as the F-1 visa, does not allow its recipients to work. International students can work on campus, but, as Ifemelu's Aunty Uju says, "You can't work with your student visa and work-study is rubbish, it pays nothing, and you have to be able to cover your rent and the balance of your tuition."[21] Despite having access to the informal knowledge networks and resources of Aunty Uju—whose friend allows Ifemelu to use her Social Security card—and her high school friend Ginika, who moved to the United States as a teenager, Ifemelu cannot find a job. No matter how many times she applies to be a waitress, a babysitter, or an at-home caregiver, none of them lead to employment through which she can support herself. If-emelu's joblessness is especially frustrating because she has no idea why she is not finding work: "At each interview, she smiled warmly and shook hands firmly, all the things that were suggested in a book she had read about interviewing for American jobs. Yet there was no job. Was it her foreign accent? Her lack of experience? But her African friends all had jobs, and college students got jobs all the time with no experience."[22] The questions Ifemelu asks in this excerpt reveal that most of her uncertainties around her unemployment would not exist if she were a citizen. As a citizen, Ifemelu would have more control over her options. She applies for jobs like waitressing, home aid work, and babysitting precisely because these jobs pay in cash, making it more difficult for businesses who hire undocumented workers to be tracked and/or punished. The most frustrating thing about her failure to find a job, in addition to having no stable source of income, is her lack of control over the process. Even with all of the privileges that she has as a young woman getting her college education, and a number of supportive family members and friends helping her to navigate the systems at work in a new place, she still has great difficulty finding employment. There is a severe domino effect between Ifemelu's emotional state, her unemployment, and her citizenship status. As a nonimmigrant, she has less control over her ability to get a job, which leaves her feeling anxious and depressed. All of these circumstances, particularly the lack of control, set the stage for the sexual assault she experiences with the tennis coach.

The first time that Ifemelu meets the tennis coach is when she travels to Ardmore, Pennsylvania, in response to an ad in a local Pennsylvania newspaper: "Female personal assistant for busy sports coach in Ardmore, communication and interpersonal skills required."[23] During her meeting with him, the coach never explains the work that Ifemelu would do aside from requiring someone to "help him relax." But the way the ad emphasizes that the assistant be female is a strong indication that the coach expects some kind of sexual contact. This is never stated explicitly in their meeting. She decides that he is "not a kind man" and she leaves. But she continues to experience the emotional fallout of joblessness, reaching her absolute limit when her roommate's dog eats her bacon. This event would be somewhat funny if she were not so desperate to hold onto every last shred of food that she bought.[24] It is also yet another moment over which Ifemelu has no control, thus motivating her to call the tennis coach again. Though she is still uncertain about what kind of work the tennis coach wants her to perform, she prepares for the possibility that it is sexual: "Whatever happened, she would approach it looking her best, she would make it clear to him that there were boundaries she would not cross. She would say, from the beginning, 'If you expect sex, then I can't help you.' Or perhaps she would say it more delicately, more suggestively. 'I'm not comfortable going too far.' She might be imagining too much; he might just want a massage."[25] Here, Ifemelu is attempting to assert control over a situation in which she has none, planning what she will say and the demands that she will make. But the actual assault does not occur precisely as Ifemelu imagines and she certainly cannot prepare herself for the absolute loss of control, bodily control in particular, that transpires.[26]

Though legal statutes around rape and sexual assault are, at best, fragile attempts at placing stark boundaries around human interactions that are often extremely complex and ambiguous, in Ifemelu's case it is helpful to look at the law. According to Pennsylvania state law (as well as most state and federal laws), Ifemelu is not assaulted. Pennsylvania specifically defines *sexual assault* as an act of "forcible compulsion" which is defined as "compulsion by use of physical, intellectual, moral, emotional or psychological force, either express or implied. The term includes but is not limited to compulsion resulting in another person's death, whether the death occurred before, during or after sexual intercourse."[27] The tennis coach does not use any force, as the narrator corroborates: "He had not forced her." But this legal statute uses a narrow definition of *force*, one that is limited to the kinds of force that an individual exerts over another individual. The tennis coach does not use any kind of force to make Ifemelu perform a sexual act, because the encounter is transactional; Ifemelu understands that she will receive money once she has performed enough "human contact" to help him "relax." Of course, to receive money for an act does not in and of itself put the performance of sex work outside the bounds of assault. But there are numerous other details that exclude Ifemelu's encounter with the tennis coach from the consideration of legal action. Ifemelu meets with the tennis coach once and then returns a second time, which means that she had time to think about his proposal, despite maintaining uncertainty of its sexual nature when, perhaps naively or optimistically, she thinks, "He might just want a massage."[28] In addition to the premeditation of her return to his office, Ifemelu has several opportunities to leave the room once she is there. But she stays and even considers leaving multiple times: "She should leave now. . . . She should leave."[29] Because she considers leaving and actively chooses not to, there is no evidence that she does not consent to her encounter with the tennis coach.

Though this may not be considered an assault according to the law, it is most certainly an emotionally and physically traumatic experience, which is especially clear when Pamela Haag's distinction between desire and consent is considered.[30] The tense line between desire and consent in this scene is articulated in two instances: during the encounter and afterward. When Ifemelu is in the bathroom cleaning up afterward, she dissociates from her body: "Her fingers felt sticky; they no longer belonged to her."[31] During the encounter itself, Adichie gives the reader access to Ifemelu's thoughts, which raises the important distinction between consent and desire once again: "She took off her shoes and climbed into his bed. She did not want to be here, did not want his active finger between her legs, did not want his sigh-moans in her ear, and yet she felt her body rousing to a sickening wetness. Afterwards, she lay still, coiled and deadened. He had not forced her. She had come here on her own."[32] Ifemelu repeatedly declares what "she did not want" to happen as it is happening; though she did not desire the tennis coach to touch her body in the ways that she describes, she is nevertheless, technically, consenting to that touch. She loses a connection to her body as it becomes the domain of a paradox: at the same time that she does not desire the tennis coach, her body responds to his touch. In addition to this mental and physical disparity and the utter loss of control, what makes Ifemelu's encounter with the tennis coach so devastating is that Ifemelu does not have language to describe what happens to her, as is clear when her friend, Ginika, expresses great concern over her severe depression: "She wishes she had told Ginika about the tennis coach, taken the train to Ginika's apartment on that day, but now it was too late, her self-loathing had hardened inside her. She would never be able to form the sentences to tell her story."[33] There are myriad reasons why Ifemelu feels that what happened to her is unspeakable, but one of the most pressing is that the encounter lies not only outside the realm of her expectations of herself, but also outside the realm of law. Part of the unspeakable nature of rape for Black women stems from the establishment of the Black enslaved person as always already criminal, but never the legitimate victim of a crime in the court of law, as Saidiya Hartman elucidates in *Scenes of Subjection*.[34] Hartman goes on to rightly assert the ways in which the sexual violation of Black enslaved women was not only not a crime but was considered a legitimate use of property and that this perspective was both deeply embedded in white supremacist myths about Black women's sexuality and baked into the structure of the legal system. "Not only was rape simply unimaginable because of purported black lasciviousness, but also its repression was essential to the displacement of white culpability that characterized both the recognition of black humanity in slave law and the designation of the black subject as the originary locus of transgression and offense."[35] The legacy of enslavement lives on for Black women, especially those whose citizenship status places them in double jeopardy: both their blackness and their migration make them vulnerable to being seen as—and seeing themselves as—nonvictims and, in Hartman's estimation, nonhumans.

You can see the assault as absolutely devoid of legal issues only if you examine it in isolation from the context, which is very easy for most lawyers and state officials to do. But it is much more difficult for the reader to erase context. Is Ifemelu forced to be there? Yes. In a convoluted way, Ifemelu is forced to be there. The forces of impoverishment and desperation that are inflicted upon her by unfair employment restrictions for people on temporary visas coerce Ifemelu to go to the tennis coach's office a second time. In addition to Ifemelu losing control over her body, the sexual encounter with the tennis coach brings our attention to the kinds of sexual acts that lie outside the legal definition of *assault*. Those encounters that lie within the parameters of the legal system are often defined by individual coercion rather than by systemic coercion. For this reason, many legal studies scholars argue for revised definitions of *sexual assault*.[36] In Ifemelu's case, though consent is difficult to trace given the larger external forces putting Ifemelu in that room, power is not so. Ifemelu notes the imbalance of power when she gives up on the idea of leaving: "There was, in his expression and tone, a complete assuredness; she felt defeated. How sordid it all was, that she was here with a stranger who already knew she would stay. He knew she would stay because she had come. She was already here, already tainted."[37] The "complete assuredness" of the tennis coach's tone demonstrates that he knows he has control over the situation. Or, at the very least, Ifemelu perceives him as having control and perceives herself as having none. And given the power dynamics that have been established by the exchange of money, by their races, their genders, their citizenship statuses, and their social statuses, the tennis coach does have all of the control. He has money, something that she needs. To get the thing that she needs, Ifemelu must do something she does not desire to do but which she seems prepared to consent to doing. It is this issue of control as well as her inability to articulate her feelings around the encounter that makes the encounter so traumatizing.

Years after her experience with the tennis coach, Ifemelu creates her blog, *Raceteenth or Various Observations About American Blacks (Those Formerly Known as Negroes) by a Non-American Black*. But it is important how slowly and with control she arrives at blogging as a form of expression to counter the lack of control that the assault incurred. During the years between the assault and the blog, Ifemelu gets a job as a babysitter for a wealthy, white family in the suburbs of Pennsylvania. Kimberly is her boss, and Kimberly's brother Curt becomes Ifemelu's boyfriend. Curt gets Ifemelu a well-paying job at a public relations office in Baltimore where they move and live together. Through this job, Ifemelu gets her green card and her life is therefore much more financially and emotionally stable. Despite this stability, through her new job and interracial relationship, our protagonist is thrust into a host of situations in which she experiences microaggressions, largely aimed at her racial and ethnic identities. White coworkers ask if her hair is a political statement when she decides to go natural, her white boyfriend's friends treat her with awe while putting her at a distance, men make comments when she and Curt walk around holding hands, and plenty of other such racialized interactions. As happens for so many black immigrants from majority black countries, such moments initiate an awakening of sorts in Ifemelu to her blackness as she navigates the American world as a black woman. One of the ways she chooses to cope with this awakening is by going through what is known as "the big chop," cutting out her relaxer in her hair and "going natural." When she has trouble figuring out how to care for her natural hair, a friend suggests that she try a website called happilykinkynappy.com. Ifemelu finds a community there, not only in the sense that she can read the posts of other women but also in the sense that she can share her own story.

Jamilah's words made me remember that there is nothing more beautiful than what God gave me. Others wrote responses, posting thumbs-up signs, telling her how much they liked the photo she had put up. She had never talked about God so much. Posting on the website was like giving testimony in church; the echoing roar of approval revived her. On an unremarkable day in early spring . . . she looked in the mirror, sank her fingers into her hair, dense and spongy and glorious, and could not imagine it any other way. That simply, she fell in love with her hair.[38]

In italics is the post that Ifemelu writes about Jamilah, another member of the natural hair forum whose story inspired our protagonist to express her own self-love. Ifemelu likens posting on the forum to "giving testimony in church," thus entering two black American institutions at once: the staid and historic black American church and the emerging, contemporary online natural hair movement. Not only is the Internet a space through which Ifemelu can heal, learning to love the body that, in some ways, betrayed her with the tennis coach years ago, but also a space through which she expresses herself as a black woman. This is the first evidence that the Internet provides Ifemelu with something that heals the wound of self-loathing that her assault incurred upon her. After her assault, Ifemelu feels such shame and disappointment in herself that she thinks "she would never be able to form the sentences to tell her story."[39] But Ifemelu's absolutist belief in her silence around her assault is only partially true. Through the natural hair online community Ifemelu begins her journey to becoming a successful black blogger. The power that she gains from this work does a great deal to reverse a lot of the pain that the tennis coach and, indirectly, a flawed immigration system inflicted upon her. However, this power ends up backfiring on Ifemelu when the blog grows so much that it is no longer under her control.

Soon after joining the online natural hair community, Ifemelu is complaining to her college friend, Wambui, about a racialized interaction she has with Curt. After ranting a bit over email, Wambui responds with praise, remarking on how much Ifemelu's email sounds like a blog post and that she should consider writing a blog. Ifemelu takes her time considering this idea, but ultimately acts upon it and creates the blog, *Raceteenth or Various Observations About American Blacks (Those Formerly Known as Negroes) by a Non-American Black*. Before we dive into the content of the blog, the title and how Ifemelu arrives at the idea of creating a blog are points that deserve analysis. It takes Ifemelu a long time to create the blog and she is hesitant about it, as is demonstrated when she publishes her first post, immediately takes it down, and then puts it back up.[40]

The form of the blog itself has liberative aspects because of how it gives Ifemelu control, but the content is also an important source of empowerment because of how specifically bound up it is in her immigrant identity. The long title hints at the content of the blog: *Raceteenth or Various Observations About American Blacks (Those Formerly Known as Negroes) by a Non-American Black*. Ifemelu's blog often relays anecdotes and/or political-social commentary from her perspective: that of a black woman living in America who was not born in America. But as much as this perspective is identity-based, the tone is also specific to Ifemelu as it is oftentimes sarcastic. She tells stories about everything from hair, to presidential candidate Barack Obama, to surprising interactions with white folks—in a way that is often sarcastic, ironic, and playful. Throughout the novel Adichie excerpts sixteen blog posts; sometimes they are directly relevant to the narrative content that appears just before and sometimes not. Aside from excerpting posts, Adichie often makes the blog a part of the narrative by alluding to post titles, such as "Not All Dreadlocked White American Guys Are Down" and "Badly-Dressed White Middle Managers from Ohio Are Not Always What You Think."[41] One blog post demonstrates the specificity of the blog content—in that it is part of a series, even though it is only one of two with the title "Understanding America for the Non-American Black"—and another post title gives a sense of the subject matter, entitled "Sometimes in America, Race Is Class." Ifemelu uses her blog to play the role of cultural critic/tour guide to other non-American black men and women who may be able to use her experiences to avoid the traps that go unspoken in American society.

The blog format has advantages for Ifemelu, specifically as a means of reversing much of the emotional pain she suffered during her assault. The blog provides Ifemelu with a space in which she has most of the control, something of which the tennis coach deprived her. Ifemelu is writer, editor, and manager of the blog content. *Raceteenth* also allows Ifemelu to undo some of the feelings of self-loathing that she learned from her assault. The encounter with the tennis coach taught Ifemelu a kind of self-loathing: she loathes herself for consenting to a sexual act despite the fact that she did not desire it. In particular, creating the blog helps Ifemelu to learn to love herself as a non-American black woman, the identity in which her sexual assault is entrenched because of her immigration status. By expressing the humor of her experience as an immigrant and poking fun at the experience of migration, Ifemelu deflates some of the horror and trauma that immigrants can endure, and in this way takes back some of the power that the tennis coach robbed her of all of those years ago. Above all, the blog gives Ifemelu a space through which to speak the unspeakable.

There is no legal term for what the tennis coach (and the U.S. immigration system) did to Ifemelu. During a scene immediately after the assault, in which Ifemelu's friend Ginika suggests that she is depressed and should seek professional help, Ifemelu refers to this problem of naming when referencing the trouble of translating mental health issues between African and American cultures. "Years later, she would blog about this: 'On the Subject of Non-American Blacks Suffering from Illnesses Whose Names They Refuse to Know.' . . . A Congolese woman . . . refused to accept the diagnosis of panic attacks. . . . It was not even that it was called by another name, it was simply not called at all. Did things begin to exist only when they were named?"[42] This question about something being real only once it is named could apply just as much to what happened between the tennis coach and Ifemelu as it does to mental health.[43] Is the assault not an assault simply because the law cannot recognize it as such?[44] Again, we must recognize the historical context and its legacy per Hartman's illumination of the U.S. legal system as a means through which to erase Blackness from the status of "human." In lieu of legal naming, Ifemelu does what little she can to use the blog as a public form of expression that acts as an indirect catharsis for the emotional trauma she incurred during her assault. As important as it is to point to the advantages of the blog format for immigrant women of color who want and/or must seek ways of healing and/or restorative justice that are in lieu of and/or that supplement legal justice, it is also important to highlight the limits of this form for doing so.

The novel confronts the limits of the blog form after *Raceteenth* becomes a success. The blog becomes so successful, in fact, that it allows Ifemelu to quit her cushy job at a public relations firm—the very job that allowed her to get her green card—and work on the blog full time. *Raceteenth* garners a large enough following that Ifemelu is able to use the blog as a launchpad for public speaking engagements on diversity at universities and corporate retreats. The blog therefore presents its limits only in its success as Ifemelu describes the blog as a monster once it has gone beyond her control: "The blog had unveiled itself and shed its milk teeth; by turns, it surprised her, pleased her, left her behind. . . . Now that she was asked to speak at roundtables and panels . . . always identified simply as The Blogger, she felt subsumed by her blog . . . at night . . . her growing discomforts crawled out from the crevices, and the blog's many readers became, in her mind, a judgmental angry mob waiting for her, biding their time until they could attack her, unmask her."[45] The vivid, embodied description of the blog, its readers, and its attending anxieties as "crawling out from the crevices" and as a "judgmental angry mob" emphasizes the intimacy between the blog, Ifemelu's body, and the illusion of control. Before its success, to have control over the blog functioned as a synecdoche for Ifemelu having control over herself. With success, Ifemelu's body becomes more public and thus no longer within her control. She fears that her readers will reveal her as a fraud, as less well-versed in the topics of race, class, culture, and nationality than she performs to be. This loss of control was by no means inevitable, nor is it inherent to the blog as a form. The blog form, in fact, inherently protects Ifemelu as she is able to maintain a great deal of anonymity because she never identifies herself by name, national origin, or image. Ifemelu continues to protect these aspects of her identity when the blog becomes successful, but she must create safeguards that she did not have to instate previously.[46] The final area of disadvantage that blogging presents for immigrant women of color who are seeking supplements to and/or replacements of legal justice is that the blog can eventually start to reinforce and/or mimic the emotional impact of the assault.

The novel explains that Ifemelu begins blogging after she sends a "long e-mail, digging, questioning, unearthing" to her friend Wambui about one of her many racialized experiences with Curt and Wambui suggests that she start a blog because "this is so raw and true. More people should read this."[47] Ifemelu goes on to explain that she creates the blog out of a longing for community: "Telling Wambui what happened was not satisfying enough; she longed for other listeners, and she longed to hear the stories of others. How many other people chose silence? How many other people had become black in America? How many had felt as though their world was wrapped in gauze? She broke up with Curt . . . signed on to WordPress, and her blog was born."[48] On the surface, the novel's logic for Ifemelu's blogging is that it is an outgrowth of typical immigrant experiences, such as being isolated and lacking an outlet for expressing frustration over cultural misunderstandings. However, below this logic is an emotional explanation that is tied to the trauma that her encounter with the tennis coach incurred. Ifemelu's query "How many other people chose silence?" can be read as an inference to how the tennis coach implanted in Ifemelu a shameful silence that was rooted in her identity as a black immigrant woman. She believes that she will never be able to tell the story of her assault, but she is able to use her blog to share the piece-by-piece story of how she became (or is in the process of becoming) black in America. Ifemelu does not become black when she is sexually assaulted, but that experience is a racialized trauma. Our protagonist can use written expression to voice the systems behind that trauma. The blog begins to fail Ifemelu—or she discovers that she no longer needs it—when it becomes a representative of the same emotional lies that her trauma taught her: that she is not valuable, that no one will believe her story, that there is no way for her to make her trauma legible in a way that would exact punishment upon her assailant.

After years of running *Raceteenth*, Ifemelu shuts down the blog. As mentioned, there are a number of ways in which the blog proves to be disadvantageous, undoing the healing that it had done originally by removing Ifemelu's sense of control over the blog as a mode of expression. In addition, originally the blog was intended to be an opportunity for her to share her story and hear the stories of others. The blog is excerpted so many times throughout the novel that it is obvious that it functions as a form of expression for her, but it is very rare that we see Ifemelu interact with her readers or hear their stories.[49] So, as a means of creating community, there is little evidence that it does so in the multidirectional way that Ifemelu had hoped. During and after her assault, Ifemelu learns to perform a version of herself that sinks into isolated depression, feels out of control of her own body, and is incapable of expressing emotions surrounding her trauma. *Raceteenth* provides an enormous antidote to the emotional and rooted-in-systemic-failures fallout of Ifemelu's assault. But, eventually, the blog compels similar if not the same feelings of isolation, depression, anxious loss of control, and concern around free expression that were incurred by her experiences with the tennis coach and with the immigration system that facilitated the assault. Ifemelu experiences these same feelings through the few interactions between herself and her readers:

> Readers like SapphicDerrida, who reeled off statistics and used words like "reify" in their comments, made Ifemelu nervous . . . so that she began, over time, to feel like a vulture hacking into the carcasses of people's stories for something she could use. Sometimes making fragile links to race. Sometimes not believing herself. The more she wrote, the less sure she became. Each post scraped off yet one more scale of self until she felt naked and false.[50]

Ifemelu begins to relive feelings that are adjacent to the feelings of self-loathing, worthlessness, and self-deception she experienced during and after her assault. Instead of being a source of healing, the blog reveals to Ifemelu that, although the blog had initially strengthened her self-worth because of the great control it gave her over her self-expression, this feeling subsequently soured when the blog, as she says, outgrew her, her audience becoming less of a source of sharing/healing and more a source of threat, waiting to reveal her as the imposter she feels herself to be. The disadvantage of the blog in this case is its audience. Even though SapphicDerrida is a fan of the blog, the user makes Ifemelu feel uneasy, out of control, and lacking in self-worth, thus reversing many of the emotional strides she made through the blog, which had been a great source of healing from her trauma. Many theorists of black studies and gender studies, such as Fred Moten, Gayatri Spivak, and Judith Butler, offer ways of thinking through linguistic failure, the places language fails to capture the traumas of those most vulnerable to violence.[51] However, Ifemelu's experience of the Internet as a potential space for healing and then as a space that fails her is not necessarily a problem of language, but rather a problem of systems. This relates more to Kimberlé Crenshaw's "Mapping the Margins,"[52] which points very specifically to the ways in which institutions for healing for survivors of domestic violence—women's shelters, the Violence Against Women Act, amendments made to immigration laws, etc.—reinforce the white supremacist heteropatriarchy that puts Black immigrant women in the position of vulnerability. These systems were never built for women of color, and therefore, by centering white women of middle and upper-middle classes, the same arenas for healing have the potential to replicate the cycles of abuse that victimize Black immigrant women in the first place.

Conclusion

The #MeToo movement, which largely centered white cis women of privilege—taking the name (without permission) of Tarana Burke's Me Too movement, which largely centered Black femmes across a spectrum of social classes—is just the latest in a long line of ways in which white feminism has used a colonialist approach to "equality." Despite both movements using the Internet to some extent, that Twitter is the most valued tool of the #MeToo movement is telling, as it reflects the ways in which traditional justice systems (and therefore mainstream activism) prioritize "the voice," "speaking one's truth," and "public testimony" as the thing that frees us all. This privileging of the voice and of telling one's story of rape so as to garner justice for that crime maintains the white middle-class fantasy that justice can be obtained by means of an individual wrong being righted. Both Ifemelu and Nafissatou Diallo are Black immigrant women who fall into this trap in very different ways, one attempting to use television media to advance a criminal justice case against her rapist and the other imagining ways in which public testimony could channel the rage from her sexual assault into some form of digital healing and formation of community. Television and the black blog present advantages and disadvantages for black immigrant women of color who have experienced sexual trauma, because they force each woman to isolate their identities from one another. Nafissatou Diallo cannot be her whole messy self nor show vulnerability around the story behind her refugee application. In order for Diallo to be coherent, she must play "good immigrant" as well as "ideal rape victim," both of which are tropes that demand certain assimilationist narratives, on the one hand an ethnic narrative, and on the other a gendered narrative. Similarly, Ifemelu no longer finds the blog she creates in America to be a useful source of healing once she begins to lose control over it. Better said, when Ifemelu no longer identifies with her audience or is no longer able to view them as her equals and they become her superiors, the blog begins to vacuum her self-worth rather than acting as a space of encouragement, validation, and sharing.

Both Diallo and Ifemelu use technology as a supplement for and/or in lieu of legal justice. Diallo opts for the televised interview in the midst of her legal case against her assailant. Specifically, television helps her to respond to allegations from other media sources that she is a "hooker." Television is helpful because it allows Diallo to express herself in a multitude of dimensions, namely visual and aural, that are particularly supplemental to her as an immigrant woman of color. The newspaper that alleges she is a "hooker" uses writing and static photographic imagery to misrepresent Diallo. Diallo sees moving image and sound as advantages, opportunities for the public to not only see her but also hear her accented English, see her brown body move through space, see how she dresses and how she wears her hair, hear how she recounts the assault and defends her side of the story. These elements are especially useful for Diallo because of her identity as a Black immigrant woman, despite the fact that the United States and its official channels of migration do not make *all* of Diallo—including her Blackness, her citizenship status, and her womanness—coherent. Neither Diallo nor Ifemelu is digestible as all three of these; therefore, each must turn to either the hypervisible to deny one or more of these identities (that is, Diallo must deny the most stereotypical and negative assumptions around Blackness through her dress, etc.) or to the invisible (that is, Ifemelu choosing a faceless, soundless form of communication such as a blog in which she is largely anonymous) as supplements and/or alternatives to the traditional avenues for justice, both of which fail. Historically, it has been difficult to live in a Black immigrant woman body—or a Black woman body, for that matter—because of the ways in which white supremacy demands a kind of singular identity in order to be coherent and because of the ways in which Black women were excluded from the sacred standards of white middle-class femininity. Despite all of this difficulty, what astonishes me are the ways in which they still searched for alternatives, determined to seek out and imagine how technology could be useful to a Black immigrant woman who is pursuing and/or refusing legal justice for her assault.

At the time of her interview, it is likely that Diallo knew she was going to have to give up on the state's criminal case against Strauss-Kahn and pursue her own civil case against him. After her televised interview aired, one of the widespread stories that came from the interview was that she was not paid for the interview.[53] The fact that Diallo did not request payment for her *ABC News* interview works to supplement her civil case. From the inception of the civil case, many accused Diallo of lying about the assault entirely as a means of extorting money from Strauss-Kahn, which is an effort to exact money from her assailant for the damages incurred by the assault as well as by the postassault trauma.

Ifemelu has a completely different experience with her blog, the mode of technology she chooses as an outlet for reversing the feelings of self-loathing, uncertainty, and loss of control that were incurred during her experience with the tennis coach. Though the blog, *Raceteenth*, at first provides a salve on these negative feelings for Ifemelu, over time it becomes yet another source of those same negative feelings. Initially, the black blog that Ifemelu creates offers her total control: as a space through which she can express her feelings about the systems of structural racism that indirectly put her in the room with the tennis coach in the first place, and as an opportunity to hear the stories of other immigrants, namely other black immigrant women. However, the blog eventually morphs into something that Ifemelu cannot control. *Raceteenth* slowly becomes a source of self-doubt and a loss of self-worth as the audience of the blog grows (both intellectually and in terms of size) beyond Ifemelu's understanding. When Ifemelu returns to Lagos, she starts a new blog, *The Redemptions of Lagos*, which seems to correct some of these elements. Notably, she hires a staff of writers rather than being the only writer; through this, she does not have to constantly bear the burden of being the expert, and the topics that she covers are far-ranging. But, just like with *Raceteenth*, the whole goal of the blog is a kind of integrity-based truth, which we get a glimpse of when Ifemelu mentions the kinds of stories she imagines will be in the new blog. She hopes to use it as a tool for uncovering the truths of Nigerian society as she experiences it, featuring people in her community who are actually helping people, offering an outlet for those in her community other than wealthy Nigerians who can afford to pay the media to portray whatever false do-gooder image of themselves they want to publicize.[54] Of course, the advantages and disadvantages for Ifemelu are different from those for Diallo, because Ifemelu is not seeking legal justice for what happens to her. In fact, she is incapable of doing so because her encounter with the tennis coach is not legally articulable. For this reason, the blog serves as a substitute for legal justice for Ifemelu, rather than a supplement as it serves for Diallo. Ifemelu is able to access some of the kinds of things that legal justice can offer victims of sexual violence: a reversal of the emotional impact of the trauma (that is, the person who took power away from you now has their power taken from them, because they will serve jail time and/or be forced to compensate you for any damages incurred) and an opportunity to join a community of survivors who can provide resources for healing. The latter occurs indirectly because Ifemelu does not create a community of survivors of violence; but she does create a community of black immigrants who have undergone all kinds of trauma (ranging in size and in level of damage) that has left their lives, as she says, "wrapped in gauze." Rather than talk only to survivors of assault, Ifemelu uses the blog as a more open space for all kinds of people who look like her, talk like her, and have traveled far to study or work or live, just like she did. The social and online aspect of *Raceteenth* can capture an even broader range of experiences of what it means to be a black immigrant woman.

There is no way for any mode of technology to provide all of the needs—emotional, physical, and metaphysical—of black immigrant women who are survivors of sexual violence. However, it is disenchanting to see how many ways each mode of technology under examination in this chapter can be exploited for the benefit of oppressive power structures. Afropessimism provides just one detour away from traditional modes of justice as it acknowledges the ways in which past harms, perhaps, can never be truly healed.

Figures 5.1, 5.2, 5.3 Nafissatou Diallo is pictured here during her *ABC News* interview detailing the crimes committed against her by Dominique Strauss-Kahn. Each image showcases how Diallo utilized her body to demonstrate the crimes as she also used her voice to describe them. These images demonstrate the ways in which Diallo's dress, hairstyle, and overall appearance do their own talking for her. (Credit: *ABC News*)

Figures 5.1, 5.2, 5.3 *(continued)*

Nafissatou Diallo and Chimamanda Ngozi Adichie, in their own Afropessimistic ways, test the limits of questions around healing for Black immigrant women who are victims of sexual crimes as well as Black women/femmes across spectra of experience. What do you turn to when there is no language for the crimes committed against you? What hope may there be in failure? And what failure may there be in hope?

NOTES

1. Alyssa_Milano (@Alyssa_Milano), "If you've been sexually harassed or assaulted write 'me too' as a reply to this tweet," Twitter, October 15, 2017, 4:21 p.m., https://twitter .com/Alyssa_Milano/status/919659438700670976.

2. Safiya Umoja Noble, *Algorithms of Oppression: How Search Engines Reinforce Racism* (New York: NYU Press, 2018).

3. "Recommendation for Dismissal," *The People of the State of New York v. Dominique Strauss-Kahn*, indictment no. 02526/2011 (August 22, 2011).

4. I say "allegedly" because it is not possible to know for sure what exactly Diallo wrote on her asylum application. Though we do not have direct access to Diallo's application,

we have some knowledge of what she wrote on it because the New York DA makes some allusions to the application in their motion to dismiss the case.

5. Diallo's image had been captured by courtroom sketch artists and published on various news shows, but she had not appeared publicly before July 25. It is worth noting that Diallo took the witness stand at Strauss-Kahn's grand jury trial and the jury swiftly indicted him. Lawyers and other witnesses attributed the swiftness of the jury's decision to Diallo's effectiveness and affectiveness as a public speaker. Others attributed the grand jury's quick response to the heft of physical evidence, as Diallo's rape kit corroborated her story as did the verified DNA evidence that Strauss-Kahn left at the scene. All of this trust that Diallo built when she was on trial basically disappeared when she admitted to the DA that she lied about several details of the assault itself as well as previous assaults she had mentioned.

6. The *Post* story opens up the crucial contemporary debate around sexual violence and sex work. By presuming that those who are paid for sex cannot be assaulted, that somehow payment erases one's right to bodily agency and/or consent, the *Post* puts Diallo in the uncomfortable position of having to defend her modesty so as to push herself as far away as possible from the negative, cartoonish associations with the word *hooker*.

7. "Dominique Strauss-Kahn's Accuser, Nafissatou Diallo, Speaks Out to 'GMA's' Robin Roberts (07.25.11)," YouTube, uploaded by *ABC News*, July 25, 2011, www.youtube.com/watch?v=lxc8rmcNr9A&t=1s, 00:03:03.

8. bell hooks, *Ain't I a Woman: Black Women and Feminism* (Boston: South End Press, 1981), 52.

9. Brad Hamilton, "Dominique Strauss-Kahn 'refused to pay' hooker maid for sex," *New York Post*, July 3, 2011, accessed May 19, 2018, https://nypost.com/2011/07/03/dominique-strauss-kahn-refused-to-pay-hooker-maid-for-sex/. See also Joe Coscarelli, "From 'Frog' to 'Fraud!': How the New York *Post* Told the DSK Story," *New York Magazine*, August 23, 2011, https://nymag.com/intelligencer/2011/08/dsk_case_new_york_post.html.

10. Evelyn Brooks Higginbotham, *Righteous Discontent: The Women's Movement In the Black Baptist Church, 1880–1920* (Cambridge, MA: Harvard University Press, 1993). Higginbotham writes extensively about the various manifestations of the politics of respectability among black women of the church, but I am attending to its uses specifically in terms of combatting myths around black female sexuality. She writes, "They felt certain that 'respectable' behavior in public would earn their people a measure of esteem from white America, and hence they strove to win the black lower class's psychological allegiance to temperance, industriousness, thrift, refined manners, and Victorian sexual morals" (p. 14). Victorian sexual morals are not precisely the expectations that the *Post* "hooker" headline captures, but they are consistent with an assumption of deviancy that the extreme sexual conservatism of black women in the Reconstruction period uses to defy notions that they are hypersexual. Many scholars have responded to and/or extended Higginbotham's theory of respectability politics since the inception of the term, but I still find the original content and context useful even when used in the distinct content and context of a twenty-first-century assault of an immigrant woman of color.

11. The few comments that do mention Diallo's looks are somewhat innocuous in that they do not relate significantly to how her characterization as unreliable and as a sex worker led to the actual demise of her case. However, one comment from user Laser Nite does link Diallo's appearance and sound to her unreliability: "If you pause the video a number of times and catch her micro-expression reactions, she looks like a liar, she sounds like a liar, she feels like a liar." The comment that "she looks like a liar" calls into question what racist assumptions may be underlying the notion that liars have a certain look. Does

she look like a liar because she is black? The user appears to be male and therefore could be linking Diallo's lying to her gender, a very common connection in all of the comments. But the comment also speaks to the notion that the average viewer was acting as judge and jury when watching Diallo's interview, using her facial expressions to determine her honesty. Appearance and truth-telling are therefore inextricably linked and help viewers build a context against which Diallo's story either aligns with or fails to align with their own worldview.

12. "Immigrant" is a loaded term and one that does not speak very specifically to people's lived experiences as those who leave their home countries to settle, work, and/or live in other countries. Diallo is a refugee, but I am asserting that viewers of her interview read her voice and accent as those of an immigrant, as a person who was not born in the country in which she lives.

13. "Dominique Strauss-Kahn's Accuser, Nafissatou Diallo, Speaks Out to 'GMA's' Robin Roberts (07.25.11)," 00:01:44.

14. Lisa Lowe, *Immigrant Acts: On Asian American Cultural Politics* (Durham, NC: Duke University Press, 1996); Mae Ngai, *Impossible Subjects: Illegal Aliens and the Making of Modern America* (Princeton, NJ: Princeton University Press, 2004).

15. As much as immigrants are put in a position in which they must prove their "goodness," they are, contrarily, put in a position in which they must distance themselves from the "bad." In a sense, what Ozawa, Thind, and many immigrants had to do, and continue to have to do, is prove to the United States that they will not be a burden on the country, that they will not extract from the United States all of its resources without contributing to a nation-building project. This need to portray themselves as figures of contribution rather than extraction is especially true for those who enter the United States on F-1, J-1, and H-1 (and H-1B) visas, because these are the visas for those who will study and/or work in the United States, usually in fields such as engineering, computer science, and/or the medical profession. The burden on them to prove that they will not be a burden is built into their application, whereas refugees do not have that same burden, despite the fact that the United States will almost definitely benefit from their presence as disposable labor.

16. The notion that people from other countries must align themselves with white, middle-class values in order to be perceived as citizens is not specific to immigrants. As mentioned in the visual analysis, black Americans have used the politics of respectability and other strategies to be perceived by the white majority as citizens.

17. "Dominique Strauss-Kahn's Accuser, Nafissatou Diallo, Speaks Out to 'GMA's' Robin Roberts (07.25.11)," 00:05:51.

18. "Dominique Strauss-Kahn's Accuser," 00:28:47.

19. Andrew Taslitz, *Rape and the Culture of the Courtroom* (New York: NYU Press, 1999), 79.

20. Adichie does not facilitate the tracking of time for the reader in *Americanah*. Events are told in a nonlinear fashion, completely out of order. The rare indications of time are the mentions of real-life political events, such as the 1983 military coup in Nigeria or the election of America's first black president, Barack Obama, in 2008. Chimamanda Ngozi Adichie, *Americanah* (New York: Alfred A. Knopf, 2013), 8, 271. Adichie never says which year Ifemelu migrated to the United States, but she drops clues by mentioning how long Ifemelu has been living there. It is likely that only upon re-reading would one be able to glean that Ifemelu migrated to the United States in the 1990s.

21. Adichie, *Americanah*, 107.

22. Adichie, *Americanah*, 147.

23. Adichie, *Americanah*, 145.

24. There are a number of moments throughout the novel during which Ifemelu highlights her sense of humor or her ability to observe the world from a somewhat cynical yet knowing distance as both a coping mechanism and as a natural part of her personality. These moments in which she finds humor are especially potent because of how they smooth the transition for the reader from her protagonist voice to her blogger voice. And I would say that this moment in which her roommate's dog eats her bacon is one such instance, because although it is not intentionally funny in the moment, it strikes an unnervingly satisfying balance between "humorous" and "painful," which is the exact tone of *Raceteenth*, the blog that Ifemelu creates years after she finishes college.

25. Adichie, *Americanah*, 155.

26. Adichie, *Americanah*, 156.

27. 18 Pa.C.S.A. § 3101, Pennsylvania State Law.

28. Adichie, *Americanah*, 155.

29. Adichie, *Americanah*, 155.

30. Pamela Haag, *Consent: Sexual Rights and the Transformation of Liberalism* (Ithaca, NY: Cornell University Press, 1999).

31. Haag, *Consent: Sexual Rights*, 191. Dissociation is one of several symptoms of Rape Trauma Syndrome (RTS), a much-debated term for the emotional fallout for victims of rape and/or sexual assault. Yxta Maya Murray outlines the debates amongst feminist scholars around this term: some find it a useful way to translate the experience of postrape trauma to a general and/or legal audience while others argue that it pathologizes rape victims, too narrowly defining their trauma. Yxta Maya Murray, "Rape Trauma, the State, and the Art of Tracey Emin," *California Law Review* 100, no. 6 (December 2012).

32. Murray, "Rape Trauma, the State," 190.

33. Murray, "Rape Trauma, the State," 160.

34. Saidiya Hartman, *Scenes of Subjection: Terror, Slavery, and Self-Making in Nineteenth-Century America* (Oxford: Oxford University Press, 1997), 80.

35. Hartman, *Scenes of Subjection*, 80.

36. See, for example, the work of Michal Buchhandler-Raphael and Hannah Brenner, who argue that consent-based definitions of *rape* and *sexual assault* are inadequate and that power-based definitions would be more holistic, placing less burden on the victims to prove that a crime occurred. Hannah Brenner, "Beyond Seduction: Lessons Learned about Rape, Politics, and Power from Dominique Strauss-Kahn and Moshe Katsav," *Michigan Journal of Gender & Law* 20, no. 2 (2014): 225–290 at 227; Michal Buchhandler-Raphael, "The Failure of Consent: Re-Conceptualizing Rape As Sexual Abuse of Power," *Michigan Journal of Gender & Law* 18, no. 1 (2011): 147–228 at 151.

37. Adichie, *Americanah*, 189.

38. Adichie, *Americanah*, 215.

39. Adichie, *Americanah*, 160.

40. Adichie, *Americanah*, 298.

41. Adichie, *Americanah*, 5.

42. Adichie, *Americanah*, 160.

43. There is plenty of room to consider the extent to which cultural differences influence Ifemelu's inability to articulate what happens to her as assault. In fact, the novel establishes the social circles in which Ifemelu and her family travel as rife with tricky exchanges between powerful men, beautiful women, and money or material goods. Aunty Uju and her relationship with The General is, perhaps, the most informed example in that we spend a good deal of time learning about that relationship, but there are several such

exchanges that Ifemelu witnesses both before Ifemelu leaves Lagos and when she returns. These exchanges are treated as nothing but normal. Yet at the same time that Ifemelu internalizes different versions of sex-as-commodity, nothing prepares her emotionally for her encounter with the tennis coach.

44. To follow the logic that things only become real once they are named is very dangerous for black women with regard to sexual violence. Especially if the word *real* is interpreted as "legible to the law." For decades, the sexual violation of black women was regarded as lawful, both within and outside of the period of enslavement. In other words, well into the mid-twentieth century it was not a crime to rape black women and/or it was difficult to prosecute men for the rape of black women.

45. Adichie, *Americanah*, 305–308.

46. Adichie, *Americanah*, 306–307.

47. Adichie, *Americanah*, 298.

48. Adichie, *Americanah*, 298.

49. Reader comments are mentioned only once, when the user SapphicDerrida laments the loss of the blog in the opening pages of the novel. Adichie, *Americanah*, 5.

50. Adichie, *Americanah*, 5.

51. Judith Butler, "Performativity, Precarity and Sexual Politics," *Antropólogos Iberoamericanos EnRed* 4, no. 3 (2009): 1–8; Fred Moten, "Blackness and Nothingness," *The South Atlantic Quarterly* 112, no. 4 (2013): 737–780; Gayatri Chakravorty Spivak, "Can the Subaltern Speak?" *Die Philosophin* 14, no. 27 (2003): 42–58.

52. Kimberlé Crenshaw, "Mapping the Margins: Intersectionality, Identity Politics, and Violence Against Women of Color," *Stanford Law Review* 43 (1990): 1241.

53. Julie Moos, "ABC Ends Checkbook Journalism, Will No Longer Pay for Interviews," *Poynter*, July 25, 2011, accessed September 23, 2018.

54. Adichie, *Americanah*, 423.

6

Slavery, Migration, and the Genealogies of Blackness in Yaa Gyasi's *Homegoing*

PAULA VON GLEICH

With its broad thematic reach and complex narrative structure, the prize-winning debut novel *Homegoing* by Ghanaian American writer Yaa Gyasi taps into and expands various genres. Central among this mix is what Ashraf Rushdy has called "genealogies or epics of location" in the American neoslave narrative tradition, exemplified by such novels as Alex Haley's *Roots* (1976) and Sandra Jackson-Opoku's *The River Where Blood Is Born* (1998).[1] But as Yogita Goyal points out, *Homegoing* demands not only to be read alongside classic American neoslave narratives, such as Toni Morrison's *Beloved* (1987), but also alongside recent Afropolitan novels, such as Chimamanda Ngozi Adichie's *Americanah* (2013).[2] After all, *Homegoing* brings together discourses around slavery and migration that until recently have been received "as two distinct stories" in the United States, and thereby the novel challenges dominant concepts of the Black diaspora and "expected ways of narrating both America and Africa."[3] Piecing together "the moment of Afropolitanism" with elements from the African American literary tradition, the novel thus also joins what Stephanie Li describes as "pan-African American literature" of the twenty-first century.[4]

In this chapter, I examine how *Homegoing* uses genre mixing, a complex narrative form, and recurring motifs, especially that of the marked body, to rethink Blackness in conversation with twenty-first-century Black feminist and Afropessimist work on notions of captivity and fugitivity in the Black diaspora. Drawing on Afropessimist theory as well as what we may call in Alexis Pauline Gumbs's words "Black Feminist Fugitivity" will shed light on how Gyasi's novel both responds to and further complicates the twenty-first-century "future" of Blackness and antiblackness that slavery "created," to paraphrase Saidiya Hartman.[5] As *Homegoing* negotiates genealogies of Blackness and antiblackness, it calls for a reconsideration not only of "the Black immigrant" but also of the conceptual differentiation between enslavement and voluntary or forced migration as part of the gendered "afterlife of slavery" that Afropessimism and Black feminist thought critically reflect on.[6] The novel shows that neoslave narratives and Black migrant stories—while indeed diverse, nuanced, and reflecting both similarities and differences on the level of experience—are ultimately linked to each other through ongoing forms of captivity and flight.

Homegoing follows six generations of Ghanaian and African American descendants of two half-sisters born to an Asante woman named Maame in the territory of today's Ghana in the early eighteenth century. Effia, the older of the two half-sisters, grows up in a Fante village before she is sold for a high bride price to the white British enslaver James Collins. She lives with him in Cape Coast Castle as his surrogate wife, and their descendants remain in West Africa until the late twentieth century. The younger half-sister, Esi, grows up with Maame in an Asante community, then is captured by Fantes, imprisoned in the dungeons of the castle under Collins's orders, shipped to America, and enslaved. The half-sisters' descendants—illustrated in a family tree that precedes the narrative—reunite in the early twenty-first-century United States when the African American descendant Marcus and the Ghanaian descendant and second-generation U.S. immigrant Marjorie meet. Covering three centuries, the novel traces the development of West African, African American, and U.S. immigrant Blackness through the trope of the split family tree, facing slavery, colonialism, and their antiblack afterlives. In doing so, the novel also tracks the antiblackness that Black people face in the United States with little distinction according to class, origin, ethnicity, citizenship, or the like, back to the history of the transatlantic slave trade and different forms of migration and mobility, insisting that both have a shared origin. Ultimately, *Homegoing* reflects interrelated genealogies of twenty-first-century Blackness through an epic family quest for escape and refuge, or the ongoing process of home*going* in the face of enslavement, colonialism, migration, imprisonment, and poverty on both sides of the Atlantic.

The novel consists of fourteen chapters, each of which focuses on one character, alternating between the two family branches. The chapters appear as small snapshots that start and end in medias res and through retrospection cover about twenty years in the life of each main character.[7] After every two chapters, the narrative moves on to two individuals of the next generation and a new historical period in what are today Ghana and the United States, with significant ellipses between. The seven chapters of Part 1 cover the historical era of the transatlantic slave trade and legal slavery in West Africa and North America, whereas the seven chapters of Part 2 are set in different times after the American emancipation declaration. With the story told from a figural narrative perspective, with a different reflector in each chapter, readers gain significant knowledge about the family history that individual characters have no access to or only limited access to. Thus, on the plot level the novel creates a polyphony of Black diasporic (hi)stories in the dispersed plural that may seem disorienting due to the chapters' short story–like appearance. Yet, the chapter arrangement, guided by a linear progression of time across chapters and by clear rules for place changes and character alternation, provides a lucid underlying structure, supported by the selective paratextual family tree.[8] Thus, the novel's form and content reflect both the antiblack realities of violent fragmentation and confinement *and* Black diasporic possibilities of reconstruction and escape from those realities. In order to examine the ways in which the novel's complex form and recurring motifs contribute to such a nuanced rethinking of Atlantic Blackness, migration, and its relation to captivity and flight, first I briefly discuss concepts of captivity and fugitivity as well as Hartman's notions of "the afterlife of slavery" and the "fugitive's legacy" in Afropessimist and Black feminist thought.[9] In the remainder of the chapter, I trace and compare forms of captivity and flight in select chapters of Gyasi's novel, set both in Ghana and in the United States during and after legal slavery, paying particular attention to their narrative form.

Captivity, Fugitive Legacies, and the "Afterlife of Slavery"

While "the immigrant" has largely been imagined as non-Black, non-white, and Latinx in the U.S. public imagination in the last few decades, in his seminal *Red, White, and Black: Cinema and the Structure of U.S. Antagonisms* (2010), Frank B. Wilderson III argues that "certainly, immigrants all over the world leave one country (or one place) for another. But only Black folks migrate from one place to the next while remaining on the same plantation."[10] According to Wilderson, when "the Black immigrant" is concerned, "the circuit of mobility is between what Jared Sexton calls the social incarceration of Black life and the institutional incarceration of the prison-industrial complex."[11] As Sexton underlines in a footnote to his article "People-of-Color-Blindness: Notes on the Afterlife of Slavery," although Black migrant communities

are distinguished often enough, and often enough distinguish themselves, from the native-born black population in the United States, black immigrants cannot avail themselves of the racial capital of nonblack immigrants of color. Instead, they find themselves consistent-ly folded back into the category of homegrown blackness, as it were, and subject to the same protocols of social, political, and economic violence, especially in subsequent generations. . . . Black immigrants do not so much disrupt the paradigm as demonstrate why it is correct to speak at this level of an irresolvable discrepancy between black-ness and immigrant status.[12]

The paradigm Wilderson and Sexton speak of here considers the ways in which antiblackness has proliferated, for example, as gratuitous violent dispersal and captivity across time and space, and how it has shaped the modern world at least from the transatlantic slave trade, chattel slavery, and colonialism to segregation, surveillance, and racialized mass incarceration in the United States today.[13] In his structural analysis of U.S. civil society, Wilderson thus differentiates between "the structural positionality" of Black people as that of perpetual "Slaves" outside of civil society on the one hand and white people as the "senior partners" of civil society on the other, with people of color acting as "junior partners" at society's inner margins.[14] In other words, Afropessimists, such as Wilderson, argue that both white and non-Black people, including migrants of color, have constructed themselves as free Human subjects through the violent "abjection" of Black people as socially dead, non-Human captives for centuries.[15]

This understanding of the abject status of Blackness builds significantly on the concept of the "afterlife of slavery" famously coined by Saidiya Hartman.[16] In her landmark monograph *Lose Your Mother: A Journey along the Atlantic Slave Route*, published in 2007, Hartman writes,

If slavery persists as an issue in the political life of black America, it is not because of an antiquarian obsession with bygone days or the burden of a too-long memory, but because black lives are still imperiled and devalued by a racial calculus and a political arithmetic that were entrenched centuries ago. This is the afterlife of slavery—skewed life chances, limited access to health and education, premature death, incarceration, and impoverishment.[17]

Blending travel narrative, historiography, autoethnography, and fiction, *Lose Your Mother* does not only spell out the concept of the afterlife of slavery in the United States that Hartman had already been developing in her earlier *Scenes of Subjection: Terror, Slavery, and Self-Making in Nineteenth-Century America* (1997).[18] *Lose Your Mother* also documents Hartman's critical reflection on the presences and absences of historical traces of slavery and its afterlife in local historical records and communal memories in Ghana. In her deliberations emerging from a research trip to the West African coast, Hartman revisits, among many other places, Cape Coast Castle, a key setting of *Homegoing* and a place where Gyasi claims to have found inspiration for her novel as well.[19] As Laura T. Murphy notes, during her reflections Hartman finds "that West African people did not mourn the loss of twelve million people in the way she, as an African American, had anticipated."[20] In fact, she realizes that during her time in Ghana she had primarily listened for the stories of "the captives" held in the dungeons of castles on the West African coast before they were "dragged across the sea." And in so doing, she had almost missed the stories that the survivors "who stayed behind" had to tell: "Theirs wasn't a memory of loss or of captivity, but of survival and good fortune. After all, they had eluded the barracoon, unlike my ancestors."[21]

But *Lose Your Mother* does not stop at observing differences in the historical record and the memorialization of slavery in the United States and Ghana. To the contrary, the monograph's last chapter, entitled "Fugitive Dreams," contains a passage of "critical fabulation" about West African "survivors" escaping the "raiders" involved in the "global trade in black cargo."[22] This speculative narrative is set in Gwolu in the north of Ghana where people went to escape the trade. It details, in Lara Choksey's words, "an imaginary collective flight, a journey away from captivity."[23] Hartman developed the technique of "critical fabulation" in response to the historical archive and historiography of slavery and what she describes in her 2008 article "Venus in Two Acts" as "the incommensurability between the experience of the enslaved and the fictions of history."[24] Thus, with the help of critical fabulation, Hartman recognizes that—in fact, very much like the formerly enslaved people in the northern states of America—the fugitives in the north of Ghana

> learned that the settlement in an outlying territory was not the guarantee of sovereignty and that flight was as near to freedom as they would come. And that the gap between what they had dreamed of and what they could have would never be bridged. . . . The bloodletting of the modern world allowed for no havens or safe places. The state of emergency was not the exception but the rule. The refuge became hunting grounds for the soldiers of fortune whose prizes were people.[25]

Similar to Gyasi's *Homegoing*, Hartman's monograph thus negotiates the "fugitive legacy" of those who escaped the transatlantic slave trade on the African continent and those sold and sent on the Middle Passage.[26] Reconstructing "a history out of escape," both texts stress the short- and long-term effects of the trade not only on those who entered but also on those who participated in the trade and/or managed to evade the Door of No Return.[27] Casting her view across centuries, Hartman also mentions contemporary undocumented migration from Ghana to the United States and Europe, with ambiguous resonances of the Middle Passage, as migrants "risked deadly voyages to escape poverty and joblessness."[28] In doing so, she seems to ask, who could truly find refuge from the antiblack forces of captivity? She defines *fugitivity* as "refusal" of captivity or the practice of moving away from one form of captivity toward a position assumed to be less confining, without necessarily being able to arrive at a position of social life and unconfined freedom outside of antiblack fragmentation and confines.[29]

Homegoing too reflects the ways in which African and African-descended people have been put to perpetual and reiterative forms of captivity and flight across the "Black Atlantic,"[30] questioning any seemingly essential differences between migration, mobility, and flight and the structural positionalities of African Americans and Black Africans, particularly in the context of the United States. As we see below, perpetual or reiterative confinement frequently questions the notion of linear progress, upward mobility, and change in the novel. West African and African American characters experience captivity as enslavement, forced labor, servitude, and incarceration, but also in arranged marriages, the domestic sphere, colonial missionaries, social isolation, or poor segregated communities. The narrative negotiates the relationship of these forms of confinement to mobility, migration, and flight as characters on both sides of the Atlantic move within and across the territories of today's Ghana and the United States, migrating from the inland to the Atlantic coast, from the segregated U.S. South to the North, between villages and urban centers, between Fante and Asante territory, and across the ocean. They move as travelers or tourists, soldiers or captives, traders or enslaved people, as students, runaways, community pariahs, or migrants. As I argue in what follows by drawing on Hartman's work, many of these movements can be understood as flights from a physical place and/or a racialized (as well as gendered and classed) position of captivity to places or positions assumed to be less confining or unfree, in search of unconfined freedom.

Genealogical Ruptures and Fugitive Fabulations

Homegoing's reflections on the riffs and relations between similar and varying West African and Africa American experiences of captivity and flight begin chronologically with experiences of slavery and its trade in West Africa in the eighteenth century. This first section of the novel fills an "aporia" in many North American slave and neoslave narratives by imagining in idiosyncratic detail generations of people who have been touched by, escaped from, or were involved in the transatlantic slave trade (and colonialism) but largely remained in West Africa.[31] The chapters of the first part of the novel, set in what is today Ghana, not only tell stories of characters who fall prey to the transatlantic trade in people, such as Esi. They also tell stories of people who remain bystanders or are used to forge trading relations, such as Effia; of some who are actively involved in the trade, such as Effia's son Quey; and of yet others who refuse to participate, such as Quey's son James Richard.[32] The latter fakes his death in order to leave his Fante community, which is involved in the trade, to "make a new way" and seek refuge in his "own nation" elsewhere with Akosua from an Asante family.[33]

Apart from different forms of involvement or refusal to participate in the capture and trading of people, the first few chapters of the novel also address the complexity and instability of what enslavement means to different individuals and communities in West Africa and how they are differently affected, not least in terms of their gender. Besides the trade in enslaved people with the British that Esi falls victim to, in the early chapters set in West Africa especially women and girls, such as Maame, Effia, Abronoma, or Nana Yaa, are captured, owned, sold, and forced into marriage or domestic service for political and financial reasons.[34] By interweaving narrative fragments about these minor characters with Effia's and Esi's more elaborate stories, the chapters attend to the similarities and differences between various gendered forms of enslavement, without losing sight of the fact that as Black African women they are all vulnerable to enslavement, notwithstanding any ethnic differences or class privileges that may also influence their lives.

Apart from the respective treatment of Effia and Esi as tradeable wife and fungible property that critics have discussed at some length,[35] Maame's and particularly Abronoma's experiences of captivity and escape have received less attention, even though they are inextricably linked to Effia's and Esi's fates. Abronoma is an Asante prisoner of war whom Maame reluctantly adopts as a "house girl" from the stream of "prisoners who were paraded through the village" frequently.[36] Maame disapproves of house servants because she herself had been a captive servant in an Asante community, was raped by her owner, and had to set fire to the village and leave her first daughter Effia behind in order to escape. Maame's second daughter, Esi, grows up without any knowledge of her mother's earlier life in captivity. From Esi's perspective, Maame "had no family, no background to speak of" and was saved by her husband from some unknown "wretchedness."[37] Thus, Esi adopts a dominant, dismissive, and dehumanizing attitude toward captives in her Fante village, until she learns from Abronoma of her mother's past. Wanting to "make amends" with Abronoma for mistreating her, Esi sends for Abronoma's father and thereby launches the events that eventually result in Esi's enslavement and the continued separation of the two half-sisters, "doomed to stay on opposite sides of the pond" as Abronoma predicts before her father raids Esi's village to rescue his daughter and to take Esi captive.[38]

The ways in which first Maame and then Esi are marked by captivity and flight, and the loss attached to their experiences, point to the roots and the local effects of slavery in West Africa that are often overlooked in well-known American neoslave narratives. Foreshadowing her own and her daughter's fate on the other side of the Atlantic, Esi tries to escape with her mother when their village is raided and Abronoma is freed. However, she quickly realizes that she has to leave her mother behind, and she recognizes the loss attached to captivity and flight because

> Maame was not a whole woman. There were large swaths of her spirit missing, and no matter how much she loved Esi, and no matter how much Esi loved her, they both knew in that moment that love could never return what Maame had lost. And Esi knew, too, that her mother would die rather than run into the woods ever again, die before capture, die even if it meant that in her dying, Esi would inherit that unspeakable sense of loss, learn what it meant to be un-whole.[39]

Esi comes to understand how having been captive, enslaved, and fugitive irreversibly changed her mother, and that she too would "inherit" that mark. Indeed, later Esi would "split her life into Before the Castle and Now. Before the Castle, she was the daughter of Big Man and his third wife, Maame. Now she was dust. Before the Castle, she was the prettiest girl in the village. Now she was just thin air."[40]

Yet, while Esi still has a sense of herself before enslavement, whose loss she mourns, her own daughter Ness grows up enslaved on cotton plantations in the American South without any experience of or frame of reference for a place and time before slavery. Instead, she describes a sense of loss and "motherlessness" in a "spacetime" that is familiar to many readers of American neoslave narratives, such as *Beloved*, and which—as we see below—recurs in many of the American chapters of *Homegoing* as well.[41] Listening to Esi's "bedtime stories" about the Middle Passage, in which people were "thrown into the Atlantic Ocean like anchors attached to nothing: no land, no people, no worth," the transatlantic slave trade and slavery form Ness's "horizon and . . . origin story."[42] Later, when she has become a mother herself, Ness and her enslaved husband Sam wish to escape the plantation and slavery before their son Kojo inherits that same loss—that is, before he is taken from them and forgets "the sound of her voice, the details of her face, the way she had forgotten Esi's."[43] Rehearsing the familiar plot of family separations and flight attempts recounted in many American slave and neoslave narratives, they try to escape "the Devil's plantation" and flee "north to freedom," but are caught.[44] Sam is killed and Ness is re-enslaved and scarred for life as punishment, after ensuring their baby's successful escape with Aku, an Asante Underground Railroad conductor and survivor of the Middle Passage.

Knowing "the way back out," Aku adopts Kojo and they settle in Baltimore, where the formerly enslaved are legally free. Kojo grows up in good care but without even the little knowledge that Ness had about their family and their "origin" on the Middle Passage.[45] Except for the insight that his mother was of Asante origin, he feels utterly disconnected:

> Jo used to worry that his family line had been cut off, lost forever. He would never truly know who his people were, and who their people were before them, and if there were stories to be heard about where he had come from, he would never hear them. When he felt this way, Ma Aku would hold him against her, and instead of stories about family she would tell him stories about nations. The Fantes of the Coast, the Asantes of the Inland, the Akans.[46]

Since Kojo has no access to the narratives of his family lineage that the novel is made of, his adoptive mother Ma Aku's stories about West African nations are needed to fill part of the void he feels. After Ness is unable to share her mother's nighttime stories about the Middle Passage with her son before they are separated, Ma Aku's stories attempt to bridge some of the gaps that the repeated separation and dispersal of family members leaves behind. As Choksey maintains, "When the force of history that keeps time moving forward forces characters to lose each other, forms of care that are on the run, outside the law, become ways of enduring the present."[47] Of course, Aku's act of storytelling, like the novel's telling of the stories discussed so far about the slave trade in Ghana and slavery in North America, may also be understood as a form of Hartman's "critical fabulation." They too "[strain] . . . against the limits of the archive to write a cultural history of the captive, and, at the same time, [enact] . . . the impossibility of representing the lives of the captives precisely through the process of narration."[48]

Besides Aku, other critical fabulators or historian-storytellers in the novel are, for example, Tansi, Esi's friend in the dungeon; the Ghanaian teacher Yaw, who writes a sweeping monograph about the colonization of Africa and its freedom struggles; and Marcus, who pursues a Ph.D. in sociology at Stanford University.[49] The latter focusses his studies on the ways in which the little he knows about his family, which he can trace back to his great-grandfather H (Kojo's lost son), can be connected to the history of structural antiblack racism in the United States—from slavery, convict leasing, and Jim Crow to the "war on drugs" and racialized mass incarceration.[50] Ultimately, Gyasi's novel itself functions as a form of critical fabulation on a metalevel, with its narrative excess of the epic family saga across centuries and continents on the one hand, and narrative restraint as the saga unfolds in elliptic, sometimes only loosely connected vignettes on the other. Together with its focus on forms of confinement and flight, the result is a narrative tug of war between creolizing and dispersing forces on the one hand and structuring, ordering, and containing tendencies on the other.[51]

Ultimately, the fragmented narrative form—born out of the violence of the trade, the Middle Passage, and slavery—asks readers to assemble knowledge about the dispersed family's history over the course of the novel. In other words, the responsibility of observing not only the nuanced differences and connections of forms of captivity but also their long-term effects and strategies of escape and reconstruction, as they play out across the Black Atlantic, is handed over to the novel's readers. As readers learn, loss largely marks the American characters' familial memory, whereas knowledge about ancestral experiences of captivity and flight as well as a consciousness about culpability in enslavement remains limited in the West African family line as well. Later generations in Ghana relate to their family's involvement in the trade of people mostly through the notion of a family curse, haunting dreams, and fire.

Akua, the fourth-generation descendent of Effia, learns from a "firewoman" who haunts her dreams and causes her to set fire to her home that "there is evil in our lineage. There are people who have done wrong because they could not see the result of the wrong." As an old woman, Akua explains to her estranged adult son Yaw, who had received severe burning scars from the fire that killed his sisters as a child,

> Evil begets evil. It grows. It transmutes, so that sometimes you cannot see that the evil in the world began as the evil in your own home. I'm sorry you have suffered. I'm sorry for the way your suffering casts a shadow over your life, over the woman you have yet to marry, the children you have yet to have.[52]

Beyond the foreshadowing of Yaw's marriage to his employed house servant Esther and the birth of their daughter Marjorie, as well as the ways in which they too will be affected by the history of captivity and flight, Akua's monologue is dense with conceptions of the captive past of slavery from the perspective of twentieth-century Ghana. Akua continues:

> When someone does wrong, whether it is you or me, whether it is mother or father, whether it is the Gold Coast man or the white man, it is like a fisher-man casting a net into the water. He keeps only the one or two fish that he needs to feed himself and puts the rest in the water, thinking that their lives will go back to normal. No one forgets

that they were once captive, even if they are now free. But, still, Yaw, you have to let yourself be free.[53]

The metaphor of the fisher fishing only to feed himself rather than for profit illustrates a misconception of the scope of the trade and the fate of the enslaved people after they left the West African shore. The metaphor clearly understates the trade's transatlantic reach, its violence and deadliness, and its ongoing effects in terms of white Western wealth and privilege on the one hand and Black physical and social death in the Americas and Africa on the other. According to Portia Owusu, however, the general emphasis on greed as well as financial and political interests as driving forces for the "evil" challenges this misconstruction throughout the novel.[54] Moreover, through its narrative structure and scope, readers receive a fuller picture of the aftermath of the trade than the individual characters receive, enabling the readers, if not the characters, to unpack Akua's dreams as well as the potential shortcomings of their imagery.

Nevertheless, by stating that "no one forgets that they were once captive, even if they are now free," Akua recognizes that captivity leaves a mark on former captives and their descendants. Setting fire to her own home, Akua—"chosen by the ancestors to hear their family's stories"—does more than reenact Maame's strategy of flight (the burning of her house).[55] She also channels lasting effects of transatlantic and intergenerational experiences of captivity by physically afflicting burning scars on her body and her son's body. In her analysis of *Lose Your Mother* and *Homegoing* as challenging "genetic accounts of historical belonging," Choksey fittingly understands "kinship as the mark of a wound left open down the generations," questioning whether there has been a true end to captivity and the need for escape:

[The] mark of property [becomes] a kind of "trait" to be passed down to subsequent generations. The system of using people as capital becomes embedded in a biological metaphor, an inheritance of anonymity and defacement (spoiling the surface, scratching out the face, reducing the body to a brand).[56]

Readers of American neoslave narratives, such as *Beloved*, will be familiar with the metaphor of the scar or brand mark for the violence and loss of family and kinship experienced during slavery and the intergenerational trauma passed on from it. Gyasi not only adopts this metaphor in *Homegoing*'s American chapters, as we see below, but also extends it in the novel's chapters set in Ghana, to those "who stayed behind." They too need to "let [themselves] be free" in an anti- and decolonial struggle against ongoing (post)colonial forms of confinement.[57]

As I have discussed so far, especially the first chapters of *Homegoing* provide stories of African traders, survivors, and differently affected captives that give voice to both the complicity with and refusal of practices of gendered enslavement, telling West African stories rarely told, especially to a North American readership. But the novel's complex and sweeping form also grants space to the split and the void that the Middle Passage and slavery produced in individual lives and across generations. It juxtaposes varied African experiences with slavery, otherwise often missing from North American narratives of slavery, with African American experiences of captivity and flight that U.S.-centered neoslave narratives have grappled with since the mid-1970s. Also, apart from the narrative structure, connections between these fragmented stories are created and reinforced in the novel through recurring motifs, such as the aforementioned storytelling, historical and literary writing, fire, and scars.

Especially with the help of the image of the scarred or marked body, the novel clearly connects the captivity and unfreedom that Akua notices and re-enacts in West Africa with that of kin in North America. Following the mark of captivity through the generations, Gyasi's novel—like Hartman's monograph—extends its perspective beyond the history of legal slavery and colonialism first to its immediate aftermaths and then to the postcolonial and post–Civil Rights era, making visible what Stephen Dillon aptly calls, with respect to Hartman's work, "slavery's mark on the now."[58] As I argue in the second half of this chapter, the physical scars on Akua's and Yaw's hands and face and the marks of captivity they discern in their family line are connected through vivid imagery and personification to those afflicted on Ness's and her grandson H's backs on the other side of the Atlantic during slavery and its immediate aftermath. But metaphorically speaking, many more characters of the post–Civil Rights era, such as Willie, Sonny, Marcus, and Marjorie, are also marked.

Captive Marks, Escape, and the (Im)Possibility of Return

In the American chapters of the second part of the novel, *Homegoing* grapples with many of the issues that Hartman includes in her definition of the afterlife of slavery quoted above. Kojo, Ness's son, experiences the precariousness of legal freedom, when his legally free wife Anna is kidnapped, taken down south, and re-enslaved while she is pregnant with their son H.[59] After legal emancipation, H too oscillates between legally free status and captive status as he falls victim to the convict leasing system on charges of having "studied" a white girl, the daughter of "his old sharecropping boss."[60] As Christine Okoth notes, "H's case exemplifies Saidiya Hartman's argument that freedom, in the case of formerly enslaved people[,] quickly turns into a different kind of servitude, where possessive individualism becomes the gateway to criminalisation" and "the extractive zone of the Alabama coal mine . . . repeats the formal logic of Black fungibility that organised the economic system of plantation slavery in the Americas."[61]

After H miraculously survives the deadly working conditions of this "other kind of servitude" in the coal mine and completes his sentence, he tries to escape the carceral environment by walking away "as far as he could, . . . until there was no mine in sight, no smell of coal clinging to his nostrils."[62] Yet, he quickly realizes that the whipping scars on his back and arms, which he received during his sentence, forever mark him as "one of them cons" so that "he couldn't go back to the free world" and instead returns to work in the mines.[63] Not only are convict leasing and hard prison labor clearly represented here as "slavery by another name," with "the belly of the mine" recalling the belly of the ship of the Middle Passage and foreshadowing the holding cell of late-twentieth- and early-twenty-first-century racialized mass incarceration.[64] The scars it leaves on H's body are also connected metaphorically to the scars left on his unknown distant kin Akua and Yaw on the West African coast and those afflicted on his grandmother Ness's body decades earlier on an American cotton plantation.

Yet, the scars are not the only marks on H's body that connect him to Ness. As his daughter Willie would remember later, the work in the mines sickened her father. H coughs severely, "as though some invisible man were behind him, hands wrapped around the large trunk of his thick neck, choking him."[65] This vivid, bodily image of the forced labor slowly killing H recalls an earlier literary personification of the scars Ness receives as punishment for her attempt to escape slavery and protect her son, H's father Kojo. While the "invisible man" of the convict-leasing era chokes H from behind, the "invisible man" of slavery appears to hold Ness in his grip from behind, with the added connotation of sexualized violence: her "scarred skin was like another body in and of itself, shaped like a man hugging her from behind with his arms hanging around her neck."[66]

In the following generations, the marks of captivity become less physical but are discernable nonetheless, especially with respect to characters living in the United States. After H's death, Jim Crow segregation drives his daughter Willie out of the Deep South to Harlem, where she envisions a better future for her husband and child, free from the grip of carceral captivity and segregation. In conversation with her son, who is active in the civil rights movement, Willie describes her participation in the Great Migration in the 1940s as her own form of protest:

You think you done somethin' cuz you used to march? I marched. I marched with your father and with my li'l baby all the way up from

Alabama. All the way to Harlem. My son was gon' see a better world than what I saw, what my parents saw. I was gon' be a famous singer. Robert wasn't gon' have to work in a mine for some white man. That was a march too, Carson.[67]

As Marcus, Carson's son and Willie's grandson, reflects later, Willie and her husband Robert were in fact "fleeing Jim Crow," only to find another form of antiblack racism in New York City that confined Black people in poor neighborhoods and drew Willie and Robert, who could suddenly pass for white, apart.[68] Poverty, police violence, incarceration, drugs, and a less formal, but no less forceful segregation of people racialized as Black and white continue to risk and confine Willie, her children, and children's children in New York City, moving from the era of Jim Crow to what Michelle Alexander has described as "The New Jim Crow."[69]

Willie's son Carson, who is mostly called Sonny in the respective chapters, becomes increasingly frustrated with the forms of surveillance and police violence directed toward Black people in Harlem and "the futility of his work for the NAACP."[70] Echoing the Afropessimist rejection of the progress narrative, Sonny/Carson doubts the transformative potential not only of activism but also of change altogether when he asks himself this:

> How many times could he pick himself up off the dirty floor of a jail cell? How many hours could he spend marching? How many bruises could he collect from the police? How many letters to the mayor, governor, president could he send? How many more days would it take to get something to change? And when it changed, would it change? Would America be any different, or would it be mostly the same?[71]

Wishing for a wholesome Black community untainted by antiblack violence and in fact fully segregated from white people, "what Sonny wanted was Africa" as envisioned by Marcus Garvey.[72] Yearning for change, but unable to bring it about with his activism, he decides to work as a bartender in a jazz club and falls in love with the young, gifted, heroin-using jazz singer Amani. In seeming response to Sonny's desire for African home*going* (which, however, remains unacknowledged between the two), Amani tells Sonny, "'We can't go back to something we ain't never been to in the first place. It ain't ours anymore. This is.'" When making this statement, Amani gestures with her hands "to catch all of Harlem in it, all of New York, all of America" before the two enter a "dope house" where Sonny starts using heroin.[73] His resulting addiction appears as a form of flight from an environment (Harlem, New York, the United States) of proliferating captivity (jail, police violence, public housing, poverty) and a lack of lasting physical and social mobility out of these confines. But the drug use can also be understood as a search for refuge that marks Sonny's body visibly as "worse than dead, . . . a dead man walking" and thereby reinforces the antiblack structures it wants to escape by feeding into the narrative of individual bad choices as the cause for structural disadvantages of Black people in the United States.[74] As Willie explains to Sonny, "'[The white man] ain't got to sell you or put you in a coal mine to own you. He'll own you just as is, and he'll say you the one who did it. He'll say it's your fault.'"[75]

Despite Amani's rejection of the possibility of return, the novel's ending strives for symbolic closure of the void that the Middle Passage produced and a sense of healing of the wounds of slavery through the Pan-African trope of return. In the last chapter of the novel both family branches metaphorically return to the place where they were separated, when Yaw's daughter Marjorie and Sonny's son Marcus visit Cape Coast Castle as tourists at the beginning of the twenty-first century. A breach seems to figuratively be sealed when both overcome their transgenerational fear of fire and water, and Marjorie hands Marcus her family's heirloom, the black stone that had been passed down through the generations from Maame.[76] As readers recall from the first two chapters but Marcus and Marjorie are unaware of, Maame had left the stones to each of her two daughters; but Esi, who is Marcus's ancestor, loses hers in the dungeons before entering the Door of No Return.[77] The rich symbolism of the joint return to the castle as a form of home*coming* and the handing over of the stone clearly drive for narrative closure of the tug of war between creolizing and fragmenting as well as ordering and containing tendencies in the novel. Still, the text seems to ask, with its broad cast and their diverse experiences and worldviews, what it means for Esi's family line to have lost the familial connection that the stone symbolizes in the first place. After all, when Esi loses her stone in the dirt of the dungeon, her half-sister Effia lives on the upper floors of the castle and does not recognize "the slaves" down below, who "spoke a different dialect than her" but "who looked like her and smelled like her," as kin "split from the same tree."[78]

Thus, the ending of the novel seems to explore whether—and, if so, how—Esi's and Effia's twenty-first-century descendants may finally rid themselves of the marks of captivity and recognize each other as the kin that they genealogically are. Fittingly, the penultimate chapter, before the fairly happy ending at Cape Coast Castle, negotiates the relation of Marjorie, as a Ghanaian second-generation immigrant, not only to a white American majority population but also to the African American community, *and* to her home country. Interestingly, the classic immigrant story of Yaw and Esther moving to the United States "landing in a country as foreign to them as the moon"[79] to presumably provide their daughter Marjorie with better opportunities is mostly left out of the novel in an ellipsis between Yaw's and Marjorie's chapters. Instead, readers only learn of Yaw's and Esther's migration, their "tiny apartment" in Huntsville, Alabama, and their humble work as community college teacher and as caretaker at a nursing home through the perspective of Marjorie, who is born in the United States to her Ghanaian parents in the late twentieth century.[80] Thus, the migration that would ultimately destabilize, if not undo, the split of the two family branches is in fact deprioritized on the plot level in favor of Marjorie's feelings of in-between-ness, of not fitting "here or there" as a Black African immigrant in the U.S. South.[81]

Growing up in Alabama, Marjorie feels like an outsider at her school, with the "only real friends she had" being "characters in novels" she reads. This changes briefly when she forms a close but short-lived relationship with another "outsider," a white boy from a military family who had just returned from a long stay in Germany.[82] Despite their mutual affection, common interests, and shared feelings of isolation, the two soon recognize the ways in which Graham can quickly blend into the white majority community at school, "slip in unnoticed, as though he had always belonged there," whereas Marjorie continues to be an outsider even in the small group of Black students who make her feel like "the wrong kind" of Black, not least because of the way she speaks English.[83] Moreover, Marjorie feels increasingly estranged from her parents' home country, acquiring English rather than Twi as her primary language and visiting her Ghanaian grandmother Akua only on summer vacations until Akua dies of old age and Marjorie does not travel back for many years.[84]

Marjorie's conflicted relationship to her Ghanaian roots and dominant conceptions of Blackness in the United States clearly plays out in a scene with her African American teacher. When Mrs. Pinkston asks Marjorie to write a poem about "being African American" for "The Waters We Wade In," a "black cultural event" scheduled to take place "well after Black History Month," Marjorie refuses to identify as African American.[85] As she explains to the reader but not to her teacher (to whom she seems to remain silent), African Americans are called "*akata*" in Ghana and are perceived as "different from Ghanaians, too long gone from the mother continent to continue calling it the mother continent."[86] Rejecting the moniker "African American" as "*akata*," Marjorie establishes a clear demarcation between herself as Ghanaian and U.S. American Blackness that echoes Amani's viewpoint. Yet, right afterward Marjorie also acknowledges that she herself feels "pulled away too, almost *akata*, too long gone from Ghana to be Ghanaian,"[87] dissolving the demarcation she had just established. Consequentially, the poem she writes is "built from the dream stories" her grandmother Akua told her about their family that, as the beginning lines read, "Split the castle open—to find me, find you."[88] Marjorie's poem, like Akua's dreams or Yaw's and Marcus's historiographical work and the previously discussed recurring motifs, connects and reconstructs the dispersed family vignettes and their Ghanaian and African American affiliations; thus it contributes to the tug of war between hybridizing and structuring tendencies, without coming down on either side.

Importantly, Marjorie's inner dispensing of her previous understanding of herself as essentially Ghanaian and not African American is further reinforced by her teacher's following Afropessimist-like statement: "Here, in this country, it doesn't matter where you came from first to the white people running things. You're here now, and here black is black is black."[89] In other words, in response to Marjorie's rejection of the African American moniker in favor of her Ghanaian heritage, Mrs. Pinkston draws her attention to the ways in which in the United States, as Sexton put it, Black people are "subject to the same protocols of social, political, and economic violence," notwithstanding their ethnicity or national origin.[90] That Marjorie owns the black stone as a literal connection to her West African ancestors and that she can share this connection at least symbolically with Marcus at the end are essential for the novel's narrative arc, its character development, and the transnational conversation about Blackness that the novel performs on the level of content and form. But it does not suggest that Black immigrant lives, like Marjorie's, are exempted from proliferating forms of antiblack dispersal and captivity in the United States, nor that narration or critical fabulation offer an ultimate route to unconfined freedom.

To the contrary, the last chapter of the novel told from Marcus's perspective—while including the aforementioned scenes of symbolic return and reunion that fulfill Sonny's dream of Pan-African home*going* in the following generation—also reflects on the captive and fugitive legacy of the afterlife of slavery that still shapes Black life in the twenty-first-century United States. Describing his father, Marcus draws on the metaphor of the stone again, but not with the previous connotation of familial relation: "Sonny was forever talking about slavery, the prison labor complex, the System, segregation, the Man. His father had a deep-seated hatred of white people. A hatred like *a bag filled with stone* [my emphasis], one stone for every year racial injustice continued to be the norm in America. He still carried the bag."[91] After one of the two stones that connected the two family lines is lost, it multiplies in North America as the weight of slavery in its antiblack afterlife—proliferating as perpetual and reiterative forms of captivity and fugitivity that Marcus studies for his Ph.D. dissertation and that members of his extended family lived through.

Without any records of his family history beyond what he learns from his father, Sonny, and his grandmother Willie about great-grandfather H, Marcus consults African American history more broadly. In doing so, he traces his people's survival in the United States back to the mere luck of having successfully escaped gratuitous antiblack violence again and again. Marcus rejects the myth of meritocracy that, not least, continues to attract immigrants to the United States, such as Marjorie's family, presumably. Questioning American exceptionalism, Marcus maintains "that he had been born, that he wasn't in a jail cell somewhere, was not by dint of his pulling himself up by the bootstraps, not by hard work or belief in the American Dream, but by mere chance."[92] He also acknowledges that the tables could turn on him at any moment, just as they had on his great-grandfather H after emancipation when he was "once slave, once free, now slave again."[93] So despite the seeming happy ending that emphasizes return, reunion, and progress, the novel "gives a fairly definitive answer as to whether newness may also signify freedom."[94] As Dominique Haensell concludes, "The same deadly fiction that put H in jail" could still mark Marcus as a threatening "angry Black man" and could imprison or kill him "if he, studying the injustices of the convict leasing system, expresses his anger in a public outburst."[95]

Conclusion

In a recent opinion piece for the *Guardian*, Gyasi commented on the fact that *Homegoing* reentered the *New York Times* bestseller list four years after its publication in the aftermath of the murders of George Floyd, Ahmaud Arbery, and Breonna Taylor:

> It is wrenching to know that the occasion for the renewed interest in your work is the murders of black people and the subsequent "listening and learning" of white people. I'd rather not know this feeling of experiencing career highs as you are flooded with a grief so old and worn that it seems unearthed, a fossil of other old and worn griefs.[96]

Gyasi comments on the role of literature in the unfinished "reckoning" of the United States with its racist, antiblack history and present. She asks, "Why are we back here? Why am I being asked questions that James Baldwin answered in the 1960s, that Toni Morrison answered in the 80s?" and adds, "Some may want to call the events of June 2020 a 'racial reckoning', but in a country in which there was a civil war and a civil rights movement 100 years apart, at some point it would be useful to ask how long a reckoning need take. When, if ever, will we have reckoned?"[97] To this white German reader, Gyasi's critical commentary clearly underlines the importance and tradition of "reckoning" with the long history of antiblack violence with the help of literary texts by and about the Black diaspora. But it also calls us to acknowledge its belatedness, insufficiency, and the unequally distributed costs of doing so at the beginning of the second decade of the twenty-first century. White read-

ers like myself need to recognize and sit with the violence our reflections (re)
produce in conversation with works like *Homegoing* as part of a longstand-
ing discourse in the United States.

Proceeding in the footsteps of intellectual luminaries, such as Baldwin,
Morrison, and Hartman as well as other Black diasporic thinkers, such as
Paul Gilroy and Édouard Glissant, Gyasi's *Homegoing* stresses that the history
of slavery and the transatlantic trade in West African and African-descen-
dant people presents diverse, but connected legacies of captivity and fugitivity for the descendants of the African "survivors" and the captives sent across
the ocean. Both Gyasi's and Hartman's work also seem to suggest that those
legacies, their connections and disconnects have to be reckoned with in cre-
ative ways on both sides of the Atlantic, considering both the time and places before and after the Middle Passage. The novel addresses the split of the
Middle Passage between its two main settings and the creolization of Blackness as illustrated in the two family branches on a thematic and formal level
by placing elements of the neoslave narrative tradition alongside past and
present stories of mobility, flight, and imprisonment through the ages. Recurring symbols and motifs, such as storytelling, historiography, fire, and the
marked body, ultimately create small bridges that enable mobility across and
beyond the void of the Middle Passage without, however, denying its existence and detrimental and ongoing effects. The novel thereby points to the
antiblackness that was with Hartman's words "entrenched centuries ago" and
still "imperils and devalues" African American and Black migrant lives without much distinction in the United States, where "black is black is black."[98]

The text clearly illustrates the ways in which racial, gender, ethnic, and
class identifications are constantly constructed, deconstructed, and recon-
structed culturally, socially, politically, and historically. It connects these re-
and de-constructions not only to the severe material consequences on individual lives but also to the larger underlying antiblack, patriarchal logic of
the modern world order as theorized and criticized especially by Black Feminism and Afropessimism. The novel's narrative strategies grapple with the
complex history of antiblack captivity and perpetual flight that work against
its push towards a closed narrative arc of reconstruction, return, and reunion.
After all, as Haensell poignantly argues, in its episodic but fragmented structure, the narrative "emphasizes rather than mends the fracturing of kinship"
caused by the trade, the Middle Passage, slavery, and their afterlives.[99] *Homegoing* "employs both the forward push of futurity and the backward pull of
historicity as a novel that flashes the hopeful potential of restoration and connection across the rupture of the Middle Passage, without trivializing the
long-lasting effects of slavery and its aftermath."[100] Through the novel's complex form, its genre mix, and its style as well as its transatlantic and transgenerational scope, *Homegoing* creates narratives of the lives and afterlives

of slavery without shying away from difficult questions of complicity, guilt, and familial kinship. Nevertheless, it does not imagine life untouched by slavery, a moment of unconfined freedom in the African homeland, nor a postracial (postcolonial, postslavery) moment in which Ghana or the United States have overcome their legacies of slavery and colonialism.[101] Instead, it illuminates the ways in which slavery and colonialism have left a mark on African Americans and Black Africans that testifies to both their experiences of perpetual forms of captivity and their shared struggles to escape.

NOTES

1. Ashraf H. A. Rushdy, "The Neo-Slave Narrative," in *The Cambridge Companion to the African American Novel*, ed. Maryemma Graham (Cambridge: Cambridge University Press, 2004), 95–96.

2. Yogita Goyal and Yaa Gyasi, "An Interview with Yaa Gyasi," *Contemporary Literature* 60, no. 4 (Winter 2019): 471–472, https://muse.jhu.edu/article/773068. For a comparative analysis of the role of immigration in *Homegoing* and *Americanah*, see, for example, Ava Landry, "Black Is Black Is Black? African Immigrant Acculturation in Chimamanda Ngozi Adichie's *Americanah* and Yaa Gyasi's *Homegoing*," *MELUS* 43, no. 4 (Winter 2018): 127–147. For a critical discussion of *Americanah* under the auspices of antiblackness and migration, see Maya Sylvia Hislop's contribution in this edited volume.

3. Yogita Goyal, *Runaway Genres: The Global Afterlives of Slavery* (New York: New York University Press, 2019), chap. 5, ProQuest Ebook Central, http://ebookcentral.proquest.com/lib/suub-shib/detail.action?docID=5844700.

4. Dominique Haensell, *Making Black History: Diasporic Fiction in the Moment of Afropolitanism* (Berlin: De Gruyter, 2021), https://doi.org/10.1515/9783110722093; Stephanie Li, *Pan-African American Literature: Signifyin(g) Immigrants in the Twenty-First Century* (New Brunswick, NJ: Rutgers University Press, 2018). For an in-depth analysis of *Homegoing* as reflecting what Dominique Haensell pointedly coins the "Afropolitan moment" and its representation of the progression and halting of time, see Haensell, *Making Black History*, chap. 4.

5. Alexis Pauline Gumbs, *Spill: Scenes of Black Feminist Fugitivity* (Durham, NC: Duke University Press, 2016); Saidiya V. Hartman, *Lose Your Mother: A Journey along the Atlantic Slave Route* (New York: Farrar, Straus and Giroux, 2007), 133.

6. Hartman, *Lose Your Mother*, 6.

7. See Goyal and Gyasi, "An Interview," 476.

8. The family tree includes only select family members. In this way, it enables readers to follow the familial relations of the fourteen characters throughout the narrative, without distraction by family strands that the novel does not detail. Sonny and Amani's son, Marcus, who is the protagonist of the last chapter, is, for example, listed at the bottom of the tree, but Sonny's sister's children or the children Sonny has with three other women, who are mentioned only marginally, are not included.

9. Hartman, *Lose Your Mother*, 6, 234.

10. Frank B. Wilderson III, *Red, White, and Black: Cinema and the Structure of U.S. Antagonisms* (Durham, NC: Duke University Press, 2010), 140.

11. Wilderson, *Red, White, and Black*, 140.

12. Jared Sexton, "People-of-Color-Blindness: Notes on the Afterlife of Slavery," *Social Text* 28, no. 2 (May 2010): 53, https://doi.org/10.1215/01642472-2009-066.

13. On forms of racialized and antiblack captivity in North America, see, for example, Angela Y. Davis, "From the Prison of Slavery to the Slavery of Prison: Frederick Douglass and the Convict Lease System," in *The Angela Y. Davis Reader*, ed. Joy James (Malden, MA: Blackwell, 1998), 74–95; Douglas A. Blackmon, *Slavery by Another Name: The Re-Enslavement of Black Americans from the Civil War to World War II* (New York: Anchor Books, 2008); and Michelle Alexander, *The New Jim Crow: Mass Incarceration in the Age of Colorblindness* (New York: New Press, 2012).

14. Wilderson, *Red, White, and Black*, 38. Wilderson's differentiation of positionalities also accounts for Indigenous people. As the title indicates, in *Red, White, and Black*, he understands the positionality of Indigenous people as separate from that of the "senior" and "junior partners," whereas in later publications he has described Indigeneity as both "a liminal category, and . . . on the side of 'junior partners' and antagonistic to Blacks." Paula von Gleich, Samira Spatzek, and Frank B. Wilderson III, "'The Inside-Outside of Civil Society': An Interview with Frank B. Wilderson, III," *Black Studies Papers* 2, no. 1 (2016): 14, http://nbn-resolving.de/urn:nbn:de:gbv:46-00105247-16. See also Wilderson, *Red, White, and Black*, 29–30, 48–50.

15. For the Black captive abject/free Human subject binary, I draw on Sylvia Wynter's key differentiation between "'the genre' of Man" as that "which overrepresents itself as if it were 'the human'" and an unrealized, all-encompassing "'genre' of the human." Sylvia Wynter and Greg Thomas, "Proud Flesh Inter/Views: Sylvia Wynter," *Proud Flesh: New Afrikan Journal of Culture, Politics, and Consciousness* 4 (2006): 24, 11, 25. Similarly, I understand with Patrice D. Douglass (who also draws on Wynter) Human gender as a performed "possession," whereas "gender for the Black exposes how Black bodies are possessed, not by their individual or collective (gender) identifications, but by the investments or valuations placed upon gender as a genre for designating Human distinction or 'kind.'" Patrice D. Douglass, "Assata Is Here: (Dis)Locating Gender in Black Studies," *Souls* 22, no. 1 (January–March 2020): 91. I take the concept of "abjection" from Sabine Broeck, *Gender and the Abjection of Blackness* (Albany: State University of New York Press, 2018).

16. Hartman, *Lose Your Mother*, 6.

17. Hartman, *Lose Your Mother*, 6.

18. Saidiya V. Hartman, *Scenes of Subjection: Terror, Slavery, and Self-Making in Nineteenth-Century America* (New York: Oxford University Press, 1997). On the influence of *Scenes of Subjection* on the development of Afropessimism, see, for example, Frank B. Wilderson III and Saidiya V. Hartman, "The Position of the Unthought," *Qui Parle* 13, no. 2 (Spring/Summer 2003): 183–201.

19. Goyal and Gyasi, "An Interview," 480.

20. Laura T. Murphy, *Metaphor and the Slave Trade in West African Literature* (Athens: Ohio University Press, 2012), 174.

21. Hartman, *Lose Your Mother*, 233, 232.

22. Hartman, *Lose Your Mother*, 226.

23. Lara Choksey, *Narrative in the Age of the Genome* (London: Bloomsbury Academic, 2021), 142, http://dx.doi.org/10.5040/9781350102576.0010.

24. Saidiya V. Hartman, "Venus in Two Acts," *Small Axe* 12, no. 2 (June 2008): 10.

25. Hartman, *Lose Your Mother*, 227. On the notion of unfreedom or confined forms of freedom for the formerly enslaved in the northern states of America as reflected in their autobiographical writing, see, for example, Paula von Gleich, *The Black Border and Fugitive Narration in Black American Literature* (Berlin: De Gruyter, 2022), 72–91, 171–177, https://doi.org/10.1515/9783110761030.

26. Hartman, *Lose Your Mother*, 232–233.

27. Choksey, *Narrative in the Age of the Genome*, 142.

28. Hartman, *Lose Your Mother*, 170.

29. Tina Campt defines *fugitivity* and *refusal* in contrast to "opposition or resistance" as "a fundamental renunciation of the terms imposed upon black subjects that reduce black life to always already suspect" and "a quotidian practice of refusing the terms of impossibility that define the black subject in the twenty-first-century logic of racial subordination." Tina M. Campt, *Listening to Images* (Durham, NC: Duke University Press, 2017), 109, 113. For more about the concepts of captivity and fugitivity in Black North American narratives and Black feminist and Afropessimist thought, see von Gleich, *The Black Border and Fugitive Narration*.

30. Paul Gilroy, *The Black Atlantic: Modernity and Double Consciousness* (London: Verso, 2002).

31. Goyal and Gyasi, "An Interview," 472–473. North American neoslave narratives have tended to neglect West Africa as a main setting and West Africans remaining on the continent as complex main characters, not least because their focus has frequently been on the loss of the knowledge of and connection to the time, place, and familial and communal relations before the Middle Passage. As Portia Owusu points out, however, to assume a complete absence of a discourse on the history of slavery in West Africa is not only factually wrong but also perpetuates the dominant Western enlightenment narrative that Africans do not have a history or are incapable of reflecting it. It seems thus more apt to speak of different cultural and literary engagements with slavery in the United States and West Africa. See Portia Owusu, *Spectres from the Past: Slavery and the Politics of History in West African and African-American Literature* (New York: Routledge, 2020), 4–6. For a discussion of hidden or coded contentions with slavery in West African literature of the twentieth century, see Murphy, *Metaphor and the Slave Trade*.

32. See Yaa Gyasi, *Homegoing* (London: Penguin Books, 2016), chaps. "Effia," "Esi," "Quey," and "James."

33. Gyasi, *Homegoing*, 107, 99.

34. See Gyasi, *Homegoing*, chaps. "Esi" and "Quey."

35. See, for example, Mar Gallego, "Sexuality and Healing in the African Diaspora: A Transnational Approach to Toni Morrison and Gyasi," *Humanities* 8, no. 4 (2019): 183, sec. 2.1., https://doi.org/10.3390/h8040183.

36. Gyasi, *Homegoing*, 35.

37. Gyasi, *Homegoing*, 35.

38. Gyasi, *Homegoing*, 39, 40.

39. Gyasi, *Homegoing*, 42.

40. Gyasi, *Homegoing*, 31.

41. Gyasi, *Homegoing*, 77. On Michelle Wright's concept of "spacetime," see Michelle M. Wright, *The Physics of Blackness: Beyond the Middle Passage Epistemology* (Minneapolis: University of Minnesota Press, 2015). On the role of motherlessness in *Homegoing*, see Owusu, *Spectres from the Past*, chap. 5. On captivity and flight in *Beloved*, see von Gleich, *The Black Border and Fugitive Narration*, 187–204.

42. Gyasi, *Homegoing*, 70; Choksey, *Narrative in the Age of the Genome*, 145.

43. Gyasi, *Homegoing*, 85.

44. Gyasi, *Homegoing*, 85.

45. Gyasi, *Homegoing*, 85, 70. It is worth mentioning that Kojo, like Ness, is cut off not only from his mother's family history but from his father's as well. Readers learn that Sam arrives on the plantation "straight from the Continent" and speaks a language Ness does not recognize. Gyasi, *Homegoing*, 80.

46. Gyasi, *Homegoing*, 130.

47. Choksey, *Narrative in the Age of the Genome*, 145.

48. Hartman, "Venus in Two Acts," 11.

49. Gyasi, *Homegoing*, 29–30, 222–223, 286. On critical fabulation in relation to *Homegoing*'s use of metafiction and the novel's take on fiction and historiography, see also Haensell, *Making Black History*, 171–172, 175–179.

50. Gyasi, *Homegoing*, 289.

51. On creolization in postcolonial and Black diasporic theory, see, for example, most prominently Édouard Glissant, *Caribbean Discourse: Selected Essays*, trans. Michael Dash (Charlottesville: University Press of Virginia, 1989).

52. Gyasi, *Homegoing*, 242.

53. Gyasi, *Homegoing*, 242.

54. Owusu, *Spectres from the Past*, 94, 96.

55. Gyasi, *Homegoing*, 274.

56. Choksey, *Narrative in the Age of the Genome*, 140.

57. Gyasi, *Homegoing*, 242.

58. Stephen Dillon, *Fugitive Life: The Queer Politics of the Prison State* (Durham, NC: Duke University Press, 2018), 98.

59. Gyasi, *Homegoing*, 129.

60. Gyasi, *Homegoing*, 158.

61. Christine Okoth, "The Extractive Form of Contemporary Black Writing: Dionne Brand and Yaa Gyasi," *Textual Practice* 35, no. 3 (April 2021): 388, 390, https://doi.org/10.1080/0950236X.2021.1886705. Importantly, Okoth also accounts for the "promise of sociality that H sees in the shafts and rooms of the mine . . . [as] partially realised in the wake of the mining workers' transition from unfree convict labourers to free miners and the successes of collective bargaining" for better pay. Okoth, "Extractive Form," 390.

62. Gyasi, *Homegoing*, 166.

63. Gyasi, *Homegoing*, 167.

64. Blackmon, *Slavery by Another Name*; Gyasi, *Homegoing*, 164.

65. Gyasi, *Homegoing*, 204.

66. Gyasi, *Homegoing*, 74. Incidentally, H's slow suffocation from black lung disease also recalls the contemporary rallying cry "I can't breathe" of the Black Lives Matter movement against fatal police violence. The connection between Ness's and H's marked bodies receives yet another layer of meaning when we consider the fact that for both of them their physical scars foreclose any improvement of their harsh working conditions, thwarting social upward mobility.

67. Gyasi, *Homegoing*, 262.

68. Gyasi, *Homegoing*, 289.

69. Alexander, *The New Jim Crow*; see Gyasi, *Homegoing*, chaps. "Willie," "Sonny," and "Marcus."

70. Gyasi, *Homegoing*, 243.

71. Gyasi, *Homegoing*, 244.

72. According to Sonny, Garvey "had been onto something." However, Sonny takes issue with the ways in which Garvey's theories were put into practice. Gyasi, *Homegoing*, 244.

73. Gyasi, *Homegoing*, 255. See also Gyasi, *Homegoing*, 247, 249.

74. Gyasi, *Homegoing*, 260.

75. Gyasi, *Homegoing*, 263.

76. Gyasi, *Homegoing*, 300.

77. Gyasi, *Homegoing*, 16, 42, 46, 49.

78. Gyasi, *Homegoing*, 25, 45.

79. Gyasi, *Homegoing*, 277.

80. Gyasi, *Homegoing*, 266, 272, 280.

81. Gyasi, *Homegoing*, 278.

82. Gyasi, *Homegoing*, 275, 271.

83. Gyasi, *Homegoing*, 280, 268.

84. Gyasi, Homegoing, 266, 264.

85. Gyasi, *Homegoing*, 273.

86. Gyasi, *Homegoing*, 273.

87. Gyasi, *Homegoing*, 273.

88. Gyasi, *Homegoing*, 283, 282.

89. Gyasi, *Homegoing*, 273.

90. Sexton, "People-of-Color-Blindness," 53.

91. Gyasi, *Homegoing*, 284, emphasis added.

92. Gyasi, *Homegoing*, 296. On the myth of the American dream and the self-made man, see, for example, Heike Paul, *The Myths That Made America: An Introduction to American Studies* (Bielefeld, Germany: Transcript Verlag, 2014), chap. 7.

93. Gyasi, *Homegoing*, 162.

94. Haensell, *Making Black History*, 182.

95. Haensell, *Making Black History*, 182; see Gyasi, *Homegoing*, 290.

96. Yaa Gyasi, "White People, Black Authors Are Not Your Medicine," *The Guardian*, March 20, 2021, https://www.theguardian.com/books/2021/mar/20/white-people-black-authors-are-not-your-medicine.

97. Gyasi, "White Peope, Black Authors."

98. Hartman, *Lose Your Mother*, 6; Gyasi, *Homegoing*, 273.

99. Haensell, *Making Black History*, 151.

100. Haensell, *Making Black History*, 55.

101. Haensell comes to a similar conclusion when she contends that "the novel doesn't construct the myth of a pure ancestral homeland or singular origin but presents the Gold Coast as a synchronic assemblage of collective histories, a complexly flavored 'pot of groundnut soup,' stirred up by the British and others before them, and already intrinsically diverse, cosmopolitan, modern (98). Even though the scope and thrust of the novel could be read as epic and thus easily reduced to a mythologized quest for origin, there is no harmonious state of innocence to return to and, crucially, also no 'classical' sense of historical or national progress." Haensell, *Making Black History*, 166.

Contributors

Jamella N. Gow is an Assistant Professor of Sociology at Bowdoin College. Her research focuses on how im/migration, race, and blackness intersect for Black migrants. Her work explores how Caribbean migrants navigate racial and ethnic identity, inclusion/exclusion, and diasporic politics through immigrant status and blackness in the United States. Her most recent publications include "Countering Anti-Blackness with Migrant Solidarity: Black and Caribbean Linkages through Racial Struggle (*Ethnic and Racial Studies*, 2023), "Race, Nation, or Community? Political Strategy and Identity-Making within the Transnational Haitian Diaspora in Miami's 'Little Haiti,'" (*Journal of Haitian Studies*, 2021) and "Reworking Race, Nation, and Diaspora on the Margins" (*Diaspora: A Journal of Transnational Studies*, 2021).

Maya Hislop is an Assistant Professor of English at Clemson University. Dr. Hislop received her Ph.D. in 2018 from the University of Virginia, where she specialized in twentieth-century and twenty-first-century African American literature. Her book project *Bodies in the Middle: Black Women, Sexual Violence, and Justice* (forthcoming in 2023 from University of South Carolina Press) moves a conversation about Black women and sexual violence forward from enslavement to consider how a history of antirape and antiracist social justice movements inform our readings of novels on the same themes. Her interests also include critical race theory, graphic novel studies, film studies, and humor studies.

Philip Kretsedemas served as Professor of Sociology at UMass-Boston for over fifteen years, achieving the rank of Full Professor. He is currently serving as Managing Director of Research, Evaluation and Data Analytics for the Acacia Center for Justice, where he continues to be involved in research on immigration law. His monographs and edited anthologies have been published by Columbia University Press, Greenwood/Praeger, Routledge, and Temple University Press. His most recent monograph is *Black Interdictions: Antiblack Racism and Haitian Refugees on the High Seas* (Lexington Books, 2022).

P. Khalil Saucier is Chair and Professor of Critical Black Studies at Bucknell University, author of *Necessarily Black: Cape Verdean Youth, Hip-Hop Culture, and a Critique of Identity* (Michigan State University Press, 2015), and editor of *A Luta Continua: (Re)Introducing Amilcar Cabral to a New Generation* (Africa World Press, 2016) and *Native Tongues: An African Hip-Hop Reader* (Africa World Press, 2011). With Tryon P. Woods, he is co-editor of *Conceptual Aphasia in Black: Displacing Racial Formation* (Lexington Books, 2016) and *On Marronage: Ethical Confrontations with Antiblackness* (Africa World Press, 2015).

Hyacinth Udah is a Senior Lecturer of Social Work at the James Cook University. He has research interests in social justice, migration, race and racism, politics of disadvantage, identity and belonging, critical race and whiteness theories, coloniality, decoloniality, and social change. He is a community change agent and an active academic citizen. He is a leading scholar in the field of African immigrant settlement and discourses of Otherness in Australia. His interdisciplinary work—on Othering, belonging, immigrant and international students' experiences, and social work education—is widely published in social work, sociology, and social science international journals.

Paula von Gleich is a postdoctoral researcher and lecturer on North American Literature and Culture at the Department of Linguistics and Literary Studies, University of Bremen, Germany. She is the Executive Director of the Bremen Institute of Canada and Québec Studies and co-editor of the open access journal *Current Objectives of Postgraduate American Studies*. She received a bridge scholarship (University of Bremen) and a doctoral fellowship (Evangelisches Studienwerk e.V.) and was visiting scholar at the Barnard Center for Research on Women at Barnard College and the Institute for Research on Women, Gender, and Sexuality at Columbia University. Her first monograph, entitled *The Black Border and Fugitive Narration in Black American Literature*, was published by De Gruyter in 2022. It analyzes concepts of fugitivity and captivity in Black North American narratives and Afropessimist and Black feminist theory. Her work has also appeared in the *Atlantic Studies* and *Current Objectives of Postgraduate American Studies* journals and in various edited volumes.

Tryon P. Woods is Professor of Crime & Justice Studies at the University of Massachusetts, Dartmouth, and Special Lecturer in Black Studies at Providence College. He is author of *Pandemic Police Power, Public Health, and the Abolition Question* (Palgrave Macmillan, 2022) and *Blackhood Against the Police Power: Punishment and Disavowal in the "Post-Racial" Era* (Michigan State University Press, 2019); and with P. Khalil Saucier, he is co-editor of *Conceptual Aphasia in Black: Displacing Racial Formation* (Lexington Books, 2016) and *On Marronage: Ethical Confrontations with Antiblackness* (Africa World Press, 2015).

Index